ENCYCLOPAEDIA OF
INDIAN GOVERNMENT:
PROGRAMMES AND POLICIES

ENCYCLOPAEDIA
OF
INDIAN GOVERNMENT:
PROGRAMMES AND POLICIES

Vol. 20

External Affairs and International Relations

Edited by

Satish Tiwari

ANMOL PUBLICATIONS PVT. LTD.

NEW DELHI - 110 002 (INDIA)

ANMOL PUBLICATIONS PVT. LTD.
4374/4B, Ansari Road, Daryaganj
New Delhi - 110 002

Encyclopaedia of Indian Government: Programmes and Policies

First Edition, 2000
ISBN 81-261-0515-1 (Set)

PRINTED IN INDIA

Published by J.L. Kumar for Anmol Publications Pvt. Ltd., New Delhi - 110 002 and Printed at Mehra Offset Press, Delhi.

Contents

Preface

Encyclopaedia of Indian Government: Programmes and Policies contains authoritative information on about fifty departmental policies and their future developmental programmes.

Organised to be completed in 40 volumes, this gigantic work covers Agriculture; Atomic Energy; Chemicals and Fertilizers; Coal; Commerce; Communication; Culture; Defence; Education; Environment and Forests; External Affairs; Finance; Food & Consumer Affairs; Food Processing Industries; Health and Family Welfare; Home Affairs and Internal Security; Human Resources; Industry; Information and Broadcasting; Labour; Law, Justice and Company Affairs; Non-conventional Energy Sources; Ocean Development; Parliamentary Affairs; Personnel, Public Grievances and Pensions; Petroleum and Natural Gas; Planning and Programme Implementation; Planning and Statistics; Posts and Telegraphs; Power; Rural Development; Science and Technology; Social Justice and Empowerment; Space; States Affairs; Steel; Steel and Mines; Sugar and Edible Oils; Surface Transport; Textiles; Tourism; Urban Development; Water Resources; Women and Child development etc.

Based on the information derived from authoritative sources, this work contains authentic facts and figures. I am deeply beholden to all the scholars whose writings are cited or substantially made use of in the present work. I am also thankful to Anmol Publications Pvt. Ltd. for undertaking publication of this encyclopaedia. I am solely responsible for shortcomings in presentation of matter.

Encyclopaedic in nature, this will prove a dependable reference work for scholars and academics besides those appearing for different competitive examinations.

—Satish Tiwari

1

India's Neighbours

Afghanistan

India closely monitored the continuing fratricidal conflict in Afghanistan, a country with which it has historical ties of friendship and cooperation. India maintained close contacts with various parties and groups within Afghanistan. India believes that there can be no military solution to the internecine war which is being fueled by foreign involvement, principally from across Afghanistan's southern borders.

The military situation remained in flux. The Taliban, consequent to the major offensives it had launched in July 1998 in Northern Afghanistan, succeeded in capturing several cities in Northern and Central Afghanistan driving out the forces of Gen. Abdul Rashid Dostum and the Hijb-e-Wahdat. However, Commander Ahmad Shah Masood put up a strong resistance to the Taliban advances to his traditional areas of influence and recaptured in October-November, 1998 from Taliban control all Takhar Province and some areas in Kunduz. There have also been reports of uprisings against Taliban rule in several parts of Northern Afghanistan, following which some more areas have been wrested from Taliban control.

India continued to send humanitarian assistance to Afghanistan both bilaterally and through the UN. After the devastating earthquake in Afghanistan on May 30, 1998, a plane load of relief material was sent on June 11, 1998. A consignment of 30 tonnes; of vegetable oil was sent through the UN in July 1998. A consignment of medical equipments, medical supplies and medicines worth Rs. 40 lakhs was sent to the Indira Gandhi Institute for Child Health, Kabul, in October 1.998. More consignments of medicines, woollens and food items will be sent in the coming months.

Iran

Based on cultural and civilisational affinities and historical interactions, India's ties with Iran continued to grow. As a part of the process of high-level exchange of visits which have contributed to build mutual trust and confidence, Dr. Seyed Kamal Kharrazi, Foreign Minister of the Islamic Republic of Iran, accompanied by a high-level delegation, visited Delhi on June 2-3,1998. He called on the Prime Minister and held discussions with Minister of State for External Affairs on bilateral, regional and international issues. Prime Minister had an occasion to review bilateral relations and to discuss issues of mutual interest with President Khatami on the sidelines of the NAM Summit at Durban in September 1998. Iranian President's Special Envoy on Afghanistan, Alaeddin Broujerdi, paid a visit to New Delhi in September 1998, for consultations on Afghanistan.

Economic and commercial interaction between India and Iran continued satisfactorily. The first meeting of the Indo-Iran joint Business Council was held in Tehran in May 1998 and the second meeting at New Delhi on February 24, 1999, with the active participation of apex Chambers of Commerce and Industry in the two countries to explore the possibilities of increased trade, investment and setting up of joint ventures Iranian Foreign Minister, Dr. Kharrazi visited India on February

23-25, 1999 to co-chair the Tenth meeting of the Indo-Iran Joint Commission along with External Affairs Minister. Besides discussions on bilateral, regional and international issues of mutual interest during Dr. Kharrazi's meetings with President, Prime Minister, External Affairs Minister, Commerce Minister and Minister of Petroleum & Natural Gas, the two side reviewed the progress of bilateral co-operation in agriculture & rural development, energy, industry, trade, transportation & communication, cultural, consular, information and science & technology areas. It was decided to further expand and intensify bilateral ties in these fields and institute a mechanism for regular consultations between the Foreign Offices of the two countries.

Pakistan

Prime Minister Shri Atal Behari Vajpayee took a historic initiative to visit Lahore on February 20-21, 1999 on the inaugural run of the Delhi-Lahore-Delhi bus service. His visit was part of India's consistent efforts to build peaceful, friendly and cooperative ties with Pakistan and establish a relationship based on mutual respect and a regard for each other's concerns. Earlier, the resumption of the official dialogue between the two countries in October 1998 marked a success in India's endeavours to engage Pakistan in a composite and comprehensive dialogue process that would build trust and confidence, explore avenues of mutually beneficial cooperation and address outstanding issues. A crucial element in Pakistan's attitude and approach towards India, however, was its engaging in terrorism, firing across the international border and Line of Control in Jammu and Kashmir and hostile propaganda.

Prime Minister's visit

India's basic policy approach towards Pakistan was

underlined by Prime Minister Shri Atal Behari Vajpayee's declaration that a stable, prosperous and secure Pakistan was in India's interest. This sentiment was reaffirmed by him from the Minar-e-Pakistan in Lahore on February 21, 1999. Prime Minister's visit was the most significant engagement between India and Pakistan in over a quarter of a century. It was also the first visit undertaken by the Prime Minister of India to Pakistan in a decade. During his visit, the Prime Minister conveyed to the Government and people of Pakistan India's deep desire for peace and friendship with them and for developing a comprehensive structure of cooperation for the benefit of the two peoples. The Prime Minister and the Pakistan Prime Minister signed the Lahore Declaration which is a landmark for peace and security of the two countries. A Memorandum of Understanding was also signed by the Foreign Secretaries under which India and Pakistan will work to enter into agreements to put into place far-reaching Confidence Building Measures. In a joint Statement issued on the occasion, the two countries also identified new and significant areas of cooperation such as Information Technology and decided to address humanitarian issues at a ministerial level on an urgent basis. India expects that the Prime Minister's historic initiative for the welfare of the peoples of the two countries will mark a new chapter in our bilateral ties.

Resumption of official dialogue

Prime Minister had met Pakistan Prime Minister Mr. Nawaz Sharif on the sidelines of the Tenth SAARC Summit at Colombo (29 July, 1998) and in New York (23 September, 1998). During these meetings, Prime Minister urged Pakistan to work with India to develop trust and confidence, avail of the many opportunities for mutually beneficial cooperation and address outstanding issues. Prime Minister also emphasised that Pakistan's instigation of and support to terrorism against India were incompatible with the development of peaceful and friendly relations and that these activities must cease immediately.

During Prime Minister's meeting with Prime Minister Mr. Nawaz Sharif in New York on 23 September, 1998, the Foreign Secretaries of India and Pakistan reported to the two Prime Ministers that they had reached an agreement on the modalities of the dialogue process. (The subjects for the dialogue were agreed upon in June 1997 and are: Peace & Security including CBMs, Jammu & Kashmir, Siachen, Tulbul Navigation Project, Sir Creek, Economic and Commercial Cooperation, Terrorism and Drug Trafficking and Promotion of Friendly Exchanges in various fields). The Prime Ministers welcomed this development and issued directions for the resumption of the dialogue.

The first round of the composite dialogue process was held in October and November 1998. The subjects of Peace & Security including CBMs and Jammu & Kashmir were discussed by the Foreign Secretaries in Islamabad in October 1998. The subjects of Tulbul Navigation Project, Siachen, Sir Creek, Economic and Commercial Cooperation, Terrorism and Drug Trafficking and Promotion of Friendly Exchanges in various fields were discussed, respectively, by the Secretary, Water Resources of India and Secretary, Water and Power of Pakistan; the Defence Secretaries; the Surveyor General of India and Additional Secretary, Ministry of Defence of Pakistan; the Commerce Secretaries; the Home Secretary of India and the Interior Secretary of Pakistan; and the Culture Secretaries, in New Delhi in November 1998.

During talks on Peace & Security including CBMs, India drew Pakistan's attention to India's security needs which were a function of its size and assets. India emphasised that its security concerns were not one-country specific and that its defence profile was non-aggressive. In this context, India proposed the upgradation of existing CBMs and the need to put in place new CBMs, ranging from information exchange and improved communication links to exchanging views on security concepts and nuclear doctrines. India also emphasised the need to build mutual confidence in the nuclear and conventional fields.

During discussions on Jammu & Kashmir, India made it clear that the legal status of Jammu & Kashmir, i.e. that the entire State is an integral part of India, is clear and does not admit of any change. India also demanded that Pakistan cease forthwith its futile instigation and sponsorship of terrorism in Jammu & Kashmir, which constituted a flagrant violation of the provisions of the Simla Agreement.

During talks on the Tulbul Navigation Project, India drew Pakistan's attention to understandings that had been reached during earlier discussions on this subject and that can be the basis for a resolution of the issue. During discussions on Siachen, India stressed the need for a cease fire in the area as a first step. On the subject of Sir Creek, India proposed that, pending agreement on the land boundary, the maritime boundary could be demarcated by starting at sea and proceeding landwards.

At the discussions on Terrorism and Drug Trafficking, India gave Pakistan detailed evidence regarding its role in sponsoring terrorism against India and demanded that Pakistan close down training camps for terrorists and hand over terrorists and fugitives from the law who have been given sanctuary in Pakistan.

During discussions on Economic and Commercial Cooperation, India emphasised that there were many avenues for mutually beneficial cooperation including in areas such as electric power and transportation. Detailed discussions on the technical, legal and financial aspects at the expert-level have taken place in Islamabad and New Delhi on the subject of purchase of power by India from Pakistan. These discussions are continuing.

On the subject of Promotion of Friendly Exchanges, India proposed a cultural exchange programme which would build on the commonalities between the two countries. India also emphasised the need of regular contacts to address humanitarian issue relating to fishermen and civilian prisoners and people-to-people contacts.

India released a total of 149 Pakistani fishermen in its custody. It also proposed to Pakistan that the fishermen of the two countries who stray innocently into the territorial waters of the other country should not be kept in custody but should be released on completion of formalities. Acting on this principle, India conveyed to Pakistan on 2 November 1998 its decision to release 40 Pakistani fishermen who were captured on 24 October, 1998. Pakistan also released 190 Indian fishermen who were held in its custody.

India took the initiative to start a Delhi-Lahore-Delhi bus service. An agreement and a protocol for the regulation of this service were signed in Islamabad on 17 February, 1999. Trial runs of an Indian bus to Pakistan and a Pakistani bus to India had been held in January 1999.

Pakistan's support to terrorism

Pakistan's support to and involvement in terrorist activities in Jammu & Kashmir and other parts of India continues unabated. This was strongly taken up by Prime Minister during his visit to Pakistan, and also by Foreign Secretary and Home Secretary during the dialogue process. It was pointed out that the atmosphere generated by the open exhortation of terrorist actions in India by fundamentalist organisations in Pakistan, many of which enjoyed official patronage, was not conducive to a normalisation of bilateral relations. India urged that Pakistan take urgent steps to demonstrate its commitment to tackling the issue of terrorism.

Pakistan's nuclear and missile programmes

India has carefully been following Pakistan's pursuit of clandestine weapons oriented nuclear and missile programmes which have been developed with assistance from abroad. On 6 April, 1998, Pakistan announced the successful test of a ballistic missile, the Hatf V (Ghauri). Pakistan also announced that it had conducted tests of six nuclear devices on 28-30 May, 1998. It said that the tests were in reaction to India's nuclear tests carried out earlier in May 1998. In response to these tests, Government of India's official spokesman said that this event vindicated India's assessment regarding the nature of Pakistani programme and policy as well as the measures India had taken. He also said that Government of India had taken all steps necessary for safeguarding the nation's security.

Conclusion

India seeks a relationship of trust, friendship and cooperation with Pakistan. Our approaches to Pakistan are rooted in our national consensus, which favours moving relations ahead with Pakistan over a broad front through the composite dialogue process. These approaches derive their strength from our confidence as a mature nation dedicated to peace, democracy and freedom. It is our earnest hope to build-on. the opportunities that are now available on account of the Prime Minister's initiative and his commitment to put behind past connections and think of the welfare of coming generations. The Lahore Declaration and the Memorandum of Understanding on Confidence Building Measures and the joint Statement are significant developments in our bilateral relations. We trust Pakistan will fully reciprocate our initiatives and abandon the path of confrontation and promotion of terrorism in India.

India's relations with its eastern and southern neighbours Bangladesh, Myanmar, Maldives and Sri Lanka - reflected a continuity of policy and approach in the development of close understanding and active collaboration in mutually beneficial development efforts. There was focus on sectors of specific interest to each of the countries concerned covering a wide range of areas. Equally important was the sustained dialogue covering ongoing matters of operational importance such as border management. The economic and social dimensions however provided the thrust for progress in increased engagement.

Bangladesh

There was mutual keenness on the part of both India and Bangladesh to promote understanding and to strengthen bilateral relations during the year. Several high level visits contributed to this process.

The foreign Minister of Bangladesh, Mr. Abdus Samad Azad, visited India in April 1998 as the Special Envoy of the Bangladesh Prime Minister, to greet the new Government. The Bangladesh Prime Minister, Mrs Sheikh Hasina. visited India on June 16,1998; at the talks held during the visit, both sides agreed on the need to intensify the existing warm and cordial relations between the two countries and to increase interaction at various levels through economic and cultural exchanges, parliamentary delegations, students, and cultural groups.

The two Prime Ministers met again on the sidelines of the 10th SAARC Summit at Colombo in July 1998. The foreign Secretary visited Bangladesh in June 1998 for Foreign Office consultations and held wide ranging discussions on bilateral, regional and international issues. Trade review talks took place in Dhaka in December 1998; the Indian delegation was led by the Commerce Secretary. The talks were positive in nature and covered a number of areas related to the growth of bilateral economic interaction and infrastructure development.

The system of institutional dialogue to discuss matters relating to security and border management continued during the year. Two sessions of talks between the Directors General of the Border Security Force and the Bangladesh Rifles were held in May and October 1998. The 5th meeting of the Joint Working Group took place in New Delhi in August 1998. The Home Secretary visited Dhaka in November 1998. Issues covered during these talks related to security, insurgency, illegal immigration, border management and the visa regime. The talks too place in a constructive spirit while taking into account mutual concerns.

Bangladesh was gripped by devastating floods for the longest duration recorded. There was widespread loss of life and property with a particularly negative impact on agriculture, and Bangladesh made an appeal for international aid. The Government of India rushed over 7.5 tonnes of medicines worth Rs. 40 lakhs to Bangladesh by air. India also gifted 20,000 tonnes of par-boiled rice worth Rs. 22 crores and over 800 tonnes of wheat and maize seeds worth Rs. 2.2 crores.

India's relations with Bangladesh are thus close, friendly and extensive. There is widespread people-to-people contact as established by the fact that the High Commission of India in Dhaka issues an average of 1000 visas daily. Thousands of students from Bangladesh pursue higher studies in India. There were many cultural exchanges both under governmental and Private auspices. India provided training to several technical personnel from Bangladesh.

The Bangladesh Prime Minister visited Calcutta to inaugurate the 24th Calcutta Book Fair on January 27-28,1999. An Indian Trade Fair is being organised in Dhaka on March 9-15, 1999.

Sri Lanka

India's relations with Sri Lanka continued to be marked by warmth and cordiality. The visits of the Sri Lankan Foreign Minister, Mr. Lakshman Kadirgamar, to India in March and June 1998, as a Special Envoy of the Sri Lankan President provided opportunities for useful, high level exchanges between the two Governments. Both sides reaffirmed the consensus prevailing in both countries on maintaining close and cordial relations. The Sri Lankan leader of the Opposition, Mr. Ranil Wickremesinghe, visited India in April 1998. The Prime Minister's visit to Colombo from 28-31 July, 1998 to attend the Tenth SAARC Summit helped to further cement the multifaceted ties between the two countries.

The President of Sri Lanka, H.E. Mrs. Chandrika Bandaranaike Kumaratunga, paid a state visit to India from December 27-30,1998, During the visit, the two sides signed an agreement to establish a Free Trade Area between India and Sri Lanka. The agreement is expected to lead to a steady growth of trade and investment through graduated reduction of tariffs. The two countries also signed a Memorandum of Understanding to set up the India-Sri Lanka Foundation. The Foundation would promote bilateral exchanges in various spheres and would be governed by an independent board.

The deliberations during the visit reflected the priority attached by both countries to sustaining the warmth and understanding that mark the India-Sri Lanka relationship.

Earlier, the fourth Session of the India-Sri Lanka joint Commissions met at New Delhi on December 18,1998. The Indian delegation was led by the Minister of External Affairs, while the Sri Lankan Minister of Foreign Affairs, Mr. Lakshman Kadirgamar led the Sri Lankan delegation. The Joint Commission reviewed the existing levels of bilateral cooperation in the areas of Science & technology, economy, trade & investment, and cultural, educational & social matters. Both sides agreed on further programmes to broaden and deepen bilateral exchanges.

Bilateral trade between the two countries showed an upward trend. India continued to provide trade concessions to Sri Lanka within the SAPTA framework with a view to improving market access for Sri Lankan products in India.

Both sides continued their dialogue on problems faced by fishermen of the two countries with a view to finding appropriate solutions to the problems. Both countries agree on the need to deal with these problems in a spirit of compassion and understanding.

Maldives

India-Maldives relations continued to remain close and friendly. India kept up assistance to the Maldives in its developmental efforts including in the area of Human Resource Development. There was regular interaction through the exchange of high level visits.

President Maumoon Abdul Gayoom visited India in his capacity as Chairman of SAARC from June 30 to July 1, 1998. The Vice President visited the Maldives from

November 10-13,1998 to represent India at President Gayoom's swearing-in ceremony on November 11, 1998, for a 5th consecutive term following a national referendum held on October 16, 1998.

Mr. Suresh P Prabhu, Minister of Environment and Forests attended the Seventh Session of the Governing Council of the South Asia Cooperative Environment Programme (SACEP) in Male from April 20-23,1998. An expert team from India visited Maldives from July 4-9, 1998 to study the feasibility of setting up in Maldives an Institute of Hotel and Catering Services. India provided technical training to a large number of Maldivian candidates in diverse fields including medicine, engineering, computer science and agriculture under its technical assistance and scholarships scheme.

Mr. Ibrahim Hussain Zaki, Minister of Tourism, Mr. Abdul Rasheed Hussain, Minister of Planning, Human Resources and Environment, Mr. Mohammed Latheef, Minister of Education and Mr. Ahmed Abdulla, Minister of Health, Government of Maldives visited India during the year for international meetings. These visits were also used for bilateral discussions.

Myanmar

India has a stable and cooperative relationship with Myanmar. Focussed efforts were made to diversify and broadbase areas of contact and cooperation. An MOU on Cooperation in the field of Agriculture and Allied Sectors was signed during the visit to Yangon (April 22-25) of the Minister of State for Agriculture, Shri Som Pal. As a follow up to the MOU, a work Plan was finalised during the visit to India (August 16-25) by the Myanmar Agriculture Minister. The Commerce Secretary led an Inter-Ministerial delegation in October and was accompanied by a business delegation to Yangon to explore ways and means of expanding trade and economic linkages including cross border projects in areas such as power, mining and oil & gas. The Myanmar Deputy Minister for Industry-2 visited India in November to identify sectors for collaboration. Possibilities of cooperation in the fields of science & technology, herbal medicines, satellite telecommunication etc. are being explored. A number of Myanmar nationals received training at Indian institutes.

In areas of vital interest such as border management and drug-trafficking, regular interaction was maintained through bilateral institutional mechanisms. The Home Secretary led the Indian delegation for the Fifth India-Myanmar National Level Meeting held in Yangon (April 26-29). The sectoral. level dialogue took place in January, 1999, to discuss issues related to border management.

India's traditional friendship and cooperation with its northern neighbours, Bhutan and Nepal, have continued to grow and strengthen over the years, reflecting the firm foundations and essential stability of the bilateral relationships. These bilateral relationships have traditionally been based on mutual understanding, respect and goodwill. Mutually beneficial economic cooperation between the two countries has grown steadily over the past few years and has provided substance to India-Bhutan and India-Nepal relations.

During the period under review several initiatives were taken with a view to further enriching and consolidating these relationships. In particular, India's economic cooperation programmes with Bhutan and Nepal, and trade and commercial relations developed satisfactorily, with steps being taken to liberalise and improve the procedures and bilateral arrangements in these sectors. The renewal of the Transit Treaty with Nepal with an automatic renewability clause, in particular, has contributed to developing business and investment confidence.

India's bilateral relationship with both Bhutan and Nepal is characterised by frequent interaction at both political and official levels, and this trend continued during the period under review with several high-level exchanges of visits served to provide direction and impetus to India's relationships with both its northern neighbours.

Nepal

The President of India Shri K R Narayanan made a State Visit to Nepal from 28-30 May, 1998. He was accompanied by Minister of Commerce Shri R K Hedge and four Members of Parliament. During his visit, the President held discussions with His Majesty the King, and received the Prime Minister and leaders of major political parties of Nepal, academics, intellectuals and business leaders.

Their Majesties King Birendra Bir Bikram Shah Dev and Queen Aishwarya Rajya Laxmi Devi Shah of Nepal paid a State Visit to India from 24-29 January, 1999 at the invitation of the President of India. The King was the Chief Guest at the Republic Day celebrations on 26 January, 1999. During the visit, the King called on the President and also had separate meetings with Vice-President, Prime Minister, External Affairs Minister, Home Minister and Commerce Minister.

Both the above State Visits were highly successful in underlining the goodwill and warmth that characterise our bilateral ties with Nepal, and have contributed to the consolidation of friendship and understanding between the two countries.

Among the other high level bilateral contacts, notable are Prime Minister Shri A B Vajpayee's meetings with his Nepalese counterpart Mr. G P Koirala on the fringes of the NAM Summit in Durban and the SAARC

Summit in Colombo. Discussions between the two Prime Ministers encompassed a wide gamut of bilateral, regional and international issues of common interest.

The 2nd Meeting of the Joint Working Group (JWG) on Border Management was held in Delhi on 16 & 17 June, 1998. A number of decisions with the objective of preventing misuse of the open border between India and Nepal by undesirable elements were taken by the two sides. The meeting was followed by HOME Secretary level talks on 18 June, 1998 that, inter-alia, reviewed the decisions taken by the JWG.

The first Director General level talks on Customs Cooperation were held in New Delhi on 15 & 16 June, 1998. The Nepalese delegation was led by their Director General, Customs and the Indian side by the Director General, Department of revenue Intelligence. It was decided that such bilateral DG level meeting should be held on a regular basis to monitor and effectively combat smuggling activities across the open India-Nepal border.

A 3-member Nepalese delegation headed by their Director General, Taxation attended the 2nd Meeting of the India-Nepal. joint Commission set up under the Double Taxation Avoidance Agreement (DTAA) held in New Delhi from 28-30 July, 1998. The Meeting was useful in so far as the two sides had an exchange of views on specific issues relating to DTAA, with the objective of further strengthening bilateral cooperation in this area.

In pursuance of the Memorandum of Understanding or Agricultural Cooperation signed between India and Nepal in December 1991, the 3rd Meeting of the India-Nepal Join Agricultural Working Group (JWG) was held in Kathmandu from 5-7 August, 1998. The Meeting reviewed the progress on the decisions taken at the 2nd JWG meeting held in New Delhi if December 1996 and finalised the biennial Work Plan for the year, 1999 and 2000.

The Deputy Prime Minister of Nepal, Ms Shailaja Acharya paid a private visit to India in September 1998, during which she called on the Prime Minister of India and discussed various bilateral issues of mutual concern. On a separate visit to Bihar from 22-26 October 1998, Ms Acharya participated in the inaugural ceremony on the occasion of the 29th Anniversary of the Vishwa Shanti Stupa at Ratnagiri Hill, Rajgir held on 25 October, 1998.

The 21st Meeting of the joint Technical Level India-Nepal Boundary Committee (JTC) was held in New Delhi on 26 & 27 November 1998. At the Meeting, the two sides reviewed the progress in the implementation of the decisions taken at 20th JTC Meeting and recommended specific actions for the timely completion of the Indo-Nepal boundary tasks. The 5th Meeting of the Joint Working Group (JWG), constituted by the Joint Technical Level India-Nepal Boundary Committee (JTC), was held in Kathmandu on 15 & 16 July, 1998. The Meeting reviewed the progress in the implementation of the recommendations of the 4th JWG Meeting, 20th JTC Meeting and Survey Officials Meeting (SOM) held during May 1998.

India attaches high priority to the development of economic and commercial ties with Nepal. Successive reviews of bilateral trade & transit arrangements were held during Commerce Secretary level talks at New Delhi in March, September and November 1998. The agenda covered a gamut of issues in this area, in particular, the operation of the new road transit route from Nepal to Bangladesh via Phulbari, and the renewal of the Treaty of Transit between the two countries.

A renewed Transit Treaty between India and Nepal

was signed on 5 January. 1999 in Kathmandu by Commerce Minister Shri Ram Krishna Hegde and his Nepalese counterpart Mr. Puma Bahadur Khadga. The renewed Treaty, valid for a period of seven years up to 5 January, 2006, will be automatically extended for further periods of seven years at a time, unless either of the parties gives written notice of its intention to terminate the Treaty six months in advance. A Protocol and a Memorandum to the Treaty containing the modalities and other arrangements were also signed. These would be subject to review and modification every seven years or earlier, if warranted.

India's contribution to Nepal's economic development in diverse areas has increased over the years. Major projects funded by the Government of India currently under implementation include the construction of 22 bridges on the Kohalpur-Mahakali sector of the East-West Highway, establishment of the B P Koirala Institute of Health Sciences at Dharan, construction of an Emergency and Trauma Centre at Bir Hospital in Kathmandu, broad-gauging of Raxaul-Sirsiya Rail Link and several other projects that form part of India's commitment under the Mahakali Treaty. A High Level Task Force (HLTF) monitors the progress in bilateral relations and oversees Indian assisted projects in Nepal.

Initiatives taken by the Government of India to liberalise the trade and investment regime with Nepal are expected to provide a boost to bilateral economic exchanges in the coming years. Indian investments as of date accounted for over 40% of total foreign investments in Nepal. Bilateral trade during 1997-98 amounted to Rs. 946 crores. For the period April-August 1998, the two-way trade was Rs. 409 crores, while the figure for the corresponding period in the previous year was Rs. 346 crores. An interesting development is the sharp increase in Indian imports from Nepal during the first five months of 1998-99, with the figure reaching Rs. 249 crores, as compared to Rs. 108 crores registered in April-August 1997.

A large number of Nepalese students continued to avail of academic and training facilities in India. Several scholarship I schemes, such as the Silver Jubilee Scholarship and the B P Koirala Foundation Scholarship supplemented normal scholarships and self-financing opportunities for studies in India offered by the Government of India to Nepalese students in diverse fields, notably engineering, medicine and technical areas. Specific professional training and orientation programmes were also conducted for select candidates from Nepal under the Nepal Aid Scheme. A large number of Nepalese students also directly sought admission to schools and colleges in India on a special concessional basis.

Bhutan

His Majesty Jigme Singye Wangchuck, the King of Bhutan visited India from 5-8 October, 1998. Discussions that the King held with the President, the Vice President, Prime Minister, External Affairs Minister and other senior Cabinet Ministers, provided an opportunity for a wide ranging overview of the bilateral relationship.

The Minister of Power, Shri P K Kumaramangalam led a high level delegation to Bhutan from 26-29 October, 1998 to discuss issues relating to development of hydel power in Bhutan.

The 5th Joint Technical Level Meeting on the Bilateral Survey Collaboration Project was held in Thimphu. from 6-9 August, 1998. This project aims at developing indigenous capacity in Bhutan for survey and mapping, and includes supply of equipment and technology transfer in this field.

To Bhutan's 8th Five Year Plan (1997-2002), as in previous Plans, Indian assistance has focussed on areas of infrastructure such as the construction of roads, bridges and hydro-power capacity. Special emphasis has also been placed on the implementation of projects in social sectors such as education and health. Larger projects that are being jointly developed with the Royal Government of Bhutan include the Tala Hydroelectric Project, Kurichu Hydroelectric Project and the Dungsum Cement Project.

Following the outbreak of fire in the famous Taktsang Monastery in Bhutan, the Government of India contributed an amount of Rs. 25 lakhs in April 1998 towards the cost of reconstruction of the Monastery.

Cooperation between the two countries in the areas of culture and education has been noteworthy. A number of Bhutanese students availed of scholarships provided by the Government of India in technical areas such as agriculture, engineering and medicine. Under the bilateral Cultural Exchange Programme, there are regular visits of cultural troupes and artistes between the two countries.

SAARC

Regional cooperation in South Asia under the framework of SAARC gained further momentum during the year 1998. The Tenth SAARC Summit in Colombo in July 1998 reaffirmed the desire of all SAARC leaders to strengthen cooperation in the region, particularly in the economic field.

India took some bold initiatives to speed up trade liberalisation in the region with the lifting of Quantitative Restrictions for SAARC countries with effect from 1 August, 1998. Cooperation in the core economic areas was further consolidated with the conclusion of the

Third Round of SAPTA negotiations in November 1998. SAARC leaders also agreed that there should be a separate Treaty for a South Asia Free Trade Area (SAFTA) and negotiations on this Treaty are to commence in early 1999.

New initiatives were taken to develop cooperation in the field of Information and the Media and in Telecommunications with the first meetings of the Ministers of Information and Telecommunications.

The gains of the past were assessed and a perspective plan for SAARC for the next two decades was provided by the Group of Eminent Persons constituted by SAARC leaders in 1997. Their Report presented at the Colombo Summit in July 1998 sets out a substantial agenda for economic integration in three phases and for cooperation in the social sectors upto the year 2020.

The range of SAARC cooperation is evident from the sixty meetings and activities that took place at various levels during the year starting from the Summit down to the Ministerial, official and technical levels. Highlights of the activities are as follows:

Ministerial and other meetings

The first SAARC information Ministers meeting, Dhaka, Bangladesh (24-25 April, 1998)

The Meeting adopted the Dhaka Communique containing a SAARC Plan of Action for developing cooperation in the field of Media and Information. This provides, inter-alia, for free flow of information, newspapers, periodicals, books and other publications, increased cooperation amongst news agencies of SAARC countries; holding of annual conferences of Editors and journalists, evolution of a SAARC Media Forum and discouraging negative projection of member countries.

The second SAARC commerce Ministers' meeting, Islamabad, Pakistan (29-30 April, 1998)

The Commerce Ministers discussed ways to accelerate the ongoing Third Round of SAARC Preferential Trade Negotiations and stressed the need to deepen tariff cuts accompanied by removal of Non-Tariff Barriers on major items of intra-SAARC trade, as well as product coverage. It stressed the need for early finalisation. of the Draft Agreement on Promotion and Protection of Investment in the Region, conclusion of Double Taxation Avoidance Agreements between the SAARC Countries, and for expanding intra-SAARC investment cooperation and joint ventures. The meeting also reviewed the progress of the group on transition from SAPTA towards SAFTA. The Commerce Ministers agreed to coordinate SAARC positions at the WTO and authorised the constitution of a Group of SAARC Ambassadors to the WTO at Geneva.

The first SAARC communication Ministers' meeting on 22-24 May, 1998 at Colombo, Sri Lanka

A SAARC Plan of Action was finalised which, inter-alia, calls for reduction of telecom tariffs to the lowest extent feasible, complete digitalisation of inter-country links amongst SAARC countries preferably by December 1999, allocation of sufficient band width for regional telecommunication links, setting up of Web Sites/data bases to exchange information on telecom standards, policies and technologies, adoption of Mutual Recognition Arrangements for equipment standards, and consultations to evolve common SAARC positions on Telecommunication issues of regional concern at international fora.

SAARC UGC representatives' meeting

The Representatives of University Grants Commissions of SAARC Countries met in New Delhi from 14-16 May, 1998 to consider ways of enhancing cooperation amongst universities in SAARC countries. Extensive deliberations were held and recommendations inter-alia, to recognise university degrees mutually, increasing the number of scholarships, review of the SAARC Chairs, etc. were made at the Meeting.

South Asian development fund

The Third Meeting of the Governing Board of the South Asian Development Fund was held at Pokhara, Nepal on 4-6 June, 1998. The Board finalised the draft operational modalities for the Window 11 and considered the modalities for Window III. It also reviewed the progress of Project Studies underway under Window I and recommended sponsorship of projects for which detailed studies had been carried. It also set up a Technical Committee to review the draft Accounting Manual and a proposal to set up a permanent Secretariat of the SADF. India offered to host an Executive Development Programme for the Development Financial Institutions of SAARC Countries in 1999.

Regional convention to combat trafficking in women and children for prostitution

An Expert Group Meeting on drafting a Regional Convention to Combat Trafficking in Women and Children for Prostitution was held in New Delhi (18-19 June, 1998). Negotiations lasting over two days resulted in a draft Convention. The salient points of the draft include severe punishment for trafficking under national laws, provisions for extradition or prosecution of offenders and mutual legal assistance. It also provides for positive measures to prevent trafficking, as well as for providing temporary care and for repatriation of the victims of trafficking.

Technical committee on education, culture and sports

The Fifth Technical Committee Meeting of SAARC on Education, Culture and Sports was held in Thimpu.

Bhutan on May 26-27,1998. Review of the activities under the SAARC Technical Committee during the past year like preparation of a SAARC Anthology, SAARC Audio-Visual Exchange (SAVE) Programme, Literacy programmes, Coaching Camps for Sports, etc. took place in the Meeting.

Technical committee on women in development

The Thirteenth Technical Committee Meeting on Women in Development was held in Kathmandu, on June 28-30, 1998. The consideration of the Regional Convention on Combating Traffickling of Women and Children for Prostitution was the major item. India offered to hold a "Workshop on Implementation of the Dhaka Resolution on Women".

Tenth SAARC summit

The Tenth SAARC Summit was held in Colombo, 29-31 July, 1998, to coincide with its 50th Independence Anniversary Celebrations. It was preceded by the 20th Session of the Programming Committee, the 25th Session of the Standing Committee, and the 20th Session of the Council of Ministers, and the Seventh Meeting of the Food Security Reserve Board. At the conclusion of their deliberations, the Heads of State or Government issued the Colombo Declaration. The Indian delegation was led by Prime Minister Shri Atal Behari Vajpayee. He was accompanied by the Commerce Minister, the Deputy Chairman Planning Commission as well as the Minister of State for External Affairs, who headed the Indian delegation for the Meeting of the SAARC Council of Ministers immediately preceding the Summit. The Summit took some significant decisions to advance cooperation in the core economic areas of trade and investment. A Group of Experts from all seven SAARC Countries will be set up to commence negotiations on an Agreement or Treaty for a South Asian Free Trade Area.

This Agreement will spell out binding schedules for freeing trade and is expected to be finalised and put in place by 2001. This would provide a predictable and transparent blue-print for achieving a Free Trade Area in South Asia. The Agreement will also include special facilitative measures for the Least Developed Countries. Negotiations for deepening and widening trade preferences under the South Asian Preferential Trading Arrangement will continue in parallel. SAARC leaders at their meeting in Colombo directed that the Third Round of SAPTA negotiations should be concluded quickly and also directed that the Fourth Round of SAPTA negotiations should commence immediately thereafter, with the mandate of extending deeper tariff concessions to products which are being actively traded or are likely to be traded. Discriminatory trade practices and non-tariff barriers are to be simultaneously removed on items in respect of which tariff concessions are granted. This would ensure that we continue to liberalise trade, even as the negotiations for a SAFTA Agreement are underway.

India took some bold initiatives to enhance access to its market, The Prime Minister announced that India would lift Quantitative Restrictions for SAARC countries with effect from August 1, 1998. This involves putting over 2000 products on Open General License for SAARC countries and has been widely welcomed. The Prime Minister also announced that the ceiling for Overseas Indian investment in SAARC countries under fast track procedures would be increased from $ 8 million to $ 15 million. This was appreciated as an indication of India's commitment to encourage a greater flow of Indian investment in its immediate neighbourhood.

India also offered to consider bilateral free trade arrangements with those countries who are interested in moving faster. This is expected to reinforce regional trade liberalisation and impart added momentum to the process. Sri Lanka has taken up this offer.

Significant decisions were also taken to strengthen cooperation in the social sectors. SAARC leaders agreed in Colombo to draw up a Social Charter for SAARC setting out regional goals in the important areas of population stabilisation, education, health, nutrition, child welfare and women's development. Particular focus has been placed on the persistent problem of poverty in the region and the leaders of SAARC countries have committed themselves to the eradication of poverty in South Asia preferably by the year 2002. A three-tier institutional structure to evolve cooperation in this field has been set up. These three tiers comprise: A Group of Secretaries to Governments dealing with Poverty Eradication and Social Development; the Group of Finance/Planning Secretaries; and SAARC Finance / Planning Ministers. This mechanism is a forum for exchange of information on poverty eradication programmes, strategies and technologies. The impact of structural adjustment programmes and economic liberalisation on weaker sections of society has been kept in focus through the involvement of Finance /Planning Ministers at the highest level.

The text of the Regional Convention to Combat Illegal Trafficking in Women and Children for Prostitution was finalised. SAARC leaders agreed that the scope of the Convention could be expanded in time to cover trafficking for other purposes. The Convention is expected to be signed at the next SAARC Summit in Kathmandu. A separate Convention on Child Welfare is also under discussion.

A new initiative has been taken to develop cooperation in the field of Distance Education. A SAARC Forum of Vice Chancellors of Open Universities will be established to develop cooperation in areas such as the sharing and joint development of programmes, credit transfers for specific programmes and the translation of existing programmes.

The Summit stressed the importance of developing a regional self-reliant capability for South Asia in scientific research and development. India will host a special meeting of SAARC Science & Technology Ministers to consider a SAARC Technology Initiative to identify and implement specific regional projects in rural areas which would have a direct impact in improving the day-to-day life of people. SAARC leaders also emphasised the need to institutionalise SAARC cooperation in the field of biotechnology and have directed that cost-effective arrangements for such cooperation should be evolved.

The Summit has also taken the initiative to develop cooperation in the field of traditional systems of medicine in which the SAARC region has a rich heritage. India will host the First Health Ministers' Conference in 1999 which would help in evolving proposals for cooperation in this field.

The Report of the Group of Eminent Persons (GEP) was presented at the Tenth SAARC Summit. The Report contains important recommendations for strengthening cooperation in the economic and social field and for restructuring the Integrated Programme of Action. The SAARC leaders directed that the Report and recommendations of the GEP should be examined in depth by the SAARC Council of Ministers at their next session.

Post-summit meetings

SAARC group on customs cooperation

The Third Meeting of the SAARC Group on Customs Cooperation was held at Jaipur from August 24-26, 1998.

Several issues including exchange of information about positions to be taken at the WCO and the WTO on Harmonisation of Rules of Origin, revisions required to be incorporated in the new version of the Harmonised System of classification, Standardisation of Forms for Customs Declaration, Draft Agreement on Mutual Administrative Assistance for application of Customs Laws were discussed at the Meeting. The Meeting agreed on coordination amongst SAARC Customs Authorities for providing inputs for the Harmonised Rules of Origin and adoption of Common Formats for import/export declarations.

Conference on multi-lingual and multi-media information technology

A SAARC Conference on Multi-lingual and Multi-media Information Technology was held from 1-4 September, 1998 at Pune, India. Various facets of Information Technology relevant t(the SAARC countries were analysed and recommendations made for the spread of Information Technology in the region.

Technical committee on rural development

The Meeting of the Technical Committee on Rural Development took place in Colombo from 24-25 September, 1998 and agreed to the Indian proposal for establishing a Network of Experts in Rural Development including housing, water, sanitation. India will host a Seminar on Rural Poverty Alleviation early next year under the Technical Committee.

Informal meeting of SAARC foreign ministers at UNGA

The Informal Meeting of SAARC Foreign Ministers on 28 September, 1998 on the margins of the UNGA focussed on follow-up of the decisions taken at the Tenth SAARC Summit in Colombo in July 1998. It was agreed that the Third Round of SAPTA negotiations should be completed quickly. It was also agreed that the meeting of the Committee of Participants to consider the proposals for a downward revision of the national content requirements of the SAPTA Rules of Origin should be held immediately following the SAPTA-III talks in Kathmandu. Both these meetings have since been held.

An important decision taken by the Foreign Ministers was to consider joint SAARC initiatives, where possible, on issues before the UNGA. It was agreed that the Permanent Representatives to .the UN be mandated to consult regularly to evolve common. positions and common strategies.

The Ministers discussed the time-schedule of the various Ministerial meetings and stressed the need for proper sequencing and preparation. It was agreed that Ministerial Meetings should be preceded by preparatory official meetings. A detailed concept paper outlining the objectives sought to be achieved should also be circulated before the Meeting.

Meeting of finance secretaries and governors of Central Banks

The SAARC Finance Secretaries and Governors of Central Banks met for the first time at the margins of the Annual Meeting of the IMF - World Bank in Washington on October 5,1998. They decided to establish a network called "SAARC Finance" for exchange of information on developments in the region, specially related to exchange of Status Papers on Payment Systems in their respective countries, so that quicker settlement could be effected in respect of cross-border Trade flows. India is to prepare a monograph on this. Two issues viz. (a) Supervision of banking and non-banking financial entities and (b) Coordination between fiscal and monetary policies - were identified to be discussed in-depth at a meeting of officials of Central Banks. India proposed to host the meeting in Mumbai.

Technical committee on environment and meteorology

The Third Technical Committee Meeting on Environment and Meteorology was held in Kathmandu from 14-16 October. A format for the State of the Environment Report was prepared. It was also agreed to convene an Expert Group Meeting for Exchange of Information on Envirormental Standards. India offered to host, during the next year, a workshop on Sharing Information on Disaster Preparedness and Mitigation and two Expert Group Meetings (i) to draft an understanding on Transboundary Movement of Hazardous Wastes in the SAARC region and (ii) Expert Group Meeting for the proposed establishment of a Networking Mechanism to assist member countries for protection and preservation of the Environment.

SAARC Law conference

The Seventh SAARC LAW Conference was held in Colombo from 23 -25 October, 1998. The Chief Justice of India, Attorney General of India, Shri Ram Jethmalani, Urban Affairs Minister and a host of legal luminaries from India participated in the Conference.

Environment Ministers' meeting

The Fourth SAARC Environment Minister's Meeting was held in Colombo from October 31 to November 1, 1 998. A draft common SAARC position on Climate Change Issues on the eve of the Buenos Aires Meeting on Climate Change was adopted at the Meeting. The common SAARC position highlights the-need for determination of equitable emission entitlements as well as transfer of new and additional financial resources and environmentally sound technologies on concessional terms to developing countries. It expresses concern a ' t the attempt of some Annex-I Parties (Industrialized Countries) to link ratification of the Kyoto Protocol to the introduction of new commitments for non-Annex-I parties which will only delay the Protocol coming into force.

The SAARC Environment Ministers agreed to direct their focus on a single theme in each of their future meetings. They also agreed that Bio-Diversity should be the theme for the year 1999. The Government of India will host a Meeting on the trans-boundary movement of hazardous wastes and dumping of such wastes in the region by other countries. This Meeting would examine the implications of the coming into effect of the Basel Convention for the SAARC countries and also explore the possibility of harmonising policies and procedures with regard to hazardous wastes.

SAARC audio visual exchange programme (SAVE)

The seventeenth meeting of the SAARC Audio Visual Exchange Programme was held in New Delhi on 17-18 November, 1998.14 Radio and 11 TV Programmes, were selected by its Screening Committee. These Programmes will be broadcast/ telecast simultaneously in all SAARC countries. The Meeting also deliberated on various means to increase the SAARC profile in the Region. India offered to host a training programme on "On line Editing" for TV technicians from the Region.

Third round of SAPTA

The Third Round of Preferential Trade Negotiations under SAPTA concluded on 23 November, 1998 in Kathmandu. A total of 3456 tariff lines were covered under concessional tariffs. India offered more than half the concessions. The cumulative total concessions offered countrywise were: India: 1917, Bangladesh: 481; Pakistan: 295; Sri Lanka: 82; Nepal: 189; Bhutan: 124; Maldives : 368.

The Third Meeting of Committee of Participants was held in Kathmandu on 24-25 November, 1998. A consensus to revise the Domestic Content Requirements under the SAPTA Rules of Origin downward by ten percent was reached at the Meeting. Goods traded under the SAPTA Agreement will be covered under the revised rules of origin after endorsement by the SAARC Council of Ministers.

SAARC visa exemption scheme

An Expert Group Meeting on review and further expansion of the SAARC Visa Exemption Scheme was held in Kathmandu (November 25-26,1998). This Scheme was initiated in 1988 with a view to promote closer and frequent contacts among the people of the SAARC region and became operational from March 1, 1992. The Meeting recommended addition of 20 categories of persons who could travel within the SAARC Countries without visas. The Meeting also suggested various measures to improve the Scheme and make it more transparent and acceptable in all SAARC countries.

Draft convention on regional arrangements on the promotion of child welfare in South Asia

The decade 2001-2010 has been designated the "SAARC Decade of the Rights of the Child". An Expert Group Meeting to consider a draft Convention on the Promotion of Child Welfare was held in Male, Maldives from December 9-10, 1998. This will be further discussed by the Technical Committee on Health, Population and Child Welfare.

The Eighth meeting of the Governing Board of the SAARC Tuberculosis Centre took place on 6-7 January, 1999 in Kathmandu, Nepal. Inter-alia, the Governing Board decided on organising a SAARC-CIDA workshop on Control of TB and HIV cases in the Region, setting up of a lab- testing facility at the Centre, SAARC Training Programmes and a Multicentric Study on Primary Drug Resistance.

A two Weeks Executive Development Programme for Middle Level Officers of Nodal Development Financial Institutions was held at the Jawaharlal Nehru Institute for Development Banking, Hyderabad from January 11-23,1999.

The First Meeting cf Vice Chancellors of Open Universities in SAARC countries was held from January 25 to 27 in Colombo, Sri Lanka. The Meeting discussed issues of regional cooperation in the areas of Sharing of Resources including course module and personnel currently available from respective institutions, joint development of programmes /courses, evolving mechanisms for credit transfer, accumulation and accreditation and sharing information technology. A Task Force of three members (Sri Lanka, India and Maldives) was constituted to work out details of a Policy Formulation Body, an Academic Body, an Accreditation Body as well as drawing up of relevant protocols and identifying sources of funding.

The Thirteenth Technical Committee Meeting on Prevention of Drug Trafficking and Drug Abuse took place at Male, Maldives from 27-28 January, 1999. The discussions covered the issue of making the SAARC Drug Offences Monitoring Desk (SDOMD) in Colombo more effective. Other issues included control of drugs and precursor chemicals and rehabilitation of drug addicts.

A Seminar on Supervision of Banks and other Financial Entities in the SAARC Region was held in Pune from January 27-30,1999. Soundness of the financial system as an essential prerequisite for successful pursuit of macroeconomic, policies, importance of supervision by Central Banks, etc. was discussed in the Seminar.

The Sixth Governing Board Meeting of the SAARC Documentation Centre was held on February 5-6, 1999, in

New Delhi. It has been decided to launch a SAARC website which will provide information on all activities that have been held under the aegis of SAARC including reports, recommendations and studies for regional cooperation. In addition, training of documentation officials in SAARC countries, development of several value added databases like scientific research institutes in the region, alternate/ traditional forms of medical systems, periodicals and books published yearly, etc. will be undertaken by the SDC during the current year.

The Third SAARC Commerce Ministers' Meeting (February 2-3, 1999), preceded by the Tenth Meeting of the Committee on Economic Cooperation at the Commerce Secretary level (January 30-February 1, 1999), took place in Dhaka, Bangladesh. The Meeting decided that two preparatory Meetings should be held for coordination of SAARC positions at the forthcoming WTO Ministerial Meeting in the USA in November 1999. India offered to host the first of these two preparatory meetings. The Commerce Ministers approved the outcome of the Third Round of SAPTA negotiations and called for issuing notifications, giving effect to the Round, not later than October 1, 1999. They also decided that the Fourth Round of SAPTA negotiations should commence by the first half of August, 1999. The First Meeting of the Expert Group to commence drafting the SAFTA Treaty would also be held immediately thereafter. The Meeting approved the revision of the SAPTA Rules of Origin reducing the domestic /regional content requirement by 10 percent. The Meeting also decided to make a formal request to the European Commission to recognise SAARC as an association for according cumulative Rules of Origin for GSP Treatment.

The Seventeenth Meeting of the Technical Committee on Agriculture was held in New Delhi from

February 15-17,1999. A Draft Regional Perspective of the Status of Agriculture ill SAARC Countries was prepared by India and was adopted at the Meeting. A detailed analysis of the position of Horticulture in the SAARC Region was discussed and a compendium of the deliberations will be prepared. India has proposed to organise a Training-cum Demonstration Programme on Watershed Management Approach for minimising soil degradation. Two workshops on Nut Cropping and Soil Fertility Management for Increased Productivity in Rice based Cropping Systems will be held in the course of the year under this Technical Committee.

The following important meetings are likely to take place during the remaining part of the current year:

(i) Sixteenth Meeting of the Technical Committee on Science and Technology from February 24-26,1999 in New Delhi.

(ii) Programming and Standing Committees and the Council of Ministers Meetings in mid March 1999 in Colombo, Sri Lanka.

Review of SAARC functioning

Two review Reports on the functioning of SAARC were prepared during the year.

The first was the Report of the Independent Group of Experts on the functioning of the Integrated Programme of Action (IPA) with its eleven technical committees comprising Agriculture, Communications, Education, Culture & Sports, Environment & Meteorology, Health & Population activities, Prevention of Drug Trafficking & Abuse, Rural Development, Science & Technology, Tourism, Transport and Women's Development. The Report has suggested a moderate restructuring of the IPA with reduction of the number of Technical Committees to seven by amalgamation of several Committees, and the setting up of a new Committee on Energy.

The other, far reaching Report was by the Group of Eminent Persons constituted by the last Summit in Male (12-14 May, 1997). The mandate of the Group was to undertake a comprehensive appraisal of SAARC and identify measures, including mechanisms to further vitalise and enhance the effectiveness of the Association and develop a long range vision and formulate a Perspective Plan of Action, including a SAARC Agenda for 2000 and Beyond, which will spell out the targets that can and must be achieved by the year 2020. The Group submitted its Report to the Tenth SAARC Summit in Colombo in July 1998.

The GEP has identified the following focus areas

Economic agenda

On the economic side, the GEP has recommended a substantive agenda for achieving economic integration in three phases:

(i) Negotiation of a Treaty for a South Asian Free Trade Area (SAFTA) by 1999 with implementation commencing 2000. Achievement of SAFTA by 2008, stretching to 2(for the Least Developed Countries;

(ii) Achievement of a SAARC Customs Union with harmonisation of external tariffs by 2015; and

(iii) Achievement of SAARC Economic Union with harmonisation of monetary and fiscal policies by 2020.

The GEP has also recommended substantial concessions for the Least Developed Countries including a longer time period freeing trade.

Other proposals in the economic field include:

- Finalisation of a Regional Investment Agreement setting up a SAARC Investment Area before t commencement of SAFTA implementation;
- Harmonisation and simplification of Customs Procedures and upgradation of Customs Infrastructure;
- Harmonisation and conformance of Standards, Quality a ,3 Measurement;
- Development of Transportation Infrastructure and Tarnsit Facilities; Social Agenda.

In the Social field, the GEP has recommended:

- Commitment to the Target of reaching a replacement level of population which translates into a birth rate of 21 thousand before the year 2020;
- Attainment of universal primary education upto the a of 15 before the year 2010. Elimination of gender disparities in access to education within the target date of 2010;
- Setting aside 6% of GDP for reducation by the year 2010;
- Reduction of infant mortality below 50 per thousand live births by the year 2005. Attainment of 100% immunisation by the year 2000 in target areas set by the UNICEF programmes;
- Empowerment of women socially, economically and politically;
- Holding of regular biennial Ministerial meetings on Women's Development;

- Each member-State to set its own time-frame for poverty eradication;
- Effective utilisation of the SAARC three-tier mechanism on Poverty Alleviation to facilitate sharing of experiences and formulation and implementation of regional policies;
- Regular meetings at political and technical levels on the Environment. Urgent follow-up on the SAARC Plan of Action on the Environment.

The two Reports will be an issue of special consideration at the next Council of Ministers Meeting and an extra day would be set aside at the next Meeting of the Standing Committee of Foreign Secretaries for their detailed consideration.

Subregional cooperation Bangladesh-Bhutan-India-Nepal growth quadrangle (BBIN-6Q) initiative

The Second meeting of Foreign Secretaries of the four countries met in Kathmandu on 17 July, 1998 and finalised Working Modalities for Sub Regional Cooperation. The Growth Quadrangle is to follow a project led approach to cooperation in the core economic sectors of Multimodal Transportation and Communication, Energy, Trade and Investment Facilitation and Promotion, Tourism, Optimal Utilization of Natural Resource Endowments and Environment. These projects would result in tangible benefits to the people in the sub-region in the form of poverty eradication, employment and income generation, social welfare and improvement in the quality of life. These projects will be supportive of and complimentary to national plans of the countries in the Growth Quadrangle, to fully utilize their talent and resources as well as mobilize the participation of the private sector in the implementation of projects and activities identified collectively. The projects will develop and make best use of neighborhood synergies and would be such that they can most productively be dealt with on a sub-regional basis. The resources and expertise within the sub-region will be given priority and used to the maximum extent possible with resort to international resources and agencies depending on the requirements of specific projects and availability of internal resources. A prioritized, practical, action-oriented, time-bound and incremental approach will be followed in selection, development and implementation of projects having immediate impact as well as large infrastructure projects with long gestation.

A three-phase plan of action involving conceptualization of specific projects in the first phase, preparation of feasibility studies and financial estimates in the second phase and implementation of projects and schemes as and when they are ready in the third phase has been agreed upon. The first phase is to last for one year, the second phase to take two years, and the third phase to take between 5-10 years.

Nepal will continue to coordinate the overall sub-regional cooperation efforts. Nepal will also coordinate projects in the area of Tourism and Multi-Modal Transportation and Communication. Projects in the area of Natural Resource Endowments and Energy will be coordinated by Bangladesh. Bhutan will coordinate projects relating to the Environment. India will coordinate projects in the area of Trade and Investment Promotion and Facilitation.

2

External Affairs Since Independence

The kingpin of India's foreign policy has broadly been dictated by a principle of equidistance form the Superpower rivalry until the dissolution of the Soviet Union. In any assessment of India's role to ensure global peace, non-aligned movement played an important part. Although the movement never functioned on any bloc concept, it became the voice of vast multitudes of people spanning four continents belonging to the developing world.

The non-aligned movement was launched in Belgrade in 1961. Eminent statesmen who pioneered the movement were Prime Minister Jawaharlal Nehru, President Tito of Yugoslavia and President Gamel Nasser of Egypt. The movement which had only a handful of members initially later grew into a formidable number. The current chairmanship of Colombia, once believed to be an Americanally in Latin America, is a clear proof that the movement's appeal was spreading to South America, usually considered as "backyard" of US sphere of influence.

The disappearance of the Soviet Union brought an end to Superpower rivalry. It had its effect on the non-aligned movement. Except the coordinating bureau of non-aligned countries at the United Nations, the movement never though it appropriate to have a headquarters. This never gave rise to absence of cohesion in the movement's functioning. In contrast, the Organisation of Africa Unity (OAU) has its headquarters in Addis Ababa, while the Arab League is located in Caero.

Non-aligned movement could have been more powerful as a political force at international level had China preferred to join it. Mao Zedong divided the world into "three worlds" according to the level of economic development. Surely, China fitted in with the concept of "third world", embracing the developing countries. But at no point of time since 1961China a expressed the desire to be part of non-aligned movement, although China rightly belongs to the developing world.

India's third conribution to world peace came from its unremitting support to the anti-apartheid movement in South Africa and its support to decolonisation. New Delhi never gave up the cause of the black South Africans and the Black Africans in the rest of the continent, despite repression on their movement and denial of basic human rights by the colonising powers. One after the other, the French, Portuguese and Dutch colonisers left territories ruled by them. But South Africans were yet to see the light at the end of the tunnel.

The paths to peace and freedom and equal rights were strewn with thorns and hurdles were placed at all steps. the White rule became a blot on the world conscience. Denial to right to live brought an upsurge among the Black South Africans. In their struggle, they found India and the Indians settled there as a great source of inspiration. It was not because Mahatma Gandhi's association with South Africa in the initial years of his political life that made India so receptive to the aspirations of the Black South Africans.

Perhaps in the South African freedom movement and

struggle for equality was seen the same psyche of the Indian people who suffered humiliation, imprisonment and torture in India during the long independence struggle. Indians felt genuinely for the Black South Africans. So did the goverment.

In less than a decade's existence as an independent nation, India brought before the world a new concept of governance based on the principle of "Panchsheel". It was but natural for a country that has a long tradition of tolerance. India with numerous languages and multiplicity of religion itself symbolises co-existence. Mutual respect for each other, irrespective of differences, demonstrates Indian ethos.

It is in this context, the Bandung conference in April 1955 that adopted "Panchsheel" created a new concept for the world already handed over to violence and turmoil. The Bandung conference had five proponents: India, Indonesia, Burma, Sri Lanka and Pakistan. The Bandung conference was preceded by the bombing of the Air India plane carrying delegates and journalists over South China sea. Evidently, forces that wanted the settlement of disputes through terrorism asserted their right to show their way of solving issue and problems.

India's main foreign policy objectives are based on peaceful co-existence, self-reliance and co-operation, non-alignment, support for de-colonisation, disarmament, restructuring of the inequitous International Economic Order and the global fight against racialism. India's first Prime Minister, Jawaharlal Nehru, laid down the basic parameters of India's foreign policy and his unique contribution was the concept of non-alignment. The fundamental aim was to preserve India's freedom of option and decision-making in an autonomous way, in a world bristling with animosities and block antagonism.

Consistent with our traditional values, Nehru ceaselessly promoted the universal cause of disarmament, racial equality, international cooperation for economc develpment and the peaceful resolution of disputes and gave India a conceptual framework which was based on cooperative and peaceful co-existence and non-violence which we continue to adopt in evolving our foreign policy. Basic considerations which governed the structuring of our foreign policy and its implementation are: preservation of India's national identity as a plural democratic and secular society, India's territorial integrity, and well-being of our people. Indian peace-keeping operations formed an element in India's foreign policy, being reflective of India's desire to play a positive role to promote normality at a time of need on the part of certain friently developing countries in difficulties.

Indo-Nepal relations which have been a long tradition of friendship and shared history and culture continued to develop smoothly during 1994-95. Several high-level visits took place between India and Nepal which include the crown prince of Nepal's first official visist abroad to India in August 1994. India-Nepal economic relations also gained from the liberalisation of both economies and from the stable and positive framework provided by the Treaties of Trade and Transit. Nepalese exports to India during 1993-94 were worth Rs. 1,176.3 million and imports from India were worth Rs. 7,874.63 million. The new Sirsiya bridge at the Raxaul border linking the two countries at the point where the traffic in goods and people is the heviest, was completed. The Rajbiraj industrial estate was formally handed over to Nepal.

Economic cooperation between India and Bhutan has provided a solid basis for a close and warm relationship marked by mutual understanding. the King of Bhutan,

Jigme Singye Wangchuk visited India privately in December 1994 when he met the President and the Prime Minister. india is actively involved in implementing portions of Bhutan's Seventh Five Year Plan (1992-97). Major projects such as the airport terminal building at Paro, Kurichu Hydel Project in Eastern Bhutan, hospitals, schools, roads and bridges, transmission lines, rural electrification, survey project, etc., are underway. India also continued to cooperate with Bhutan in the field of higher education, survey and training, and for renovation of culturally important places.

The level of interaction between India and Bangladesh remained high during 1994-95 by exchange of several high level visits. The first meeting of Indo-Bangladesh Joint Working Group took place in New Delh to discuss, *inter alia,* security-related issues, cross-border movements, the existing visa regime, and the situation along Indo-Bangladesh border. The Border Security Force and the Bangladesh Rifles also held talks in New Delhi and Dhaka to discuss illegal immigration of Bangladesh is into India, trans-border crimes and repatriation of Chakma refugees from Tripura to Bangladesh. During February to August 1994, 5,198 Chakma refugees from Tripura were repatriated to Bangladesh strictly on voluntary basis.

Inspite of India's efforts for arriving at a long-term comprehensive and equitable arrangement on water-sharing, Bangladesh continued to raise the issue in international fora. On 20 December 1994, the Bangladesh Festival of Arts was inaugurated jointly by the Bangladesh Ministry for Cultural Affairs and India's Deputy Ministry of Education and Culture in New Delhi. The second meeting of the Indo-Bangladesh Joint Business Council was held in Dhaka in August 1994. On 4 January 1995, Bangladesh Railway signed a US dollar 10 million agreement with RITES to purchase 10 diesel metre gauge locomotives. India's exports to Bangladesh in 19930-94 were valued at Rs. 1,349.69 crore while imports from Bangladesh were Rs. 56.09 crore.

India's working relationship with Myanmar continued to improve during 1994-95. There were several exchanges of visits between India and Myanmar. During the visit of a Survey delegation from Myanmar to India, operational matters relating to boundary demarcation were discussed. Official level talks with Myanmar for operationalisation of the Border Trade Agreement were held in January 1995. Twenty-eight trainees from Myanmar came to India in 1994-95 for course on farm machinery, computers, news agency operations, journalism, survey, diplomacy, banking, railways and telecommunications. India continued to support the restoration of democratic government in Myanmar.

Relations with Sri Lanka continued to be based on friendship, understanding and good neighbourliness. India conveyed her interest in further boosting bilateral ties to Chandrika Bandarnaike Kumaratunga who assumed office as Prime Minister in August 1994. India also expressed her shock at the tragic assasination of UNP Presidential candidate and offered the forensic and ballistic assistance in the investigation of the assasination. The Sri Lankan Foreign Minister visited India in October 1994 and briefed the Indian leadership about the Sri Lanka Government's agenda including the peace process, constitutional reforms and economic policies and stressed Sri Lanka's keenness for sound and cordial relations with India and the Government of India fully reciprocated these sentiments.

The second session of the Indo-Sri Lanka Joint Commission held in New Delhi in April 1994 decided on several measures such as the restoration of preferential tariff margins on Sri Lankan cloves, reduction in tariffs on select items of export interest to Sri Lanka such as ceramic tiles, glycerine, graphite and rubber; extension of a new line of dollar-denominated credit; permission to Bank of Ceylon to open a branch in Madras; and enhanced seat capacity for airlines following civil aviation talks in July 1994. Indo-Sri Lanka trade stood at Rs. 877.3 crore from January to August 1994 with exports valued at Rs. 830.8 crore and imports from Sri Lanka valued at Rs. 46.5 crore. About 8,000 Sri Lankan Tamil refugees returned to their home country in 1994 on a voluntary basis.

The traditionally close and friendly relations with Maldives were further strengthned and consolidated during 1994-95. President Maumoon Abdul Gayoom pad a State visit to India in March 1994 and held wide ranging talks with Indian leaders. There were also visits by a parliamentary delegation led by the Speaker of the Citizens' *Majlis,* Maldives Minister of State for National Defence and Security for discussions regarding the operations of Air Maldives to India, which began shortly thereafter, and by Minister of Health and Welfare of Maldives. Ships of the Indian Coast Guard visited Maldives in April 1994 and conducted joint exercises with the ships of Maldivian National Security Service. The Indira Gandhi Memorial Hospital at Male commenced out-patient work on 15 October 1994 where 56 Indian deputationists are stationed to help start work in the hospital. Fifty-nine Maldivian nominees received training in India during 1994-95 in various fields such as medicine, nursing, etc.

India-Pakistan bilateral relations continued to show a downward trend. Pakistan's sustained efforts to internationalise the Kashmir issue, its unabated support to subversion and terrorism directed against India, its intransigence on the issue of resumption of a bilateral dialogue with India, and its persistent negative approach have vitiated the atmosphere and prevented and meaningful progress in bilateral relations. In addition to training, equipping, funding and guiding militants, Pakistan has stepped up its transborder terrorism by inducting mercenaries from third countries into Jammu and Kashmir. India has strongly urged Pakistan to conduct inter-state relations as a responsible member of the international community and to eschew the threat of terrorism held against India. Consistent with her policy to resolve defferences with Pakistan bilaterally and peacefully in accordance with the Shimla Agreenment, India has conveyed to Pakistan on several occasions her readiness for the resumption of bilateral dialogue without any preconditions. In March 1994, Foreign Secretary renewed the offer for the resumption of Foreign Secretary-level talks. The Minister of State for External Affairs, Shri R.L. Bhatia reiterated India's offer of dialogue when he met Pak Foreign Minister in July 1994 at Dhaka. Foreign Secretary followed this up with a letter to his Pakistan counterpart inviting him for talks. On 3 November 1994, India once again formally conveyed to Pakistan her offer for dialogue. During his visit to Islamabad in November 1994 to attend the Commonwealth Senior Officials Meeting (COSM), Foreign Secretary conveyed to his Pak counterpart India's readiness to discuss all bilateral issues. The Human Resource Development Minister during his visit to Pakistan to attend the Common-wealth Education Ministers Meeting (November 1994) reiterated India's desire for normalisation of relations. Unfortunately, Pakistan's response has been conditional and negative.

India propose on 7 April and 12 July 1994 to hold consultation for a review of the implementation of the Code of Conduct for treatment of diplomatic/consular personnel in India and Pakistan, in the light of numerous incidents of intimidatory surveillance and harassment meted out to the Indian diplomatic officials and their family members posted in Indian Missions in Pakistan. This proposal, however, did not find favour with Pakistan. Pakistan has persisted with her restrictive visa policy and other negative measures which further impeded people-to-people contacts between the two countries. On 17 March 1994, Pakistan unilaterally and without justification announced the closure of its Consulate in Bombay. Subsequently, on 26 December 1994, Pakistan asked India to close down the Indian Consulate General in Karachi. These actions of Pakistan are regret-table and are patently designed to create perception of tension between the two countries. Pakistan also assumed an exaggerated air of panic towards the isolated reports of incidents of plague in India.

Pakistan's campaign to internationalise and communalise the Kashmir issue continued. At the 50th session of the UNHRC (March 1994), Pakistan had decided to move a resolution on the Human Rights situation in Jammu and Kashmir and aggressively campaigned for support but, subsequently, withdrew its resolution at the behest of a number of friendly countries. At the 49th session of the UNGA, Pakistan made yet another attempt to table a resolution. However, this attempt also failed. In the face of Pakistan's campaign of Jammu and Kashmir issue, India apprised the international community of the politically motivated act by Pakistan and emphasised that all outstanding issues between the two countries need to be resolved peacefully and bilaterally within the framework of the Shimla Agreement.

There have been some high level exchanges with Afghanistan in 1994 in spite of the unstable conditions in that country. Afghan Minister for Civil Aviation visited New Delhi twice in Macrh and July 1994 as a Special Envoy of Afghan President. Afghan Ministers for Martyrs and Disabled Affairs and for Agriculture paid visits to

India in 1994. India has been able to resume some technical cooperation (training facilities, scholarships, medical facilities, etc.) during 1994. India has an abiding concern for welfare and prosperity of the Afghan people. During 1994, India supplied tea, medicines, etc., worth Rs. one crore as relief assistance to Afghanistan. India stands for a united, stable, non-aligned and independent Afghanistan, and supports a peaceful political settlement which is acceptable to all sections of the people of Afghanistan and the ongoing peace initiative of the UN, and stands ready to make a contribution to peace efforts.

In 1972 Prime Minister Indira Gandhi emphasized at the UN Conference on Human Environment at Stockholm that the removal of poverty is an integral part of the goal of an environmental strategy for the world. The concepts of interrelatedness, of a shared planet, of global citizenship, and of 'spaceship earth' cannot be restricted to environmental issues alone. They apply equally to the shared and interlinked responsibilities of environment and development. The global community must address the issue of global development in order to move towards and environmentally sound planet.

But the problem of poverty remains as serious today as it was then. Speaking recently at the opening meeting of UNCTAD at Colombia, UN Secretary-General Boutros Boutros Ghali emphasized poverty as one of the most urgent issues facing the international community. It is the goal of removing poverty, of development at the global level, which must be addressed if environmental problems are to be tackled.

The South has a difficult task ahead of it. It has to achieve economic development with minimum damage to its environment, for this alone can sustain development. Unlike colonial powers that could exploit the vast resources of their colonies and industrialize rapidly, and pollute the global ecosystem, the developing countries today are searching for more sustainable and environment friendly solutions. But these solutions have a cost. The developing countries would require access to the latest technologies that would enable them to avoid the dirty-industry route to development.

History has led to vast inequalities, leaving almost three—fourths of the world's people living in less developed countries and one-fifth below the poverty line. The long—term impact of past industrialization, exploitation and environmental damage cannot be wished away. It is only right that development in the remaining part of this century and in the next be more conscious of its long—term impact. Our common future can only be achieved with a better understanding of our shared responsibility. Shared responsibility for the present and the past.

At a global level, the common future depends on sustaibable use of natural resources. The current pattern of development based on high resource consumption, high waste and low recycling, as practised in the North, is not sustainable and yet it is in this direction that much of the South is heading.

The alternative paradigm of improving standards of living without inflicinting heavy environmental damage poses its own problems. Many of the technologies required are new, some are as yet being developed. the major costs of pollution control, and the limiting options from an environmental point of view, are factors that the early developing countries in the North did not have to consider. However, it is the cost of these more stringent norms that is the price of development today. These costs need to be shared if the developing countries of the South are to follow an alternative path. A path that bypas the route of severe environmental damage.

Sharing responsibility means sharing costs, rather than charity or aid. Funding mechanisms that are essentially donor driven need to be replaced by moe open participatory mechanisms which involve developed and developing nations. It si inherent in the concept of shared responsibility that funding becomes obligatory, rather than an optional charity. It is only on this basis that we can approah the building of a common future.

Developing countries are equal partners in any process that discusses global issues like environment and development. Their inputs are essential in decision—making to bring in local perspectives and to prevent generalized solutions. Evolving alternatives can only be done through a proper understanding of the local situation. This is best done where decision-making is not centralized.

Environmental standards and mechanisms to deal with environmental issues also need to be worked out on a country by country basis, if not in a more decentralized way. An international funding mechanism or a trade policy should not become the insturment to impose environmental conditionalities.

The countries of the south are among the richest in terms of biodiversity. This biodiversity is the source of a number of products that today benefit all humankind. Advances in biotechnology have increased the range of products in pharmaceuticals, agriculture etc. by modifying and combining the genetic resources collected largely from the South. With the much greater financial and research capability in the North, these new products are being made available through companies of the developed world. When the original genetic resources was collected there was no payment made to the country from which it came.

Today these living resources are being patented and sold aback, often to the very countries from which the original genes may have been taken.

Issues of biodiversity must be discussed along with the sharing of biotechnology, sharing of the results of R & D and the commercial benefits derived from the bio-materials. The traditional knowledge base of the rural and indigenous communitites is usually the starting point for identifying particular species for particular applications. This must be kept in mind in any discussion of intellectual property rights (IPR) related to biotechnology. Indigenous communities have over centuries worked towards developing and improving crop varieties. For instance the more than 50,000 varieties of rice found in India have provided a tremendous base for research on rice. One recognizes that biotechnology research must be adequately compensated. But mechanisms other than the presently prevalent system of intellectual property rights are required. The researcher has to be compensated without restricting use as implied in IPR.

Access to environment friendly technologies also needs to be easier and much more widespread. In many cases, existing technologies would need to be replaced. The cost of the new technologies and of pollution control mechanisms is likely to be higher than that of the older processes. However it is important that the wrong decision is not taken owing to short—term financial constraints faced by developing countries. Mechanisms would therefore have to be found to subsidize this change over.

India shares the concern about ozone depletion and understands the need for coordinated action in this area. But it also recognizes that the problem has essentially been created by the developed countries who must also accept the principal responsibility for it. A situation cannot be accepted which while reducing emission levels of CFCs in the North, prohibits even the small levels of CFC-use that arise from refrigeration and other requirements which are, if anything, more necessary in the much hotter tropical countries of the South. The solution is in terms of a quicker and less costly method of transferring the newly developing alternative technologies to the South with international funding mechanisms bearing part of the costs.

India has expressed these concerns in relation to the Montreal Protocol, and now amendments have been made to enable countries such as India to sing it. Of course it must be realized that even today India's CFC consumption is far below levels presecribed by the Protocol. But India has constituted a task froce to draft its own strategy for containing CFC consumption within the country.

Global warming is another concern that India shares with the international community. The scientific basis for calculating some of the figures related to this issue are being debated at the international level and India is bringing its perspective into this discussion. But apart from the details, India is of the view that developed countries, whose total emissions are far larger than those of the South, must shoulder the principal burden of bringing down emissions so that there is a uniform, sustainable per capita emission level. It is inevitable that in this process, countries which are developing will invariably have an increase in emission levels of greenhouse gases arising out of the development process.

In the final analysis, as Mr. Kamal Nath, India's Minister for Environment and Forests, said at the special session of the UNEP Governing Council at Nairobi in February 1992, "It is not a question of assistance or aid, but of global partnership in working towards making our planet healthier, safer and more productive."

International Cooperation

India realizes the vital need for international cooperation, bilateral and multilateral programmes and regional initiatives in dealing with issues of environment and development. At the governmental level, the Ministry of Environment and Forests acts as a nodal agency for relations with international agencies like UNEP, SACEP, IUCN, World Bank, FAO, UNDP, SAARC and EEC, Independently, NGOs in India have taken several initiatives towards global cooperation and exchanges of ideas. They have, through dealing with international NGOs and participation in international forums, created awareness of a South perspective. They have played an important part in highlighting some inherent shortcomings in international thinking and in international conventions.

India acceded to the Vienna Convention for the Protection of the Ozone Layer (March 1985). Under this framework Convention, the Montreal Protocol on Substances that Deplete the Ozone Layer was adopted in September 1987. This Protocol lays down a timetable for the phasing out of the more widely used CFCs. The Protocol came into force on 1 January 1989. India refused to sign it because of the regional treatment given to developing countries and the large economic burden which would have to be borne by them even though they have contributed almost nothing to the problem. In June 1990 the parties tot he Protocl agreed to comprehensive amendments so that developing countries such as India could participate in the global action without deterimental effects to their economies. India would be able to accede to the Protocol once the London amendments came into force. In any case, India is at present far below the targets specified by the Montreal Protocol.

India signed the Convention on the Conservation of

Migratory Species of Wild Animals (the Bonn Convention) in 1979. The convention came into force on 1 November 1983. The Convention on Protection of Migratory Birds between India and the former USSR was retified by both countries and came into force in 1986.

India has received financial and technical support for environment related projects from multilateral institutions like the World Bank, FAO, UNDP, UNIDO and EEC. On a bilateral basis, USA, UK, Japan, Canada, Sweden, Germany, the Netherlands, France, Norway, Australia, and some other countries have been collaborating extensively with India.

India is signatory to the International Convention for the Prevention of Pollution of the sea by Oil, 1954 (LOndon); the international convention on Civil Liability for Oil Pollution Damage (as amended), 1969 (Brussels); the International Covention on the Establishment of an International Fund for Compensation for Oil Pollution Damage (as amended), 1971 (Brussels); the Protocol of 1978 relating to the International Convention for the Prevention of Pollution from Ships; the United Nations Convention on the Law of the Sea, 1982 (Montege Bay); and the Basel Convention on the Control of Transboundary Movements of Hazardous Wastes and their Disposal.

To further India's efforts toward South cooperation and to evolve a common strategy among the developing countries to deal with global environmental issues, and international conference of 21 developing countries was hosted by India in New Delhi in April 1990. As a follow-up to this, a ministerial level Conference of Developing Countries was organized by the People's Republic of China in Beijing in June 1991, which was the first such conference of developing countries. At this conference, the 41 participating countires adopted a declaration which articulates the concerns of these countries. India participated actively in putting forward the concerns of the Group of 77 countries. G-77's initiatives at the Preparatory Committee Meeting held in Geneva in 1991 have emphasized the centrality of certain developmental considerations in the agenda of UNCED.

In the formulation of foreign policy of any nation, the determining principle is its long-term goal. A large degree of flexibility and predictability is its final reliance and resource.

India's foreign policy, in this broad perspective, has been guided by its commitment to world peace. It is little wonder that India should choose the path of non-alignment right from the beginning as a free nation since 1947.

While assessing India's contribution to world peace over the past half a century, I have chosen to concentrate on the principal pillars on which rest the edifice of foreign policy that has stood the scrutiny of the Indian people. Indian domestic policy has been subject of intense debate by diverse political entities but the foreign policy has almost enjoyed a monopoly of public opinion based on the principle of consensus.

In the order of importance, Indian policy on nuclear-free world and elimination of nuclear weapons aimed at achieving a comprehensive disarmament within a time-frame has been widely acclaimed all the world over.

It is an unequal world in which we live, and also a world in which political expendiency is placed above morality. The 15th century born Italian statesman and political philosopher Machiavelli may have died his physical death in 1527. But his spirit lives on and his doctrine of statecraft indealing with foreign relations still is a guidding star for many nations.

The latest battle that India fought was on the issue of Comprehensive Test Ban Treaty (CTBT) at Geneva and New York. Almost single-handed India put up a lone fight against virtually the rest of the world with the exception of a few likeminded countries. It looked like an instance of being stonewalled by representatives of countries led by nuclear-haves both at the United Nations and at the Conference on Disarmament in Geneva.

Even when it was known that India under no circumstances would agree to the CTBT draft, rest of the delegates representing their respective countries listened to India's point of view with bated breath. Till the last moment India stubbornly stuck to its policy decision that there was no in-between position on total nuclear disarmament.

Critics of India accused it of being inflexible, and the main charge against New Delhi was that it lacked realism in asking for disarmament under a time bound programme. Instead, experts argued that a time-frame of 10 years was realistic. Between now and the end of cold war with the collapse of the Soviet Union in 1991, the global nuclear arsenal has come down to half. Interestingly, the former Soviet President Mikhail Gorbachev's last call for total elimination of nuclear weapons had also set a time limit for 10 to 12 years. In the early nineties nuclear warheads were put at 57,000. This means that more than 28,000 nuclear weapons are still in the possession of nuclear weapon states.

While advocating a step-by-step approach to eliminate nuclear weapons, none of the states possessing them has ever wished to take the first step and make any firm commitment for their elimination.

Among the five permanent Security Council members, China is the only Asian nuclear weapon state. In his analysis of India and the CTBT, Director of Institute for Defence Studies Analyses Jasjit Singh said in the Institute's September 1996 issue, "there are major uncertainties about the future strategic scenario (in Sino-Indian relations)."

Jasjit Singh says: "it needs to be recalled that China carried out a nuclear test within hours of giving a commitment (during the NPT extension conference in 1995) that required the utmost restraint in carrying out nuclear explosions. It has continued to test since then at sites less than 1,000 kilometres from India. According to reports, the US Defence Secretary stated that China has been providing nuclear weapon technlogy to Pakistan in the recent past."

The world knows that India's concern about nuclear proliferation relates to China possessing a nuclear arsenal. That China's sole objective was to become a nuclear weapon state is evident from the fact that China neglected the peaceful use of neclear energy until late eighties. Ten years after China had experimented with its first successful nuclear test in 1964, India entered the nuclear scene for the first time in 1974 and there it has ended,. Besides, Pakistan has a clandestine nuclear programme fully assisted by Chinese technology. For the first time, China publicly asserted that India must ratify the CTBT. A conclusion is inescapable that those who wanted India to ratify the CTBT would have liked to see that India's security interests are mortgaged to other countries.

As the set of Asian economies achieving impressive economic performance has expanded from the Gang of Four (Korea, Taiwan, Singapore and Hong Kong) to many more (e.g., Thailand, Malaysia, Indonasia and that largest of them all, China), the South Asian region is more of an exception in not participating in this economic transformation in the continent. As the economies to India,

Pakistan, Bangladesh, Nepal and Sri Lanka adjust to the requirements of the newly emerging global economic scenario and restructure their economies of face the new challenges, is there any scope for co-operation and co-ordination? The answer is unambiguously yes. The South Asian Association for Regional Cooperation (SAARC) was born of such perception in December, 1985.

Whatever the achievements and weaknesses of SAARC there is not denying that this regional organisation has created an overall atmoshphere in which it is possible to communicate on regional perspective as viewed from each nation's vantage point. Placed below are a few important economic issues which should be on the agenda for co-operation among the nations present at this conference.

Promoting trade and investment between the countries of the South Asian region is a venture which will benefit them all in course of time. Intra-regional trade is not only less than 3 per cent of the total foreign trade of these countries at present but the share has declined in the eighties. India has large trade surpluses with individual countries in the region. There are pressures from neighbouring countries on India to throw its markets open. While India is passing through a phase of lowering its foreign trade barriers as part of the ongoing process of globalisation, promotion of trade with the SAARC countries is better pursued within the framework Sapta agreement such as (South Asian Preferential Trade Agreement). A framework agreement of SAPTA was signed by SAARC countries and adopted in April, 1993, and concessions by individual countries are to be worked out by December, 1993. Progress on this front, however, has been slow, and Pakistan in particuar has been very slow in the follow up.

An active exploration of trade possibilities and choices within the region does not preclude the option of globalising the individual economies to gain access to investment, technology and markets. Working within a regional framework creates an atmosphere in which some bilateral irritants (e.g., Pakistan's refusal to grant Most Favoured Nation Treatment to India) are easier resolved. Growing economic inter-dependence among countries of the region is also in the long run interest of peace in the region.

The importance of regional infrastructure utilising the enormous potential provided by the resources of the region cannot be emphasised enough. The possibilities and potential in the area of water resources has been extensively analysed in numerous studies at the Centre for Poicy Research. The most recent study concludes that the differences that divide the nations which share the Ganga-Brahamputra-Meghna basin and the quantitative values involved in their water disputes are relatively small compared to the far greater benefit that each of them could realise through co-operation. It recommends that numerous trade-offs can be considered in order to even out specific gains and losses so that South Asia will emerge a stronger region.

In the critical area of food security, steps have already been taken to build a SAARC Food Security Reserve which came into force on August 12, 1988. The Reserve consists of 241,580 tonnes of foodgrains of which India's contribution has been 63 per cent. While the Reserve has not been utilised so far, it holds out the promise of crucial assistance in critical times of need.

As for the common goal of poverty alleviation from the region, there is need for exchanging information and experience in direct programmes for poverty alleviation. The Report of the Independent South Asian Commission on Poverty Alleviation (1992) which was discussed at the

7th SAARC summit in April, 1993, is a good beginning. It was agreed at the summit that a national level pro-poor plan would be drawn up by each member state and the experience and progress will be compared at the next SAARC summit. Co-operation and concerted effort to fight poverty in the region must remain the top priority for the countries of the region.

Objective conditions are emanating from international change for building a conflict-free cooperative South Asia. Subjective inputs are still lacking, but those who have the destinies of one-sixth of humankind in their hand are coming under increasing pressure from the objective realities that are pathways to a new world order.

The world's growth area has shifted from Europe to the Asia-Pacific. The EEC has shown the way how nations, despite their resistance to parting with national sovereignty, are laying the foundations of economic and technological supranationalism, leading, sooner rather than later, to the foundation of willingly diminished political sovereignty. The Asia-Pacific region is much more diverse and larger than Western Europe. It is a region mostly of newly independent states who carry on their bodies the scars from their struggles for national revolution. In this region, too, several cooperative groupings are either in the process of forming or are conceptually in the air. President Clinton talks of a new Pacific Community and has plans to convene an informal summit next year of the members of the Asia-Pacific Economic Community, which is still to be formally launched. Japan's diplomacy is now vigorously seeking an area of "PARTNERSHIP" with ASEAN and other Asia-Forum with which several non-ASEAN countries like the Indo-China states, China, Japan, the US and even Russia are linked. It is committed to the creation of an ASEAN common market. Gorbachev's cry for an Asia-Pacific Helsinki is now echoed faintly by Bill

Clinton and loudly by President Nazarbayev of Kazhakstan. The US, Japan and Korea, together with Taiwan and Hong Kong, are thinking in terms of setting up an East Asian caucus. In the Western hemisphere the U.S. Canada and Mexico have signed an agreement to establish a North American Common Market. Nations of Latin America are in the process of engineering two or perhaps three regional grouping. To be sure, none of these groupings, whether formed or in the process of forming, are from those who have had the old order in their grip for several decades.

South Asia, home of one fifth of human kind, is still lagging behind other regions in coming together for faster economic development and common security. However, SAARC is now committed to create the region as a preferential trade bloc by 1997. Not al SAARC members are equally ethusiastic about the idea, but the fact that none has rejected it is evidence enough to forecast that this conflicted region too cannot live in conflict and in isolation from one another for a long time. The convergences that we see around South Asia cannot skip over our region. In the medium run, Indians and Pakistanis will become good, if not friendly neighbours. Regional cooperation in peace, development and security is now on the agenda of each nation of South Asia and of the region as a whole. As and when the South Asians build their own regional system of economic and security cooperation, they will have to learn from the history of conflicts and from their own indigenous civilsations and heritages. They will need to renounce the use or even the threat of use of force to settle disputes and differences. They will have to resolve their territorial disputes through negotiations. They will not interfere in one another's internal affairs nor allow their respective territories to be used against the inerest of other members of the regional community. Bilateral and regional treaties of cooperative security will guarantee their individual and collective territorial unity, integrity and soveregnty. This will make it possible for them to do with the minimum essential defence expenditures and harvest a peace dividend that will be used to improve people's, conditions of living.

Mass poverty is a cause for insecurity of regimes and states, and South Asia has the dubious distinction of being the home of the world's largest mass of poor and deprived humanity. The countries of South Asia must rebuild their own domestic orders with creation of wealth. From a preferential trade area in theory as well as practice, they have to graduate to a South Asian common market. They will have to create a South Asian pool of technologies and share the benefits of imported high technology. They must learn that improvement in living conditions in any one of the countries countributes to the advancement of the region as a whole. Freindly competition must be the other side of the coin of friendly cooperation.

In a new South Asian order, no nation must aspire after hegemony or sphere of influence. Each one will be the equal of the others. In building relationships with extra-regional powers, each member of the South Asian community will ensure that the interests of no other members are hurt. The weak in the community must receive the constant attention of the strong in the filed of economy and technology. To the extent possible, the community must coordinate and harmonise their increasing international trade. To the maximum degree possible, they must trade directly with one another. Customs barriers will be gradually lifted. South Asians must be able to travel freely with dignity and honour throughout the region, and build regional tourist facilities so that the region a whole becomes a major international tourist attraction. Differences will always arise between and among nations. Cooperation, practised for long years, will minimise differences, as it has happened in ASEAN.

Finally, South Asia will have to fall in line with regional and global trends. One of the most important trends is that institutions, practices and outlooks are becoming more alike across national frontiers. Economic and technological convergences are pressing for national political and defence convergences. Governments are being judged not by their claims to ideological enthusiasm or rectitude, but by their performance. Performance is now determined by answers to a set of questions. Are governments practising or inhibiting development? Are they ensuring a fair distribution of the benefits of development to the weak and are they protecting those who need social protection? Are they improving the quality of life of ordinary people and protecting the environment for their children? Are they conducting foreign policies in ways that reinforce the security and national pride of their regional collectivities. Are the governments being run for the benefit of the governed?

South Asia must leave behind its legacy of confrontations and conflicts and import from the world and retrieve from its own ancient heritage and culture qualities of cooperative peace, development and security, its leaders and peoples must take up in earnest the long-delayed task of resolving bilateral differences and disputes, and impart to SAARC the synergy of creative regionalism. All countries of South Asia are now democracies. It is imperative therefore of each nation and of the region as a whole to improve the quality of life of its teeming poor and deprived humanity. More than one-half of the billion-plus population in the region lives in abject conditions. South Asia has lived for almost fifty years obsessed with its historical cleavages. Now, as the planet moved towards the third millennium, South Asia must look to the future and build itself as a peer of other regions, which have joined the efforts of likeminded nation-states in collective endeavours to improve the quality of life of the governed.

South Asia is unaware of the rich natural and human resources of the seven nations that constitute the regional community. Now, in the post cold war world, the region is baffled and bewildered by the complexities of its humanscape. Its governments are strained by confrontations and conflicts at the bilateral level, weakened by the failure of the member states to build bridges of cooperation, and afflicted by domestic ethnic and religious cleavages that take a heavy toll of human life. While several other regions of the world have made impressive progress in regional cooperation for development and security, South Asia, home of ancient civilisations and great religions, lags behind them in making the best use of economic and technological convergences that are the hallmark of the era initiated by the end of the cold war.

Insurgencies, ethnic conflicts, caste clashes, sectarian violence, drug traffic, custodial deaths, violation of human rights, and religious fanaticism conspire together to keep South Asia in the backwoods of the modern world. Behind these effusions and fusillades of blood and hatred, however, lies an uprecedented awakening of the long-inert poor and deprived in a region whose societies are mutli-lingual, multi-ethnic, multi-cultural and multi-religious. A South Asia governed on the high principles of social justice and human resource development, will also be a South Asia of good neighbourliness and regional cooperation.

Leadership failures over a long period of time has created a broad divide between People and Power. Entrenched power structures resist participatory democracy with the principle of self-government extended to the frontier village. These interests, sometime linked with external forces, have places a high premium on conflicts and cleavages between South Asian countries. Power structures are often uninterested in horizontal development and unwilling to part with the enormous power and privilege they have enjoyed since independence.

It is the imperative of the presenet and future generations of South Asian peoples to work for a region that will match ASEAN and other regional communities in cooperative development and security. South Asian leaders must without further loos of time address themselves earnestly to conflict management, control and resolution, peaceful solution of divisive issues, the formation, stage by stage, of a common market and a free trade area, giving protection at the same time to weaker industries, and establishing a regional pool of technologies. South Asians must be able to resolve their differences without the intervention of outside powers. Peace is always an offspring of give-and-take, live-and-let-live, of compromises with dignity. Absolutist positions do not make peace.

Above all, South Asians must develop an elevating vision of the future. Their visions must be hewn from the constructive, integrative and cooperative trends and processes released by the collapse of the Berlin Walls of the cold war, not from the rhetoric of threats, and conflicts that still proliferate in the planet. Only united and together can South Asia, in cooperation with other regional organisations in the developing world, sucessfully frustrate efforts by the developed to keep the developing majority of the international community at a level of technological and economic inferiority.

All national constitutions have something akin to a bill of rights, howsoever named. Derogations are permitted but the frequency and facility with which these have been resorted to calls for introspection and review. South Asian nations should be urged to subscribe to various international covenants and instruments and, having done so, must ratify them expenditously. National laws should be reviewed and, where necessary, upgraded to measure up to these international commitments.

The right to development and poverty alleviation is imperative. South Asia must cooperate to improve the quality of life of its people. But all rights are indivisible and there is no hierarchy of rights.

It would be useful to establish links between official and NGO human rights organisations in the region. SAARC could consider an initiative in this regard by establishing a small human rights cell. Strengthening and closer monitoring of the criminal justice system in countries of the region would go far towards underpinning human rights. Special courts could be one remedy. These could promote specialisation and avoid undue delay. Cross-border violations, drug traffiking and migration pose common problems and common danger. Mutual discussion and special mechanisms might be considered to concert action and defuse tensions.

Awareness and legal aid are prime factors in promoting human rights and environmental protection.

Primary education and health and population control are of fundamental importance for the region. They merit the highest priority in national planning, investments and implementation.

South Asia should develop a common approach to the protection and advancement of its tribal populations who should be encouraged to develop in accordance with their own genius without being treated as separate groups divorced from the mainstream of national life and aspirations of which they are an integral and equal part.

South Asia is made up of plural societies embracing a rich diversity. This plurality, including all minorities, must enjoy equal rights and opportunities.

South Asian societies are deeply religious. There must be respect for all faiths, cultures and traditions. Fundamentalism of whatever brand, poses a threat to harmony and stability in each country and must be constructively countered through education and dialogue.

The environment is a trust. The countries of the region must work to pursue and accelerate policies that will stem degradation and start a restorative process. All new programmes, equipment and infra-structure should be based on upgraded environmental norms. All must strive to conserve nature, promote sustainability, avoid waste and ostentatious consumerism, and ensure greater equity.

While South Asia's environmental concerns are linked to subsistence and survival, it must be willing to cooperate to ameliorate global environmental problems. SAARC should endeavour to evolve a common aproach towards dealing with these global issues and environmental protocols under discussion.

The foregoing discussion would re-emphasise our contention at the beginning of this paper that the choices available to South Asia are plainly evident. It could either proceed to deepen its ties in various spheres of their bilateral relations, especially lower key areas like cultural, economic, social and academic activities to erode the edges of suspicion and mistrust that afflict political relations between the South Asian countries. It would be tragic if, on the other hand, mutual differences continue to exist, and bedevil the relationships between the sub-continental neighbours, and they persist in wasting their resources on activities that have no useful result.

Above all, it requires greater understanding that the locus of tensions and instabilities has shifted from the external to internal polity, and the roots of the problems of internal security, whether they arise from ethnic, communal or socio-economic causes, lie in the absence of a just order. The various forms of deprivation, that include the denial of political, economic or social rights, need to be more seriously addressed by the countries of South Asia in the interests of managing their internal polities in the years to come. For this purpose also, it is very necessary that the tensions and instabilities that confront their external polities from within the region are sought to be resolved by patient and earnest endeavours.

The South Asian Association for Regional Cooperation

The 14th session of the SAARC Council of Ministers held in Dhaka in July 1994 reviewed the progress in the implementation of the Agreement on SAARC Preferential Trading Arrangement (SAPTA). A report adopted by the SAARC Workshop held in New Delhi in March-April representing a collective position was presented at the World Conference on Natural Disaster Reduction held in Yakohama, Japan in May 1994. The Meeting of Finance/ Planning Ministers of SAARC countries held in Dhaka in July 1994 decided that a mechanism should be set up for exchange of information on experiences of the SAARC countries in the implementation of poverty alleviation programmes. The SAARC Ministerial Conference on Youth held in Male in May 1994 adopted a resolution known as "Male Resolution on Youth". SAARC Documentation Centre (SDC) has been established and located at the Indian Scientific and Documentation Centre, New Delhi. India organised a SAARC Meeting of Experts on Rehabilitation Techniques for Disabled Persons from November-December 1994 at the National Institute for Mentally Handicapped, Secunderabad.

In keeping with India's desire for greater integration with the Asia Pacific, South-East Asia continued to be an area of prime focus during 1994-95. Numerous high-level contacts helped to rekindle interest in India in those countries. Efforts to synergise the complementarity in the economies of India and the region succeeded in numerous productive ventures in both sides. There are 96 joint ventures in countries in South-East Asia. Currently, India's exports to the region are in the range of Rs. 5,500 crore, a little less than 10 per cent of her global exports.

India's bilateral relations with Singapore continued on a dynamic course. Prime Minister's visit to Singapore in September 1994 was instrumental in turning a new chapter in India's relations with Singapore. Public housing, power generation, telocommunications, tourism and civil aviation were identified as sectors for possible cooperation with Singapore in India. The Prime Minister suggested Singapore's involvement in commercialising new technologies developed by CSIR and also flagged India's interest in further strenthening defence cooperation in areas such as training and equipment. a Memorandum of Understanding on Foreign Office Consultations and a dozen corporate agreements were signed during the visit. Prime Minister Goh Chok Tong's visit to India again in January 1995 after his earlier visit in January 1994 signified the growing informality and closeness in the relationship of mutual benefit.

Prime Minister's visit to Vietnam in September 1994 reaffirmed India's traditionally warm and close relationship in the changing environment. While acknowledging the strength and continuity of bilateral relations between India and Vietnam, both sides agreed that there was need to upgrade economic linkages. Several new areas including sugarcane cultivation and processing, dairy farming, rubber plantation and manufacture, vegetable oil production, leather processing, etc., were identified. Four agreements were signed during the visit on Avoidance of Double Taxation, Facilitation of Visas, Defence Cooperation and Foreign Office Consultations. The visiting Indian business delegation also signed six corporate agreements relating to investments and joint ventures in Vietnam.

With Thialand, there is an excellent understanding at the political level reinforced by periodic exchange of high level visits which include the visit of the Thai Parliamentary Committee of Religion, Art and Culture in September 1994, Thai Deputy Foreign Minister's visit in October 1994 and Deputy Prime Minister of Thailand's visit to Calcutta in January 1995 in connection with Confederation of Indian Industries (CII) Centenary celebrations. Secretary-level talks between India and Thailand were also held in January 1995 in New Delhi. The first meeting of the India-Thailand Joint Business Council aslo took place. India's bilateral trade with Thailand showed a welcome sign of growth with the overall value reaching US dollar 601.60 million (approximately Rs. 1,800 crore) during 1993-94. From Thialand, investment proposals worth US dollar 120 million (approximately Rs. 360 crore) were approved in 1993. The Aditya Birla group is the largest Indian investor with three joint ventures.

India's close relations with Indonesia continued to be strengthened during 1994-95. The visit, of President Soeharto to New Delhi for the reconvened G-15 Summit in March 1994 offered a fresh opportunity for bilateral exchanges and interaction in diverse fields. The volume of trade in 1993-94 was US dollar 354.36 million against the previous year's figure of US dollar 197.19 million. India has 15 joint ventures in Indonesia with investments worth US dollar 189 million.

Prime Minister Mahathir's special gesture of visiting India in March 1994 for the reconvened G-15 Summit after his visit in the same connection three months earlier, contributed to the strengthening of India's bilateral relations with Malaysia. Several major projects involving Indian companies have been cleared over the last year. There are 18 Indian joint ventures in Malaysia and another 14 under various stages of implementation. Malaysian investment in India continued to look up with approved investment reaching Rs. 830 million in 10 projects in various areas. Over 100 Malaysian Air Force personnel are currently undergoing training in India as per the defence cooperation between both the countries.

With the Philippines, India's relations have remained cordial and friendly. The Foreign Office Consultations in Manila in November 1994 underlined the need to step up bilateral economic cooperation and a Joint Business Council was set up. Meat exports from India to the Philippines resumed after a gap of almost thirty years. Senator Leticia Shahani, President Pro-tempore of the Phillippines Senate visited India twice during 1994-95.

India's relations with Brunei Darussalam are also gathering momentum. Brunei's Minister of Communications visited India in January 1995 when a Memorandum of Understanding was signed to discuss matters relatingto the conclusion of an Air Services Agreement and introduction of scheduled air services between the two countres.

With Camboida, India continues to enjoy close and cordial relations. Former Deputy Prime Minister and Foreign Minister visited India in June 1994. A Memorandum of Understanding on Foreign Office Consultations was signed. It was also decided to establish a centre for artificial limbs in Cambodia.

The Lao Foreign Minister visited India in August 1994 and a Memorandum of Understanding on Technical Cooperation and a Cultural Agreement were signed. The visit imparted a much-needed impetus to the bilateral relations.

Relations between India and Australia continued to be cordial. Vice President Shri K.R. Narayanan visited Australia in April 1994 where he inaugurated the Festival "India Today 1994" a two-month long diversified programme of events featuring arts, music, culture-organised by the Austrialia-India Council. Former Deputy Premier of Victoria visited India in February 1994 to identify specific areas for expanding trade an investment and the Australian Chief of Defence Forces visited in April 1994 besides several business/trade delegations also visited India. The third meeting of the India-Australia Joint Ministerial Commission was held in February 1994 in Sydney. A business cum investment seminar was organised in Sydney and the India-Australian Joint Business Council's meeting held in Perth in April 1994. The bilateral trade during 1993-94 was worth Rs. 2,855.08 crore with adverse balance of trade against India. Australian investment in India has been rising steadily and during January-September 1994 it was Rs. 385 crore, the fourth largest after USA, Germany and NRIs. An Honorary Consul General of India was appointed in Melbourne in November 1994.

The traditional friendly relations between India and New Zealand were maintained. Bilateral consultations at Secretary-level were held in April 1994 in Wellington. Bilateral trade registered an increase of 20 per cent in 1993-94 to Rs. 342 crore. About 12 joint ventures in various fields have been launched. The fourth meeting of the Indo-New Zealand Joint Business Council was held in Auckland in April 1994 while the fourth meeting of the India-New Zealand Joint Trade Committee was held in Wellington in June 1994.

India has declared that the Fijian Government should accelerate the review process of the racialy-biased 1990 constitution with a view to achieving an early solution acceptable to all the sections of the Fijian population and

India has decided to establish diplomatic and consular relations with Federated States of Micronesia, a UN member.

If some prominence has been given here to Indo-Pak tensions it is because they constitute the overarching reason for SAARC not developing faster to knit together a pattern of regional cooperation in the region.

Apart from the Indo-Pak contention, in its various dimensions, the other sources of tensions in South Asia that could escalate to inter-State conflict might be recognised to arise from:

(i) Territorial disputes arising from divergent claims over areas in the region;

(ii) Ethnic tensions within nations that spill over inter-State boundaries; and

(iii) Population flows within the region reflecting inter-State tensions and leading to refugee exodus, or voluntary emigration in search of socio-economic betterment.

Territorial disputes are, prominently, a potent source of tensions and conflict in South Asia and, in a manner of speaking, Kashmir quintessentially represents a territorial dispute of massive dimensions, which remains unresolved and could be the cause of conflict between India and Pakistan. So does Siachen, and the absence of any agreement about delineation of the border in this area has led to a confrontation between the armed forces of the two countries that has occasioned a great deal of expense in terms of finance and lives lost to the extreme climatic conditions on the glacier. Lesser territorial disputes have obtained between South Asian countries focussing upon the Kachativu and Moore island controversies, or relating to the demarcation of naval boundaries in the Sir Creek between India and Pakistan, or in the Bay of Bengal between India and Bangladesh, but have a limited potential to ignite inter-State conflict.

The growth in ethnic-consciousness and resultant tensions in South Asia are of greater consequence, and could be placed within a theoretical construct, as being occasioned by the zeitgeist, which favours the assertion of sub-national particularities withn domestic polities. The spread of democratic forms of governance gives strength to ethnicity. Similarly, the rise of religious fundamentalism as part of a global phenomenon, would heighten this sense of ethnic particularity. These aspects of current international developments are apparent withn South Asia, in ethno-political movements ranging from Sindh to Kashmir/ Punjab/Assam to the Chittagong Hill Tracts to the Tamil majority areas in Sri Lanka. In the historical perspective these entho-political movements represent the disintegrative processes that have traditionally affected the integrity of political structures in South Asia. It provides a powerful rationale for the SAARC modelity to enable an integrative process take shape in the region that would preserve the structure of the various nation-States by submerging their sub-national ethnicity in a larger supra-national identity.

The danger to South Asian peace from this resurgence of ethno-nationalism and inter-State conflicts ensuing therefrom springs from these which impinges on the latter's political economy. This occurred most recently with the ethnic Tamil crisis in Sri Lanka, and its spillover into Tamilnadu, which created its own political dynamics for the Indian federal system. More generally, ethno-political movements in one South Asian country can spill over its borders and adversely influence the politics, apart from the economy of the neighbouring country. This calls for greater inter-State cooperation in the resolution of such problems. Else the possibility obtains that both countries involved would be embarked on a collision course as occurred in the crisis of 1971. It might be added that the instrumentality of militarily assisting a particular ethnic group to reach a favourable solution of its demands vis-a-vis the national government is fraught with unpredictable consequence, as India discovered following its deployment of the IPKF in Sri Lanka to bring peace and stability into the Tamil majority in Tamil province of Sri Lanka.

Inter-State population flows of migrants in search of a better way of life in a neighbouring country or as refugees also has the potential to endanger inter-State tensions and conflicts in South Asia. It is worth remarking that all such population flows have taken place into India over the decades following partition, that would include emigration from Nepal, Bangladesh, and most recently, Sri Lanka. Clearly, the population outflows from Nepal and Bangladesh have a nexus with the aspirations of the migrants to improve their socio-economic condition in India. It is unfortunate that such migrants do become socio-economic problems for the receiving country and can become the pawns of domestic politics by their mobilisation into vote-banks, as occurred with the East Bengal/Bangladesh migrants in the Indian states of West Bengal and Assam. After a process of time the indetification of migrants presents growing problems as India is discovering in its efforts to pushback Bangladesh entrants. This issue has polarised the national political arena with the BJP making the forced return of these migrants a major plank in its foreign policy agenda. Any attempt to evict large populations by force clearly has the potential to engender inter-State tensions and conflict.

A different situation arose with regard to the Tamil refugees fleeing Sri Lanka in the wake of the SLAF campaign against militant groups in the Tamil-majority areas of Sri Lanka. Fortunately, the 1,000,000-1,50,000 Tamil refugees that still remain in India are being repatriated in terms of an agreement reached between the two countries. Earlier, the conflict potential of the fleeing Tamil refugees lay in the ethnic Tamil problem in Sri Lanka political issue in Tamilnadu leading to competitive jingoism by regional parties demanding the use of force to settle the issue. Further, this question became an issue in Centre-State relations. A similar problem of population outflows, and related to ethno-political tensions, is occurring with the ouster of the Nepali-origin population from Bhutan, and Chakmas from the Chittagong Hill Tracts. Any possible solution to stem these outflows, whether they are natural or forced, would require bilateral negotiations between the countries affected to contain the influx. The question does arise as to what should be done if these efforts fail.

The empirical evidence would suggest, however, that external intervention into Intra-State ethno-political and/or migratory issues could produce wholly unitended effects for the intervening power. India's utilisation of the Tamil militants has lever to resolve the ethinic crisis in Sri Lanka has resulted in a marked deterioration in the law and order situation in Tamilnadu and, to an extent, in other South Indian States. They are believed to have been used by political parties in Tamilnadu to further their electoral prospects. A similar entree of the Afghan mujahideen into the body politic of Pakistan ensued following their utilisation to serve Pakistan's foreign policy interests by assisting the American strategy of arming the mujahideen to wage war against the occupying Soviet forces in Afghanistan. Pakistan is now left with an excerbation of its law order problem and the establishment of a Klashnikov culture in the country. The empirical evidence strengthens the need therefore for South Asian countries to seriously discuss this new set of issues because they have the inherent potential to destabilise border areas in the region.

Any process of bilateral or multilateral dialogues within

the South Asian region needs to appreciate the reality that serious political differences exist between them, that hinders the possibilities of greater cooperation in the sub-continent. These differences cannot be wished away and need to be firmly brought on the agenda for discussion and the search for solutions. The other reality which cannot be wished away is the looming (hegemonic) image of India. No doubt, India must understand the right of the South Asian countries to be apprehensive about it; but is equally the obligation of the other regional countries to appreciate the assurances given by India. There remains the question of underlying doubts and suspicions, which points again to the relevance of the SAARC forms to articulate apprehensions, and declare reassurances.

More specific measures can be suggested to further these objectives:

(1) Regular intervention in the public debate through all media forms to engender a greater awareness of how the existing and newer sources of tensions and conflicts are bedeviling the region, affecting the developmental process and, at one remove, subverting the processes of democratic governance.

(2) Highlight in public forums the value of multiateral/bilateral dialogue between South Asian countries and the SAARC process, to erode tensions in the region. Apart from suggesting newer cooperative instrumentalities for this purpose, the existing agreements reached by SARRC, but lie dormant, like the Terrorism Convention and Agreement on Narcotic Drugs/ Psychotropic Substances need being recognised as steps requiring vigorous implementation to clear the regional atmosphere of lurking doubts and suspicions

(3) The appreciation could also be underscored that certain natural channels of commerce have traditionally obtained in South Asia, and artificial barriers in their way have only succeeded in directing them into informal and illegal routes. This is occurring with regard to trade via third countries, that is within the knowledge of the countries concerned; hence the need to make overt what is the obtaining reallity. Besides trade these natural channels of commerce would include both capital and labour flows that need to be freed. The logic of commerce points to South Asia developing into a common market. The politics of the region will not permit this dispensation at present, but the strategic direction required might be recognised more clearly.

(4) Academic needs to be more greatly sensitised to the need for undertaking conflict resolution studies relating to the South Asia, pertaining especially to ethno-political and migration issues in the region, which seems destined to become significant in future. It would serve this purpose admirably if joint studies were undertaken by scholars belonging to the countries affected by these problems, as is being attempted by the newly established Regional Centre for Strategic Studies. Furthermore, the possibility of establishing positions for visiting scholars in the prestigious institutions represented in the South Asian Dialogue to undertake such studies could be another modus to achieving this end.

The Second South Asian Dialogue of 1992 had emphasised the need for stabilisation and structural adjustment in the countries of the South Asian region, particularly in the context of the changing global scenario. Emphasising that the agenda for economic reforms should be defined domestically, the Indian experience was extensively discussed and analysed for possible lessons in economic policy making for other countries of the region. An active domestic debate on the various policy options and an emerging consensus were seen as key ingredients for the success of the economic policy reforms within a democratic polity.

Against the background of this discussion, the developments in policy making and economic performance in India during the last year are sketched out here with a view to updating the record. This is followed by a broader discussion of the nature of regional co-operation and economic integration required to bring about the overall development of the countries of the South Asian region.

The obtaining nuclear overhang in South Asia can now be discussed. The Report on Regional Non-Proliferation in South Asia submitted by the White House to the U.S. Congress in May holds that India and Pakistan have established the capability to manufacture nuclear weapons at short notice and also prossess credible means of delivery to attack value targets. This conclusion is in line with independent Russian assessments. Estimates of the nuclear capabilities available to the two countries have also been made by several organisations based on the quantities of fissile material believed to be in their possession. India and Pakistan are, uniquely, the only adversary but cryptonuclear powers in the world. There are other unique aspects of the nuclear situation in South Asia. India's present policy of keeping its option open which, incidentally, seems to have informed Pakistan, without either expressing or foreclosing that option is singular in the so-called non-proliferation regime.This policy enjoys wide domestic support in the two countries, but it also needs greater appreciation that they could only possess crude fission devices with their means of delivery premised on aircraft. It would require a series of tests to miniaturise nuclear warheads and gain assurance about the reliability/accuracy of their missiles, apart from the political/military leadership acquiring confidence that such last-resort weapons will function when they need to be utilised.

Despite these technological constraints there is a considerable body of opinion which holds that the present ambiguous nuclear situation in south Asia has led to a stabilisation of the mutual relationship. Witness the caution displayed by the armed forces of the two countries and their political leaderships during the various crises in relations during the last few years, e.g., Brasstacks Exercise (1987), Kashmir-related escalation of border tensions (1990), and the recent (1992-93) attempts by JKDA activists to violate the Line of Control. There are contrary arguments to suggest that availability of nuclear weapons at short notice constitutes a dangerous situation, with the likelihood of a nuclear exchange being triggered by inadvertence, if not design, and being occasioned by an escalation of conflict from the conventional level. It could, however, be argued that this entire question is somewhat irrelevant, since the primary threat to India arises from ethno-political and other domestic tensions in the polity, which can be inflamed by external powers intervention, and the nuclear weapons provide no defence against this range of problems. It might be further added that the economic costs involved would constrain any overt deployment of nuclear forces. These economic costs would not merely involve the expenses, incidentally, on establishing a nuclear force which, in the case of India, most address the presence of a nuclear China on its security horizons, but also the likelihood of bilateral/ multilateral financial assistance getting prejudiced by such proliferation actions.

A word about the present state of the non-proliferation regime. There is optimism about its growing acceptability by events like the accession of France, China and South Africa to the UNP, Argentina and Brazil agreeing to a system of mutual inspection of their sensitive nuclear facilities, signing of major arms control agreements like START-I and START-II, withdrawal of tactical nuclear missles by the U.S., Russia and U.K., and moratoria placed by these nuclear weapons powers on nuclear testing and so an. At the same time, developments in the former Republics of the Soviet Union must cause the most profound concern. All tactical nuclear weapons have reportedly been shifted into Russia. There is no assurance, however, that fissile material, nuclear cores, if not entire nuclear weapons, are fully accounted for. Indeed, materials accounting procedures in the erstwhile Soviet Union were neither detailed nor strict because the nature of its political system permitted confidence that theft or misappropriation of such materials were not possible and could be easily detected. No such confidence is presently available with the break-up of the Soviet Union and the autonomy of its former Republics. The possibility of fissile materials, nuclear cores, if not entire nuclear weapons, remaining unaccounted for is real, and points to the extraordinary-danger of their falling into the hands of nuclear aspirants. There is besides newer problem accosting the non-proliferation regime after South Africa's self-confessedly admitting to making and, thereafter, dismantling six nuclear weapons. There can be no assurance that all its nuclear weapons have been uncovered and/or the fissile materials to produce a further number have been satisfactorily accounted for North Korea has highlighted the escape route available to NTP-signatories to withdraw from the Treaty whenever they chose; Iraq has revealed the clandestine path to the nuclear capabilities. These developments must be construed as adverse to the non-proliferation regime's containment.

The foregoing discussion provides the backdrop against which proposals for controlling, limiting and eventually eliminating nuclear weapons from the region must be considered. This parallels the American objective to "cap, then over the time, reduce, and finally eliminate the possession of weapons of mass destruction and their means of delivery" in South Asia. The technical implications of this measure would require ceasing production of fissile materials and work relating to missiles. It would also require that imports of materials, equipment or tecnnology that could further the military nuclear or missile programme should be stopped. Equity demands that all such proposals should be universal and non-discriminatory. Restricting these proposals to particular regions does not address the true nature or dimensions of the non-proliferation problem, especially in a milieu wherein the dilemma of fissile materials, nuclear cores/weapons/technology, apart from unemployed nuclear scientists and engineers, seeping out of the erstwhile Soviet Union and becoming available to nuclear aspirants has not been credibly resolved. There is, besides, the related dilemma of defining regions. In India's security perceptions the region must include China for the purpose of evolving any methodologies to control, reduce and eliminate nuclear weapons from South Asia.

There remains, however, the question of managing the nuclear situation in South Asia and, in particular, the crypto-nuclear adversarial relationship between India and Pakistan. The various confidence-building and tension-reducing proposals that could build upon existing arms control/ confidence-building agreements in the nuclear and conventional areas, could comprise the following:

(1) Extending the agreement not to attack each other's identified nuclear facilities and installations to designated population and high value economic assets;

(2) The "hot-line" communications between the military leaderships could be extended to the political leaderships at the highest levels and upgraded with multiple-redundancy linkages to permit fail-safe communications at all times. This becomes of extreme importance in the ambiguous state of the nuclear relationships;

(3) Periodic meetings of military officials could be formalised into regular meetings at fixed intervals to sort out subsisting border problems, apart from ad-hoc flag meetings to settle local dispute between field commanders;

(4) The agreement for providing advance information on troop movements/military exercises could be widened to include deployments of offensive weapons systems like tanks, combat aircraft, and surface-to-surface missiles within specified border zones to reduce the likelihood of surprise attacks, apart from allowing military observers to be associated with field exercises;

(5) Similarly, the agreement to prevent violations of air space could be broadened to an "open skies" arrangement that would permit aerial reconnaissance of the specified border zones to be mutually undertaken for gaining confidence that no unwarranted military movements and force re-deployments were taking place.

There are further confidence-building measures at the declaratory level that could be considered for unilateral action like no-first-use pledges, no-nuclear-test declarations, promises to adhere to the guidelines of the Nuclear Suppliers Group and the Missile Technology Control Regime, besides innovative measures like sharing information on the location of strike corps elements, and so on.

It would, indeed, be advancing a counsel of perfection to suggest that all these measures are subsumed within the need to normalise bilateral relations between India and Pakistan. One pathway for proceeding purposively here would be to widen people-to-people contacts by meetings at various levels between academicians, journalists, professional and business groups, and increasing the two-way flow of information through various media channels, apart from bilateral trade via formal ageements. In short, the measures enuisaged in Article III of the Shimla Agreement need to be seriously implemented.

At the official level, however, the need for dialogue between the two countries cannot be over-emphasised and this must be extended to the nuclear dimension. Indeed the gaps in understanding and the dangerous consequences of misunderstandings stand accentuated by frequent statements made by Pakistan's leadership about their nuclear prowess and India's reticence in this regard. Why such inflamatory rhetoric is deemed necessary could be considered in this dialogue. There is besides the impermissible actions that could lead to an overt expression of nuclear capabilities, the peronage(s) designated to exercise release authority and so on. The nuclear game has it own rules and nuclear weapons possess their own intrinsic logic. Consequently, these measures, that were found necessary by the existing nuclear weapons powers, cannot be inapplicable to crypto-nuclear powers. Hence the need to address these basic issues relating to the military atom within the structure of an Indo-Pak dialogue.

There are different strands in Indo-Pak relations that give rise to cautious optimism in the possibilities of their betterment, which includes the signficant confidence-building measures that have been reached between them, and have been detailed above. some cause for greater optimism is possible from the manner in which the JKDA attempts to cross the Line of Control had been prevented with firmness by the Pakistan army but, more importantly, in close collaboration with the Indian army. This reinforces the belief that major crises in Indo-Pak relations like the Brasstacks affair and build-up of tensions in 1990 were handled by both countries with considerable adroitness and maturity. These sensibilities lie dormant presently, but are available to address the larger issues of adversarial Indo-Pak relations, if the political will could be generated on both sides.

Moving to the sources of inter-State tensions and conflicts in South Asia, and ways to mitigate them, it requires early recognition that the spirit of detente has not struck roots yet in the region. Neither has the example of neighbouring ASEAN, which shares many geo-political similarities with South Asia, like the preponderance of Indonesia in the region, established a standard for emulation by SAARC. We might question here ingrained beliefs that the dominance of India over the South Asian polity is the chief reason for concern, and the major impediment to its greater integration. Admittedly, India is the focus of the foreign policies of the smaller nations in the sub-continent some further reflection, however, on the causes for tensions and conflicts in the region would isolate the Indo-Pak contention, which possesses historical, political, religious and geo-strategic dimensions, and has now acquired a worrisome nuclear dimension. This needs to be discussed at greater length.

This would not be the place to detail the entire gamut of Indo-Pak disputes that have emerged since their independence, but we may identify the Kashmir issue as the principal contention between them that could escalate to armed conflict. The relative merits of the case pesented over the years by India and Pakistan to press their claims are too well-known to bear reiteration. The danger from the continuance of the Kashmir issue arises from its latent possibility of triggering violence, and it bears recognition that Kashmir has been either the cause or the chief theater of conflict between the two countries in the past Indo-Pak wars. A low intensity conflict proceeds at present in Kashmir, which has its roots in the partition of the country and certain errors made by India in the past. It cannot be the case, nevertheless, that external intervention by the provision of moral and material assistance and sanctuaries to Kashmiri militants would help in evolving a solution. Beliefs, morever, that the low intensity conflict in Kashmir would become India's Spanish ulcer do not acknowledge that India cannot abandon Kashmir to be either integrated within Pakistan or become an independent state. Any such action would raise several contentious questions, and, more significantly, the reliquishment of a Muslim-majority area would have serious repercussions for India's secular polity and might lead to extensive communal violence engineered by nationalistfundamentalist forces in the country.

It must be conceded that Pakistan also has a national position on Kashmir. A serious dialogue would seem to be the only way out, and, perhaps, by recognition of the Line of Control as the de jure division of the historical State of Kashmir. Of course, dialogues with the indigenous populations of the historical state of Jammu and Kashmir, and of the different regions comprising it, are essential as well, and matters like the sequencing of all these dialogues will also have to be considered at the proper time. But an over-riding necessity is that the leaders and peoples of India and Pakistan should realise that non-resolution of the Kashmir issue is bleeding both the countries by their common need to station large forces in this area, and their requirement for large armed forces to be maintained, equipped, modernised and expanded due to the prevailing atmosphere of tensions in the bilateral relationship.

Even if it was argued that India's other security concerns

warrant periodical upgradations of its armed forces, it might be appreciated that a major portion of its military expenditure is designed against the threat assessed from Pakistan, whilst the security threat from China is reducing, and might largely recede as the recently-signed peace and tranquility agreement. Expenditures being incurred by India and Pakistan deriving, from their adversarial relationship, bear significant opportunity costs in terms of development outlays otherwise possible. A compromise on the Kashmir issue, preceded by a disengagement in Siachen, would permit the relationship to develop within more normal channels of international behaviour, and erode the most prescient cause for inter-State conflict in the sub-continent.

This focus on the Kashmir issue might be enlarged now to consider it within the larger international context, and the peace dividend promised by the end of the Cold War. The spirit of detente apparent in the international system has permitted various stubborn regional conflict situations being addressed towards evolving a solution eg., Cambodia, Namibia and Cyprus, the long-outstanding problem of apartheid in South Africa and enfranchisement of its black population is on the way to resolution. Of particular relevance to the Indo-Pak adversarial situation is the agreement signed between the PLO and Israel to usher peace into the most disputed area in the world. The conflict between them involved disputed territory and contention between opposed ideologies viz., nationalism and Zionism.

The rhetoric on both sides had traditionally argued for maximalist solutions to the problem e.g., refusing to accept ground realities like the entity of Israel (PLO), and the recognition of the Palestinians as a people (Israel). Assuredly, there will be many difficulties in translating the different steps envisaged in the peace agreement into political action, and there are powerful domestic constituencies that firmly oppose the agreement and would make strenuous efforts to obstruct its fruition. But, the significance of this momentous first step to bring peace into the Middle-East cannot be minimised, nor its promise disregarded, to resolve a most obstinate regional security problem. Without straining the simile too greatly there are important lessons in this event for India and Pakistan. First, that compromise in long-held maximalist positions in regional disputes is essential to break from sterile unproductive controversies. Second, there is wisdom in not seeking outside intervention, but not rejecting it either to promote the principle of bilateralism in Indo-Pak relations. Third, there would be value in quiet, low-profile discussions, perhaps in another country between duly accredited representatives of India and Pakistan to find solutions. Fourth, and this is central to the exercise, the realisation must dawn, as it did with the PLO/Isreal, that it was not possible for them to destroy each other and, therefore, necessity requires seeking the path of reconciliation.

National budgets, including defence allocations, are under considerable strain in India and Pakistan. The two defence establishments are, besides, finding it progressively more difficult to maintain the operational status of their weapon systems due to problems in arranging for their maintenance, spares and ancillaries from their principal suppliers viz., Russia and the United States. These constraints might assist this process of realisation in the wisdom of reconciliation. It is also conceivable that an additional factor in promoting this realisation might be renewed pressures from the international community to compose the Kashmir issue specifically and Indo-Pak disputes generally. The recently negotiated agreement in the Middle-East highlights the value of quite diplomacy and a step-wise methodology to reach the ultimate objective, besides the possibility of transcending U.N. resolutions.

The process of continuing change in post-cold war

Europe and in India's own external environment has provided an impetus for internsification of relations between India and countries of this region based on complementarity of interests and mutual benefit. India's historical and cultural interaction with Europe also provides a unique dimension that further serves to strengthen mutual understanding and affinities. Over a million persons of Indian origin live in Western Europe, a tenth of them Indian citizens. Both the European Commssion and individual members of the European Union evolved new strategies to strengthen political dialogue and economic relations with Asian countries, including India. This trend was compelmented by India's economic reforms and efforts to globalise the Indian economy.

India's trade with the EU countries increased by 20 per cent over the previous year to reach dollar 14.89 billion in 1993; this upward trend continued during 1994. Collectively the largest trading partners of India, the EU countries accounted for 30 per cent of India's exports and imports. Similar progress was registered on the investment front. The share of West European countries in FDI approvals went up from 20 per cent in 1993 to 30 per cent in 1994. Actual investment inflows from Western Europe since the launching of India's economic reforms in July 1991 comprised 31 per cent of total inflows. West European countries also continued to be a leading source of development assistance, technology and collaborations and joint ventures.

The new Cooperation Agreement between the Republic of India and the European Community on Partnership and Development came into effect on 1 August 1994. The 8th Session of the India-EC Joint Commission was held in Brussels in October 1994. The broad principles of a strategy for economic and development cooperation with the EU up to the year 2000 was agreed on, focussing on continued assistance from the EU to India's development efforts.

India's relations with Germary, India's leading economic partner in Europe, was given further impetus through the exchanges of high level visits during 1994-95. German Minister for Development Cooperation visited India in February 1994. The German Minister for Economics attended the 11th Session of the Indo-German Joint Commission held in New Delhi in April 1994. An Indian Parliamentary delegation led by the speaker of the Lok Sabha, visited Germany in June-July 1994 and interacted with a wide cross-section of German Parliamentarians and leaders of various political parties.

The Vice-Chancellor and Foreign Minister of Germany visited India in July 1994 accompanied by a high-level business delegation. He underlined the central position occupied by India in terms of Germany's "Asia Concept Policy" and stressed the importance attached by Germany to developing closer relations with India on the basis of partnership in political, economic and cultural fields. He also reaffirmed Germany's support for the resumption of Indo-Pak bilateral dialogue and welcomed India's policy of transparency on human rights. He expressed support for a permanent seat for India in the UN Security Council. The German business delegation accompanying him evinced keen interest in increasing their presence in the Indian market through investments, particularly in the fields of power, chemicals and transportation infrastructure.

The Indo-German-Consultative Groups, which has emerged as a strong catalytic force in Indo-German reactions, held its Third Session in Bonn in August and submitted recommendations covering bilateral cooperation in political, economic, scientific, cultural and media fields.

Prime Minister paid a visit to the UK in March 1994. The visit marked a new era of relations between the UK and India, reinforcing trends towards a long term partnership based on mutual confidence and trust, shared values and mutual benefit. A Bilateral Investment Protection Agreement was concluded with the UK during the visit.The Indo-British Partnership Initiative (IBPI), launched in January 1993, extended for another year, achieved major success in promoting awareness of opportunities for trade and investment opened up by India's economic reforms. Indo-British trade continued to register a high rate of growth during 1994. There were several exchanges of visits between India and UK during 1994-95. Instruments of ratification of the Indo-UK Bilateral Investment Protection Agreement were exchanged during British Foreign Secretary's visit to India in January 1995. During the year, a Commercial Office of the British High Commission was opened in Bangalore and a decision taken to establish a Consulate General of India in Glasgow.

A delegation of the French Senate led by President of the Senate Committee for Foreign Affairs and Defence visited India in February 1994. In a letter to the Prime Minister, the French Prime Minister Edouard Balladur affirmed the desire of the French Government to impart new momentum to Indo-French relations in the political, economic and cultural fields. French Foreign Minister visited India in April 1994. He expressed French resolve to intensify relations with India particularly in the economic field. From the Indin side Ministers for Agriculture, External Affairs and Health and Family Welfare visited France.

President of the Italian Senate visited India in Februray 1994. Trade and economic relations with Italy, the fourth largest market for Indian exports to Europe, continued to expand. Commerce Minister visited Italy for the 11th meeting of the Indo-Italian joint Economic Committee. The Italian President paid a State visit to India in February 1995 coinciding with the participation of Italy as partner country in the Indian Engineering Trade Fair. A Memorandum of

Understanding concerning cooperation in the field of defence equipment was concluded between India and Italy on 4 November 1994.

Minister of State for External Affairs paid official visit to Ireland and Spain in October 1994. The visits focussed on strengthening bilateral trade and economic relations with these countries. A partimentary delegation led by the Speaker of the Lok Sabha visited Ireland in July 1994. A Consulate General of Portugal was opened in Goa in April 1994 to promote Indo-Portugese relations in the areas of trade, tourism and culture. The 11th Session of the Indo-Swedish Joint Commission for Economic, Industrial, Technical and Scientific Cooperation was held in Stockholm in May 1994. The Indian delegation was led by Minister of State for Industry. The meeting provided impetus to trade and economic relations between India and Sweden.

Minister of State for Communications visited Denmark in May 1994. Ministers of State for Surface Transport and for Petroleum visited Norway. The Norwegian Minister for Development Cooperation visited India in May 1994. Official level consultations between India and Norway on economic, industrial and technicasl cooperation were held in New Delhi. Minister of State for Defence paid a visit to Greece in October 1994. The visit coincided with the first ever participation by India at the Defence Production Fair "Defendory" which was held in Athens in October 1994. Shri Mallikarjun's visit and India's participation in "Defendory" strengthened prospects for Indo-Greek cooperation in the field of defence production. In November 1994, protocols were concluded with the principality of Andorra establishing diplomatic and consular relations between India and Andorra. During 1994-95, double taxation avoidance agreements were conceded with Malta, Cyprus and Switzerland.

There was considerable interaction between India and the countries of the Commonwealth of Independent States (CIS) as well Central and Eastern Europe during 1994-95. With practically all these countries, India has had longstanding relations of friendship and cooperation based on trust and confidence. The evolution of these countries in direction of democratic pluralism and market-oriented economic structures has brought them closer to India in terms of basic orientation. India has established a mutually beneficial economic and commercial interation with all the countries in East Europe. Direct contacts between the Indian Parliament and the parliamentary systems in many of these countries are emerging as an important new dimension in the bilateral relationships.

India's relations with the Russian Federation are friendly and multifaceted, encompassing political consultation on matters of mutual interest, significant economic and commercial interation and cooperation in science and technology, defence, atomic energy, space, culture and education.

Prime Minister, Shri P.V. Narasimha Rao visited Russia from 29 June to 2 July 1994. He was accompanied by the Ministers for Commerce, Civil Aviation and Tourism, the Ministers of State in the Prime Minister's Office, and for External Affairs Shri R.L. Bhatia and senior officers. The Prime Minister had separate delegation level talks with President Yeltsin and Prime Minister Chernomyrdin. Deputy Prime Minister and Culture Minister called on the Prime Minister. The Prime Minister addressed a representative group of Parliamentarians from both Houses of Russian Parliament.

The visit ushered in a qualitatively new stage of Indo-Russian relations. The Moscow Declaration on the Protection of the interests of Pluralist States sets out the post-cold war challenges posed to the viability of large, multi-ethnic, multi-lingual, multi-cultural and multi-religious states by the forces of aggressive nationalism, religious and political extremism, terrorism and separatism and the need to combat these challenges thorugh democracy, tolerance, secularism and the rule of law. It is recognised as a unique document in international relations and has subsequently been circulated as a UN Document at the joint initiative of India and Russia. The Declaration on Further Development and Intensification of Bilateral Cooperation underlines the broad identity of views of the two countries on important regional and international issues, and identified priority areas and directions of cooperation between the two countries. In addition, Agreements and Protocols were signed on cooperation in tourism, environment, space, science and technology, standarsation and metallurgy. The 1992 Agreement on defence credit was extended for a further period of two years and an agreement on setting up of a joint venture in military aviation was signed. The first meeting of the co-chairmen of the Inter-Governmental Joint Commission, Indian Minister for Commerce and Russian Deputy Prime Minister was held in Delhi in June 1994. Priority areas of cooperation were identified and the Joint Commission held its first meeting in Moscow in September 1994. Nine Working Groups-on Trade and Economic Cooperation; Power and Non-Conventional Sources of Energy; Petroleum; Ferrous and Non-Ferrous Metallurgy; Science and Technology; Culture; Coal; Information Technology; and Environment-held meetings and identified their respective areas of cooperation.

The Home Minister visited Russia during August-September 1994. The visit gave a fresh impetus to bilateral cooperation, particularly in areas such as combating terrorism, organised crime and narcotics trafficking. Leader of Opporsition in Lok Sabha and Chairman of the Standing Committee on External Affairs headed a Parliamentary delegation to Russia in January 1995 and had a number of high level meetings.

A nine-member Parliamentary Delegation led by the Chairman visited India in November 1994 while the Russian Prime Minister VS Chernomyrdin visited India on 23 and 24 December 1994 along with a high level delegation. He had discussions with Prime Minister followed by delegation level talks and also called on President and Vice President. Eigth documents, including agreements in promotion of mutual protection of investment, shipping, exploration and peaceful uses of outer space, implementation of the programme of defence cooperation upto the year 2000 and purchases of commodities in India for the period 1995-97 were signed. During the year several rounds of Foreign Office Consultations were also held between the two countries.

Indo-Ukrainian relations were given direction and impetus by the visit of Foreign Minister Zlenko in April 1994. During the visit, three agreements were signed: Protocol of Consultations between the Minister of External Affairs of India and the Minister of Foreign Affairs of Ukraine; Agreement on the Inter-Government Joint Commission on Trade, Economic, Scientific, Technological, Industrial and Cultural Cooperation; and Agreement on Economic and Technical Cooperation. The first meeting of the Indo-Ukrainian Joint Commission and the Foreign Office Consultations were held in Kiev in December 1994.

The State visit by President Dr. Shanker Dayal Sharma from 26 to 29 May 1994 emphasied the importance India attached to relations with Bulgaria. The President had discussions with President Zhelev, addressed the Bulgarian National Assembly and was awarded an Honorary Doctorate by the University of Sofia. During the visit six Agreements on Quarantine and Plant Protection; Veterinary and Sanitary

Agreement; Avoidance of Double Taxation; Combating Organised Crime, International Terrorism, Illegal Trafficking in Narcotics and Psychotropic Substances; Protocol on Foreign Office Consultation and Cooperation; Cooperation in Tourism–were signed and a Joint Statement was issued. Bulgarian Culture Minister paid an official visit to India during February-March 1994 and the Cultural Exchange Programme for 1994-96 was signed.

President Dr. Shankar Dayal Sharma paid a State visit to Romanian from 30 May to 2 June 1994. The President held discussions with President Iliescu; addressed the Joint Session of the Romanian Senate and the Chamber of Deputies; and received an Honorary Doctorate from the University of Bucharest. During the visit, an Agreement on Combating Organised Crime, International Terrorism, Illicit Trafficking in Narcotics and Psychotropic Substances and other Illegal Activities; an Agreement on Cooperation in Tourism; a Declaration of Principles and Directions of Cooperation and the Cultural Exhchange Programme for 1994-96 were concluded.

President of the Republic of Poland Lech Walesa paid a State visit to India in March 1994. Delegation-level talks led by the Prime Minister on the Indian side and by President Walesa on the Polish side were held and were followed by a tele-a-tele between the two leaders. Minister of State for Defence visited Poland in June 1994 to discuss further prospects for cooperation in defence.

Hungarian Political State Secretary for Defence visited India in March 1994 and State Secretary for Foreign Affairs paid and official visit to New Delhi in September 1994. A Protocol on Foreign Office Consulations was signed during the visit. A Hungarian Parliamentary delegation led by the Speaker of the National Assembly visited India in November 1994.

Minister of State for Defence visited the Czech Republic in June 1994 and Foreign Secretary visited Prague on 9 August 1994. The Czech Republic upgraded its diplomatic representation in India to that of Ambassador Extraordinary and Plenipotentiary. The Joint Trade Committee on Economics, Trade and Technical Cooperation held its first meeting at Prague in January 1995.

Minister of State for Defence visited the Slovak Republic in June 1994. He called on Slovak President and Prime Minister and Foreign Minister. Prime Minister of the Slovak Republic, Jozeh Moravcik paid an official visit to India in June 1994. He called on the President, Vice President, and had talks with the Prime Minister and he also met Indian businessmen and industrialists. A Protocol on Foreign Office Consultations; a Memorandum of Understanding on Cooperation in Science and Technology; and a Memorandum of Understanding concerning Indo-Slovak Joint Committee on Trade were also signed. It was also agreed to open a resident Indian Mission in Bratislava. The Union of Slovak Industry and CII also concluded a Memorandum of Understanding. The Slovak Republic upgraded its diplomatic representation in India to that of Ambassador Extraordinary and Plenipotentiary and also established an Honorary Consulate in Calcutta.

An Armenian delegation led by Minister of Science and Higher Education visited India in March 1994 and held discussions with Minister of State (Prime Minister's Office and Science and Technology). An Agreement on Cooperation in Science and Technology, a Memorandum of Understanding on concluding an Agreement on Economic and Technical Cooperation were signed. Armenia established its diplomatic representation in India by appointing an Honorary Consul. India has offered humanitarian assistance of medicine valued at Rs. five lakh to Armenia.

Deputy Prime Minister of Moldova paid an unofficial visit to New Delhi in May, 1994 and held discussions with Minister of State for External Affairs, Shri Salman Khurshid. A Lithuanian delegation led by the Minister of Energy visited India in March 1994. He held discussions with Minister of State for External Affairs, Shri R.L. Bhatia and senior officers in the Ministry of Power. Lithuania established its Honorary Consulate in New Delhi in October 1994. India kept a close watch on the developments in the Former Yugoslavia, particularly the continuing criss in Bosnia-Herzegovina. India supports the efforts of the Interanational Conference on Former Yugoslavia, basically because to-date it is the only attempt at finding a settlement that is based on regard for legitimate aspirations and interests of all parties to the conflict. India recognised Bosnia-Herzegovina on 11 May 1992 along with the Republic of Croatia and Slovenia but not as a Muslim State.

India's Ambassador to Croatia, presented his credentials in June 1994. Commerce Minister visited Croatia on 17 September 1994. An Agreement on Trade and Economic Cooperation was signed during the visit and the Croation Assistant Minister of Economic Affairs led a delegation to India in November 1994 during the India International Trade Fair.

The year 1994-95 witnessed rapid and diversified growth in the Indo-US relations following Prime Minister's visit to the USA from 14 to 20 May 1994. Prime Minister Shri P.V. Narasimha Rao and President Clinton promised to cooperate in the search for solutions to global challenges posed by weapons of mass destruction, AIDS, environmental degradation, population growth, poverty, international terrorism and narcotics trafficking. Agreement was also reached to expand the pace and scope of high level exchanges on the full range of political, economic, commercial, scientific, technological and social issues. The two leaders agreed to seek ways to expand their cooperation at the United Nations. Two Memoranda of Understanding-on Cooperation Measures to Increase Awareness and Support for Efforts to Combat Production, Distribution and Use of Illegal Drugs and on Planning, Conservation and Management of Natural and Cultural Heritage Sites-were also signed.

Commercial and economic interaction remained the most vital sector of Indo-US cooperation through 1994-95. Bilateral trade in 1993 equalled US dollar 7.3 billion with a trade surplus of US dollar 1.8 billion in India's favour. The USA remained the single largest investor-country in terms of direct foreign investment in India, with approved investments from the US between January to September 1994 amounting to Rs. 14,302 million. Actual FDI inflows from the USA from 1991 to September 1994 amounted to Rs. 2,039 million. US Energy Secretary visited India in July 1994 leading a large Presidential Mission when four joint statements were signed and 11 cooperative projects between private companies of the two countries were announced. US Commerce Secretary led a Presidential Business Development Mission to India in January 1995 and during the visit the two countries signed a Memorandum of Understanding setting up the Indo-US Commercial Alliance.

Minister of Power visited USA in November 1994. Several agreements were signed during the visit. Minister of State for Non-Conventional Energy Sources visited the USA in December and a number of Memoranda of Understanding for cooperation between Indian and the US institutions/firms were signed during the visit. Air Chief Marshal visited US in August 1994 while Chief of Army Staff visited in September 1994. The second round of talks on a new Indo-US Extradition Treaty was held in Washington in October 1994.

Democrat Congressmen Gary L Ackerman, Jim MC Dermott accompanied by Congresswoman Barbara-Rose

Collins visited India in November 1994 while Commander-in-Chief of the US Pacific Command visited India in December 1994. In September 1994, the Indian and US Navies conducted a joint Special Operations exercise at Ratnagiri (Mirya Bay). Defence Secretary visited India in January 1995 and an Agreed Minute on Defence Relations between India and the USA was signed. It was agreed that growth of bilateral defence relations would be evolutionary and related to convergence on global and regional issues.

India and the US held a further round of discussions on non-proliferation regional security and disarmament in London in April 1994. The two countries also agreed to intensity cooperative efforts to achieve a Comprehensive Test Ban Treaty (CTBT) and a verifiable global ban on the production of fissible material for nuclear weapons purposes. US pronouncements on the human rights situations in India gave rise to considerable misunderstanding. Differences in perception continued over Pakistan's support to terrorism. However, the situation improved later in the year as a result of greater restraint and objectivity exercised by US authorities.

Indo-Canadian relations witnessed greater interation, especially in the economic and commercial spheres. From January to September 1994, foreign direct investment approvals for Canada amounted to Rs. 417 million as against the total Canadian investment approvals for 1993 of Rs. 300 million. Canadian imports from India during January to May 1994 totalled Canadian dollar 178 million, registering an increase of 30.5 per cent as compared to the imports during the same period last year. Canadian exports to India during January to May 1994 registered a marginal increase of 5.1 per cent as compared to the same period last year. The Canadian Minister for International Trade accompanied by a large Canadian business delegation visited India in October 1994. Home Minister visited Canada in October

1994 and Mutual Legal Assistance Treaty on combating terrorism, drug trafficking and organised crime was signed during the visit.

India maintains very good relations with all the Latin American and Caribbean countries. During 1994-95, India's relations with these countries were consolidated by several exchanges of high level visits, joint commission meetings and contacts at various levels. The Foreign Minister and Minister of Environment of Brazil also visited India. Minister of Civil Aviation and Tourism visited Brazil and discussed various means of close cooperation in tourism. Minister of Textiles, Deputy Minister for Education also visited Brazil in 1994, the latter to participate in the Conference on 'Education for All.'

A three-member delegation led by Minister of Parliamentary Affairs attended the inauguration ceremonies of the new President of Mexico. President Dr. Carlos Saul Menem of Argentina visited India in March 1994 to take over Chairmanship of G-15 and extended his stay to pay a bilateral visit. The leaders of India and Argentina discussed important international issues and matters of bilateral importance. Several agreements on bilateral cooperation were signed during the visit. Minister of Civil Aviation and Tourism visited Argentina in June 1994 to promote tourist traffic from South America to India and Minister of Communications visited Buenos Aires during March 1994 to attend the first World Telecommunication Development Conference organised by the ITU. The then Chief Justice of India visited Buenos Aires in August 1994 as the leader of the Indian delegation to the International Law Association Congress. The Embassy in Bogota which was closed down in 1993 was reopened in October 1994. Both India and Colombia have expressed a desire to have close cooperation and similarity of views in relations to the Non-Aligned Movement and the next Summit. Venezauelan Minister of

State for Foreign Trade participated in the G-15 Conference held in New Delhi March 1994. Minister for Legal Affairs of Jamaica participated in the G-15 Conference held in New Delhi in March 1994. During the year, a few Indian companies signed Memoranda of Understanding with Guyanese companies for establishment of joint ventures, ITPO participated in the international fair, EXPOCOMER' 94, held in Panama and diplomatic relations were established with Honduras.

Vice President and Foreign Minister of Suriname, where 40 per cent of the population is of India origin, paid a State visit to India during November 1994 and held bilateral discussions with Indian leaders. India agreed to donate an agricultural project, a home gardening project and 10,000 bicycles to Suriname. The first Joint Commission meeting between India and Suriname was held in November 1994.

APEC organised a buyer-seller meet in May 1994 in Chile. Supreme Court Justice Kuldip Singh and Delhi High Court Justice Y.K. Sabharwal visited Chile in August 1994 to attend the post-meet of the International Law Conference.

Minister of Planning and Development of Trinidad and Tobago visited India and discussed matters of bilateral interest with Indian leaders. Government of Trinidad and Tobago has given five acres of land on a 99-year lease to Government of India for setting up Mahatma Gandhi Institute for Cultural Cooperation. ITPO arranged participation of 19 firms at the third International Exposition 94, held in Port of Spain in April 1994.

Cuban Foreign Minister visited India in March 1994 and held discussions with Indian leaders on ways of expanding bilateral cooperation and trade. Minister of State for Non-Conventional Energy Sources visited Cuba in June 1994 to attend Solar Energy International Conference. India has donated a 11 kw solar energy plant to Cuba to electrify a village. Minister of State for Commerce led the Indian delegation to the second session of the Indo-Cuban Joint Commission held in June-July 1994 in Havana. A four-member delegation from Cuba visited India for exploring possibilities of import of sugar mill machinery and spares from India. A four-member CSIR delegation also visited Cuba to discuss nickel extraction.

India enjoys warm relations with the African countries and has always attached special significance to her relations with Africa. Africa continues to be a major thrust area under the Indian Technical and Economic Cooperation (ITEC) and Special Commonwealth African Assistance Programme (SCAAP), executed by the Ministry of External Affairs. Out of a total of 1,350 slots allocated for training in Indian civilian institutions under ITEC for 1994-95, 768 (more than 50 per cent) were reserved for countries in Africa. Twenty-eight Indian experts are also in station in various African countries as of December 1994. Out of 250 slots offered to friendly developing countries for training in Indian defence establishments under the ITEC Programme, more than 150 were allotted to countries in Africa.

The changed politicl scenario in Southern Africa, the integration of South African and Namibian economies, the entry of South Africa into Southern Africa Development Community (SADC), the revival of the Eastern Africa Community among Kenya, Tanzania and Uganda, and greater cooperation among countries of the southern and eastern regions are positive developments and could be expected to play a vital role in the economic regeneration and development of Africa.

Vice President, Shri K.R. Narayanan accompanied by Smt. Usha Narayanan, Smt. Sonia Gandhi and Minister of State for Commerce, represented India at the inauguration of Dr. Mandela as the first President of the new South Africa. Dr. Mandela paid a State visit to India January 1995 and was the Chief Guest at the Republic Day celebrations. During his visit, India and South Africa signed a Treaty on Principles of Inter-State Relations and Cooperation, an Agreement to set up a Joint Commission and a Protocol providing for regular consultations between the Foreign Ministries of the two countries. The Indian Emabssy established in Pretoria in May 1994 was redesignated as High Commission with South Africa joining the Commonwealth on 1 June 1994. India also established a Consulate General in Durban in May 1994, and the Indian Cultural Centre in Johannesburg was converted into a Consulate General Indexpo '94, the largest single country trade exhibition ever organised in South Africa was held in Johannesburg in August 1994. The Indian naval ships, *INS Gomati* and *INS Khukri* visited Durban and Simonstown in December. The South African Deputy Foreign Minister visited India in November 1994. A bilateral agreement to set up the India-South Africa Joint Commission and a Protocol providing for regular consultations between the Foreign Offices were initialled.

During the visit of President Mugabe in March 1994, India agreed to cooperate with Zimbabwe in the informal sector particularly in the development of small and middle enterprises. Smt. Sonia Gandhi attended the ceremony to mark the reintegration of Walvis Bay and the off-shore Islands into Namibia as Special Guest of President Sam Nujoma. A Namibian Parliamentary delegation led by the Chairman of the National Council visited India in September 1994 followed by Defence Minister for purchase of defence equipment. The visit of Finance and Communication Minister of Seychelles in January 1994 has raised hopes of improved trade relations between India and Seychelles. Two Indian navalships-*INS Gomati* and *INS Khukri*-paid a goodwill visit to Port Victoria from 23 to 26 November 1994. India deputed seven experts to Seychelles under the ITEC

Programme. Following the death of President Juvenal Habyarimana of Rwanda in an air crash on 6 April 1994 and the outbreak of ethnic violence in that country, all the Indians there (300 in number) migrated. India supplied relief materials worth Rs. five lakh to Rwandese refugees in Tanzania. An Indian army battalion to United Nations Aid Mission in Rwanda (UNAMIR) reached Kigali on 10 Novermber 1994. Rwanda has shown interest in increasing and strengthening economic and technical cooperation with India. The Angolan External Affairs Minister paid an official visit to India in April 1994. Compaore, President of Burkino Faso paid a visit to India in July 1994. India announced a grant of Rs. 15 crore approximately for setting up an agricultural development project in Burkina Faso.

The traditionally close and friendly relations between Mauritius and India have deepened further during 1994-95. Vice President leading a high-level delegation visited Mauritius for one day in May 1994. Other visits included those of Mauritian Vice President, and Ministers of External Affairs and Finance. Bilateral trade has increased by almost 30 per cent in 1994 and a number of new joint ventures in different fields were established. Mauritius has emerged as the main centre for channelising investments into India through off-shore funds as a result of the advantageous provisions of the treaty for Avoidance of Double Taxation. Twenty-nine civilian training slots were utilised by Mauritius under the ITEC Programme during the year.

Indo-Kenyan relations continued to be warm and friendly, characterised by mutual regard. President Moi stopped over in Delhi on his way to Beijing in May 1994. India donated 476 metric tonnes of rice to Kenya for the drought-affected areas. A Cultural Exchange Programme was signed between the two nations in May 1994. Minister of Civil Aviation and Tourism visited Tanzania in January 1994 and the Tanzanian Home Minister-cum-Deputy Prime

Minister visited India. Tanzania utilised 23 civilian training slots under the ITEC Programme. India's relations with Uganda witnessed positive developments during 1994-95. President Museveni led a high-powered trade and investment delegation to India in September 1994. In December, Ugandan Minister of Education and Sports visited India while several Indian business delegations visited Uganda.

General Gnassingbe Eyadema, President of Togo, paid a State visit to India in September 1994. This opened a new chapter in mutual relations and added an impetus to bilateral cooperation between the two countries. India also announced a grant of Rs. 10 crore approximately for setting up of an agricultural project in Togo and agreed to cooperate in the fields of city transportation, healthcare, scientific research, trade, industry and agriculture. India and Togo also decided to set up a Joint Commission and signed a Memorandum of Understanding on Economic and Technical Cooperation. General Sani Abacha, Head of State of Nigeria visited India in March-April 1994 to attend G-15 Summit and also held bilateral discussions with Indian leadership. Nigeria utilised 10 civilian training slots under the ITEC Programme during 1994-95.

President Diouf of Senegal visited New Delhi in March 1994 to attend the G-15 Summit and had wide-ranging bilateral discussions with the Prime Minister. Foreign Minister also attended the G-15 Troika and Ministerial level meetings. An eye clinic in Ghana is under execution by India. Ghana utilised 13 civilian training slots while two Indian experts were deputed there under ITEC Programme. In Mozambique, after decades of civil war, the ruling Frelimo Party and the main opposition Renamo signed a Peace Accord in 1992 and participated in the country's first multi-party elections in October 1994 under UN supervision. Frelimo Party leader, Joaquin Chissano was re-elected as President. India welcomed this development.

3

South East Asia and the Pacific

India's relations with the countries in the South East Asian region have expanded and diversified and more so since the conscious adoption of our 'Look East' policy which sought to strengthen existing linkages and forging new ones with the ASEAN countries. The closeness of relationship was reflected in the exchange of visits with these countries, including visit of H.R.H. Crown Prince of Thailand to India and holding of joint Commission Meetings with Laos and Vietnam. Total bilateral trade with ASEAN countries in 1997-98 was US $ 5.98 billion compared to US $ 5.99 billion in 1996-97. The marginal decline in bilateral trade can be largely attributed to the fall in the value of the currencies of ASEAN countries and contraction in imports from India. The economic difficulties facing these countries have posed new challenges and we offered to cooperate with these countries in finding ways and means to ensure that the crisis does not adversely impact on our economic & commercial relations.

Our ties with ASEAN have been developing satisfactorily since India became a Full Dialogue Partner of the ASEAN in 1996. The ASEAN India Joint Cooperation Committee Meeting held in New Delhi in April 1998 provided important mechanisms for implementing various decisions. India has a fundamental interest in the regional security issues as we share maritime boundaries with several ASEAN countries and land and maritime boundary with Myanmar. India sought to promote wider and deeper contact with ASEAN countries in the ASEAN and ARF framework to promote peace development and security in the region. Shri Jaswant Singh, Deputy Chairman, Planning Commission and a special envoy of PM led the Indian delegation to the 31st ASEAN Post Ministerial Conference (PMC) and the 5th ASEAN Regional Forum (ARF) meetings held in Manila in July 1998. The ARF Meeting was significant for India as it was the first time after our nuclear tests that all nuclear weapons States were interacting in a security related forum. The meetings provided opportunities for important bilateral interactions with ASEAN and ARF members.

Following our nuclear tests in May last year, Australia had taken several measures including ban on visits to India of Ministers and senior officials and suspension of defence cooperation and non-humanitarian aid. In response to the Australian measures Indian Government took reciprocal actions. The Australian government in December, 1998 decided to relax the suspension on Ministerial and senior officials' visits, but the other restrictions remained in place. The Australian Government has recently been trying to start official contacts at high level. Australian deputy PM and Minister of Trade Tim Fisher is scheduled to visit India from February 25ù27,1999 to co-chair the Joint Ministerial Commission Meeting with Commerce Minister.

Cambodia

After months of infighting and violent incidents, general elections were held in Cambodia on July 26 to elect a 122 member National Assembly. These elections were the first since a UNùorganised vote in 1993 which followed years of war and political upheaval. In the five years since that poll, Cambodia witnessed further violence and bloodshed. The National Election Committee of Cambodia declared the poll results on 1 September showing that the Cambodian Peoples Party (CPP) led by Hun Sen had won 64 seats, followed by Prince Norodom Ranariddh's FUNCINPEC with 43 seats and the SAM RAINSY's party with 15 seats. At a summit held on 12 &13 November, under the auspices of King Norodom Sihanouk, the CPP and the FUNCINPEC reached an agreement, to form Cambodia's next coalition government ending a deadlock of almost three months since the declaration of the results. In accordance with the deal, Mr Hun Sen was appointed as the sole Prime Minister; Prince Ranariddh as the President of the National Assembly and Mr Chea Sim, President of CPP becoming the Chairman of a newly created Senate.

India maintained friendly and close relations with Cambodia. On Cambodian Government's request, a team of five officials led by Shri Sayan Chatterjee, Deputy Election Commissioner from the Election Commission was deputed to Cambodia from 19-29 July as Observers to observe the elections. Bilateral trade during 199798 amounted to Rs. 10.3 crores. India donated medicines worth Rs. Five lakhs for humanitarian assistance to the internally displaced persons in Cambodia. As part of the Celebrations of the 50th Anniversary of India's Independence a Photo Exhibition was organised in July 1998 and Leela Samson's Group gave two dance performances.

General Ke Kim Yan, Chief of General Staff, Ministry of Defence of Cambodia led a 3-member delegation for participation in the AeroIndia'98 at Bangalore from 6-14 December, 1998.

The UN General Assembly, on the recommendations of the Credentials Committee decided (December 7) to give Cambodia's seat in the UN to the new coalition government after keeping it vacant for fifteen months.

At the 6th ASEAN Summit held in Hanoi on 15-16 December, 1998, it was decided to admit Cambodia as the ASEAN's tenth member at a special admission ceremony to be organised in Hanoi on a subsequent date.

Lao people's democratic republic (Lao PDR)

India's relations with Lao People's Democratic Republic (Lao PDR) continued to be close and cordial with Laos showing considerable understanding on matters of importance to India. Dr Souli Nanthavong, Vice-Minister of Science, Technology and Environment of Laos visited India from 1-4 April to participate in the Global Environment Facility Conference at New Delhi. Shri S T Devare, Secretary (ER) visited Vientiane from 5-6 July, 1998 and had detailed discussions with the Lao Deputy Prime Minister, Vice-Minister of Foreign Affairs and other officials. Lao Vice-Minister of Commerce, Mr Siaosavath Savengsuksa visited India from 15ù17 November to attend the India-G77 and China Trade Conference.

Bilateral trade with Laos during 1997-98, while remaining at a modest level, showed a healthy increase, at Rs. 2.9 crores compared to Rs. 1.3 crores, in 1996-97 and maintained the trend during 199899. Several Indian companies such as Kirloskars, Tatas, BHEL, PEC etc. evinced keen interest in exploring the Lao market. Kirloskar Bros. Ltd., which exported irrigation pumps worth about US $ 30 million to Laos, set up a showroom-cum-service centre in Vientiane.

As part of 50th Anniversary Celebrations of India's Independence, an exclusive Indian Photo Exhibition was held at Savannakhet from 24-26 July; a Seminar titled

'India and Laos: Areas of Understanding and Cooperation' was held in Vientiane from 27-29 July; a Bharatnatyam dance recital by Ms Leela Samson and her troupe was held in Vientiane on 12 August and a Hindi feature film 'Aasman Se Gira' was screened in a prominent auditorium on the eve of the Birth Anniversary of Maulana Abul Kalam Azad on 10 November. 21 officials of the Lao Government attended training courses in India under ITEC and Colombo Plan. In one of the major archaeological findings in the southern Champassak Province, Hindu religious relics and symbols (Shiva Lingam) were discovered in September, reinforcing the strong cultural and civilizational links between the two countries between 5th and 17th century AD. Three Lao artisans visited Bhopal in May at the invitation of the Indira Gandhi Rashtriya Manav Sangrahalaya to participate in the Workshop & Exhibition of Folk and Tribal Artists from South East Asia and India.

Smt Vasundhara Raje, Minister of State for External Affairs visited Laos from 17-20 January, 1999 to co-chair the Second Meeting of the India-Laos Joint Commission (JCM) held in Vientiane on 18-19 January, 1999. The Lao delegation was led by H. E. Mr Phongsavath Boupha, Vice-Minister of Foreign Affairs of The Lao's People's Democratic Republic. In their discussions at the JCM, the leaders of the two delegations reviewed the overall state of bilateral relations and agreed to further strengthen and upgrade the existing economic and cultural relations which will be commensurate with the excellent political bilateral relations. During her visit to Laos, MOS called on the President and the Deputy Prime Minister and the Foreign Minister of Lao PDR. An Agreement for US $ 2 million soft credit to Laos and a Protocol to renew the Cultural Exchange Programme for another three years (1999-2001) were signed during the visit.

Vietnam

India and Vietnam continued to work towards further strengthening and diversifying the existing traditionally close and friendly relations. The 4th session of the India-Vietnam Joint Working Group Meeting (JWG) was held at Hanoi from 25-27 April and co-chaired by Shri S T Devare, Secretary (ER) from the Indian side. During the JWG detailed discussions were held with the Vietnamese side on promotion of bilateral trade and expansion of cooperation in agriculture, science and technology and small and medium industries. Smt Vasundhara Raje, Minister of State for External Affairs paid a visit to Hanoi on 18 & 19 June and had detailed discussions with Deputy PM and Foreign Minister Mr. Nguyen Manh Cam. In October 1998, Smt Suseela Gopalan, Minister of Industries of Kerala led a four-member delegation to Hanoi and had high level discussions with the Vietnamese ministers, for enhancing trade between the two countries. Shri Dilip Ray, Minister of State for Coal, accompanied by a high level delegation paid a visit to Vietnam from 4-7 November to discuss programme of cooperation between India and Vietnam in the field of coal trade

Bilateral trade during 1997-98 (Rs. 478.2 crores) registered a marginal increase of 12.5% over the 1996-97 volume of Rs. 425.2 crores and continued to grow further during 1998-99. The Embassy of India, Hanoi organised the Second Pride of India Exhibition at Hanoi from 23-26 October, 1998 in which 28 Indian companies, both from private and public sector displayed state-of-the-art products in various industries and services. Coinciding with the Exhibition were: the 3rd Meeting of the India-Vietnam Joint Business Council in Hanoi and a visit of nine-member delegation from Engineering Export Promotion Council to Hanoi and Ho Chi Minh City for business promotion.

Funds were raised in April 1998 for upgrading a School in Nam Mao Commune and with the approval of the Vietnamese Government the school was renamed 'The Vietnam-India Friendship School'. Three Vietnamese artists visited Bhopal in May at the invitation of the Indira Gandhi Rashtriya Manav Sangrahalaya to participate in the Workshop & Exhibition of Folk and Tribal Artists from South East Asia and India. The Leela Samson dance troupe visited Vietnam in August and gave performances at Hanoi, Ho Chi Minh City and Da Nang. A 12-member team of Indian scientists participated in the 5th ASEAN Science & Technology Week held at Hanoi from 5-15 October. The 2nd session of India-Vietnam joint Commission for Science & Technology (JCST) was held on November 2 & 3 in New Delhi. A Seminar on India-Vietnam Studies was organised in Ho Chi Minh City on 5 November. Six Indian scientists visited Vietnam from 10-12 November to participate in the first ever joint seminar on biotechnology. A delegation from Vietnam's Institute of Oceanography visited Goa in October to participate in the International Symposium on Information Technology and discuss bilateral cooperation. Historic photographs of President Ho Chi Minh and Nehru taken on the occasion of Nehru's visit to Hanoi and Ho Chi Minh's visit to Delhi in 1958 were presented on Children's Day (14 November) to Ho Chi Minh Museum for permanent display. Three Indian Naval Ships - INS Rajput, INS Delhi and INS Khanjar paid a Goodwill visit to Vietnam from 1-4 October. Regular exchanges of armed forces delegations from both sides took place.

The Cultural Exchange Programme between India and Vietnam for the years 1998-2000 was signed at Hanoi on 14 December, 1998.

Vietnam hosted the 6th ASEAN Summit at Hanoi on 15-16 December, 1998. The Summit leaders outlined a

'Hanoi Plan of Action' for the period 1999-2004 indicating measures aimed at enhancing intra-regional economic integration, trade liberalization and financial cooperation and to establish an ASEAN free trade area by 2002.

An 8-member Vietnamese Parliamentary delegation visited India from 13-22 December, 1998 on a study tour on population and development policy under UNFPA Hanoi - Country Programme.

Dr R Chidambaram, Chairman, Atomic Energy Corporation of India led a six member delegation to Vietnam from 14-19 January, 1999 to discuss bilateral cooperation programme with Vietnam Atomic Energy Corporation.

H. E. Mr Nguyen Manh Cam, Deputy Prime Minister for Foreign Affairs of the Socialist Republic of Vietnam visited India from 30 January, 1999 to co-chair the 9th meeting of the India-Vietnam joint Commission held in New Delhi. During the visit H. E. Mr Cam called on the President and the Prime Minister. At the joint Commission Meeting, discussions were held on bilateral, regional and international matters of mutual interest and for reviewing the ongoing cooperation and identifying fresh areas with a view to enhancing bilateral interaction. An agreement for extending soft credit of Rs. 47 crores to Vietnam and a Work Plan for 1999-2000 in the area of agriculture were signed during the visit. The two sides agreed to setting up a Working Group on coal for cooperation in the sector. Besides the officials, a 5-member business delegation accompanied the Vietnamese dignitary for interaction with Indian businessmen.

Indonesia

During 1998-99, there were major economic and political

upheavals in Indonesia, which became the biggest victim of the economic crisis that hit the East Asian countries in late 1997. The economic downturn resulted in depreciation of over 70% in the value of the Indonesian Rupiah, sharp rise in the prices of food and other essential goods and massive layoffs. Succumbing to internal and external pressure in the wake of worsening economic crisis, students unrest and rioting in Indonesia, President Soeharto resigned on May 21 after being in office for 32 years, and handed over power to Vice-President B J Habibie. With President Habibie at the helm of affairs, Indonesia entered an era of greater openness and political freedom, which saw a proliferation of political parties. A special session of Indonesia's highest constitutional body, the People's Consultative Assembly (MPR) was held from 10-13 November to approve a framework for political reform. MPR Session was opposed by various groups seeking immediate removal of the Indonesian Armed Forces (ABRI) from the House and investigation into former President Soeharto's wealth. Failure of MPR Session to accommodate people's demands and fulfill their aspirations led to huge demonstrations and widespread rioting during the month. During the Special Session, MPR endorsed twelve decrees which pledged to hold elections in May/June 1999; to limit President's and Vice-President's tenure to two terms in office; to reduce armed forces' allocation of seats in the House gradually and a decree on good governance free from corruption, collusion and nepotism.

Bilateral relations between India and Indonesia, which have been traditionally close and cordial, continued to progress satisfactorily with bilateral exchanges and Indonesia showing understanding on issues of vital interest to us. Prof Dr Farid Anfasa Moeloek, Minister of Health of Indonesia, visited New

Delhi from 3-7 September, 1998 to attend WHO Conference during which he had discussions with our Minister for Chemicals & Fertilizers, Shri Surjit Singh Barnala. Shri Madan Lal Khurana, Minister for Parliamentary Affairs & Tourism led a ten-member parliamentary delegation to Jakarta (September 22-25). The delegation had meaningful exchanges with Indonesian Ministers for Population, Education and Tourism besides interacting with the Indonesian parliamentarians. The delegation also met prominent Buddhists and representatives from travel industry in Indonesia in connection with the Buddha Mahotsav organised in India from October 24ùNovember 8, 1998. Prof Dr Juwono Sudarsono, Minister of Education and Culture of Indonesia visited New Delhi from 11ù14 October, 1998 to deliver a lecture under the 'India-ASEAN Eminent Persons Lecture Series'. During the visit Prof Sudarsono called on our Minister of Human Resource Development, Dr Murli Manohar Joshi.

Shri S T Devare, Secretary (ER), MEA visited Jakarta from July 9-11 for bilateral consultations and met the Indonesian Foreign Minister, the Education Minister, ASEAN Secretary-General and senior Government officials. Dr J S Djiwandono, Professor of Economics and former Governor of Bank of Indonesia visited Delhi from 12-13 September to deliver a lecture for the ASEAN-India Eminent Persons Lecture series. Shri Virendra Dayal, Member, National Human Rights Commission visited Jakarta from 6-10 September to participate in the Third Annual Meeting of the Asia Pacific Forum of Human Rights. Shri Sayan Chatterjee, Deputy Election Commissioner paid a visit to Indonesia from 29 Novemberù6 December, 1998 to participate in bilateral and multi-lateral conferences on electoral law reforms arranged by the International Institute for Democracy and Electoral Assistance (IDEA)'s Mission to Indonesia.

Bilateral trade between the two countries during 1997-98 amounted to Rs. 4330.3 crores as compared to Rs. 4226.2 crores during 1996-97. With a view to strengthening trade relations with Indonesia (which registered a declining trend during 1998-99 due to the economic turmoil being faced by Indonesia for the past one year), a delegation led by Shri Nripendra Mishra, Additional Secretary in the Ministry of Commerce visited Indonesia from 1214 July and had meetings, inter alia, with Indonesian Minister of Trade and Industry. During this visit counter-trade arrangements as well as export from India of rice and bulk drugs were discussed. In September 1998, a delegation from the Indonesian pharmaceutical industry visited India to explore the possibility of import of bulk drugs from India. Indonesian State Logistic Bureau (Bulog), which is responsible for rice imports, sent a delegation to India in November 1998 for further discussions on rice imports.

As part of the celebrations of the 50th Anniversary of India's Independence, various functions were organised in Jakarta and other major cities in Indonesia. These included a Photo Exhibition, a Bharatnatyam dance performance by Ms Leela Samson and a Kuchipudi dance recital by Ms Swapan Sundri. Mr Nurcholish Madjid, an economic scholar visited India at the invitation of ICCR from 2-6 September to participate in an international seminar on India's Islamic Heritage.

Cooperation in the scientific and technical areas also continued. Over 63 Indonesian candidates received training in India under the Colombo Plan, ITEC and other schemes. Under the MOU signed by ISRO and LAPAN of Indonesia the construction of Telemetry, Tracking and Command (TIC) ground station at Biak (Kalimantan) for continuous monitoring ISRO's Geosynchronous Satellite Launch Vehicle (GSLV) was completed satisfactorily. As regards defence cooperation, an Indonesian Naval Ship visited India from 25-28 April to participate in joint exercise 'Madad'98'.

The next general elections in Indonesia will be held on June 7, 1999 to elect 500 members of the Lower House (DPR). The new DPR would be convened on August 29, 1999 and election of the President and Vice President would be held on November 10, 1999 after the consultation of the Upper House. Anti-government agitation and demonstration by students, communal strife between Christians and Muslims have continued unabated in various parts of Indonesia. Former President Soeharto was questioned by the office of the Attorney General on the charges of corruption.

India provided humanitarian assistance worth US $ 56,000 consisting of 18 tonnes; of baby milk powder to Indonesia. The consignment was handed over by our Ambassador to the Indonesian Minister of Health on 16 December, 1998.

Brunei Darussalam

Relations with Brunei Darussalam remained friendly and cordial. Shri S T Devare, Secretary (ER), Ministry of External Affairs, visited Brunei in early July for bilateral consultations on matters of mutual interest as part of the ongoing process. An Indian cultural week, first of its kind, was held in Brunei in June, in celebration of the 50th Independence Anniversary. The events included a Kathak dance performance, a photo exhibition, and a film festival.

Philippines

A new administration under President Joseph E Estrada took over in Philippines following elections in May 1998. The new administration addressed itself to the continuing economic and financial problems caused by the regional monetary and financial crisis, while maintaining continuity in external relations. Ties with India remained friendly and registered favourable trends during the year.

The 5th ASEAN Regional Forum (ARF) was held in Manila in July 1998. Philippines was in Chair. Earlier, Minister of State for External Affairs Ms Vasundhara Raje visited Manila from 17&18 June, 1998 in the course of which she conferred with President-elect Joseph Estrada and Foreign Secretary Domingo Siazon Jr.

The 3rd India-Philippines Foreign Office Consultations were held on 23 & 24 April, 1998 with the Indian delegation led by Secretary (ER) and the Philippine delegation by Undersecretary Mr Lauro L Baja, Jr. The consultations covered the whole range of bilateral relations besides regional and international issues.

The Indo-Philippine Agreement on Promotion and Reciprocal Protection of Investment was initialled in Manila in April 1998.

India-Philippines trade showed a downward trend during the year, with India's exports to the Philippines at $ 90 million from January to July marking a 31.36% decline from the same period last year. The decrease is to be mostly attributed to the impact of the regional monetary and financial crisis on the Philippine economy, causing reduced demand for industrial and consumer goods. A commercial delegation from India headed by Commerce Secretary visited the Philippines from 31 August to 1 September to hold discussions with the Philippine government officials including Secretaries (Ministers) of Trade, Agriculture and the Governor of the Central Bank of various matters pertaining to trade and economic relations including institutional and financial arrangements in sustaining bilateral trade, prospects for counter-trade and the possibility of using national currencies in trade exchanges. Two important trade issues which figured in discussions during the year related to Indian rice and buffalo meat exports. Greater market access for these products was sought and some gains were achieved.

Three Indian naval ships-INS Delhi, INS Khanjar and INS Jyotiûvisited Philippines from October 24-27,1998. The ships were visited by the Philippines Defence Secretary (Minister) and high-ranking officials of the Philippine Navy. They also held joint exercises units of the Philippine Navy.

Singapore

Close relations between India and Singapore have been underpinned by a steady growth in as East Asian economics potentialities shrunk. A large number of high level visits have been exchanged to demonstrate the political commitment of both governments to further India-Singapore relations. Important visits, Included visit by MOS of External Affairs in June 1998 and Secretary (ER) MEA during April 1998. In August 1998, Commerce Minister and a seven-member CEOs delegation of the Confederation of Indian Industry (CII) visited Singapore and called on Prime Minister, and Foreign Minister. During September 1998, Minister of Parliamentary Affairs and Tourism led a parliamentary delegation and interacted with the Speaker and inaugurated the International Buddha Festival. Four Indian naval ships paid a goodwill visit in September 1998. Minister of Power represented India at the East Asia Economic Summit organised in Singapore by the World Economic Forum in October 1998. Other important visitors in October included the Minister of Surface Transport as also Chief Commissioner (Investment and NRIs) and

Chairman IIC. In November 1998, Minister of State for Finance (Revenue, Banking and Insurance) held meetings with the Forum of Indian Banks and Insurance Companies in Singapore.

From the Singapore side, in July 1998, Mr Davindar Singh Member of Singapore Parliament, led a delegation of senior businessmen from the Indian Business Group of the Singapore Trade Development Board (TDB). He paid a courtesy call on the Prime Minister.

Indian exports to Singapore in Sing-dollars terms grew by 26% during January-November, 1998. Bilateral trade, however, remains in Singapore's favour at the ratio of 16:5. An important feature in bilateral trade was the entrepot role played by Singapore. with approximately 40% of trade-flow both ways comprising as re-exports. Singapore is a trading hub for Indian trade with South East and East Asian countries and a window for India's counter-trade in the region.

Thailand

India continued to maintain warm and friendly relations with Thailand. Bilateral cooperation continued in all fields. The two countries co-operated actively in the regional economic cooperation grouping. BIMST-EC, iaunched in June 1997.

Bilateral trade between India and Thailand was US $ 650 million in the year 1996-97 which declined to US $ 567 million in 1997-98. In 1998, this trend continued. The economic crisis in the region would seem to have affected the trade turnover. However, the surplus is still in favour of India, though reduced.

There were several high level visits to Thailand during this period. Commerce Minister led a delegation in April 1998, to attend the 54th Annual Session of ESCAP. During this visit, Commerce Minister met Thai

Deputy Prime Minister and Commerce Minister Dr Supachai Panitchpakdi and had useful discussions on various bilateral issues. Commerce Minister also led a delegation to Thailand in August, to participate in the Economic Ministers' Retreat of the BIMST-EC. Commerce Secretary led a business delegation to Thailand in September to explore ways and means of promoting trade and investment linkages. Shri Baba Gouda Patil, MOS for Rural Areas and Employment visited Thailand in June. He met the Thai Minister for Agriculture and Cooperatives, and visited various programmes being implemented by the Thai Government in the rural areas.

Shri Madan Lal Khurana, Minister of Parliamentary Affairs and Tourism visited Thailand in September 1998, as the head of a Parliamentary delegation. He held discussions with the President of the National Assembly of Thailand and the Chairman of the Foreign Relations and the Parliamentary Affairs Committee of the House of Representatives of the Thai Parliament. The Minister also utilised the opportunity to meet the Governor of the Tourism Authority of Thailand and to invite high level participation from Thailand for the Buddha Mahotsav which was celebrated in India in November 1998.

Both the National Assembly of Thailand and the newly established National Election Commission of Thailand interacted with the Election Commission of India on various aspects of the rules and procedures on conducting of elections and the electoral system in India.

H. R. H. Crown Prince Maha Vajiralongkorn of Thailand, along with his two daughters and Minister of Foreign Affairs of Thailand, paid a 7-day State visit to India (December 23-29) at the invitation of the Hon'ble Vice-President of India. During the visit, the Crown Prince held discussions with the President, Vice-President and Prime Minister in New Delhi.

Malaysia

India and Malaysia continued to maintain close and friendly relations. A number of important visits took place from India to Malaysia during this period. Dr Murli Manohar Joshi Minister of Science and Technology and Human Resource Development, led a delegation for the Commonwealth Games held in Kaula Lumpur from 11-21 September, 1998, and attended the inauguration of the sports event. He was accompanied by eight Members of Parliament and three Ministers from different States. During the visit, Dr Joshi also signed an Agreement of Cooperation with Malaysia in the field of Science and Technology. Shri Madan Lal Khurana, Minister of Parliamentary Affairs and Tourism headed a Parliamentary delegation to Malaysia from September 25-26, 1998, and had meetings with Malaysian Minister of Tourism and Speaker of the Senate. Shri Siddaramaiah, Deputy CM of Karnataka along with four other Ministers from the State, led a delegation to Malaysia to promote investment in the State. A business delegation headed by Commerce Secretary, P P Prabhu and comprising representatives from Ministry of Commerce, EXIM Bank, RBI, ECGC and FICCI visited Kuala Lumpur in August 1998. The delegation met with the Minister of International Trade and Industry Rafidah, Samy Vellu, Minister of Works etc. A 3-member delegation headed by Shri C M Udasi, Karnataka Minister of Public Works, visited Malaysia from June 25-29, 1998 and interacted with senior level officials including Malaysian Minister of Works and Malaysian Deputy Minister of Domestic Trade and Consumer Affairs Dato Subramaniam. He also invited Malaysians to invest in Karnataka, specially in developments of roads and highways and water supply projects. Prof U R Rao, Member, Space Commission of India, visited Malaysia July 14-19, 1998 and delivered addresses on space development at various apex institutions in Malaysia.

From the Malaysian side the Hon'ble Chief Minister of Penang, Tan Sri Dr Koh Tsu Koon led a business delegation to India on November 2-6,1998.

Australia

Relations between India and Australia were cordial and friendly before India's nuclear tests. Bilateral cooperation had been in full swing and was slated to grow in diverse fields but suddenly hit a lull, after India's nuclear tests of 11-13, May 1998.

Government of Australia reacted strongly to our nuclear tests. It recalled temporarily it's High Commissioner for consultations. Other measures directed against India were, suspension of bilateral defence relations with India, recall of Australian defence adviser and of Australian defence personnel currently training in India and Indian defence personnel undergoing training at Defence College in Australia, cancellation of ship and aircraft visits, suspension of non-humanitarian aid, and suspension of Ministerial and Senior Official Visits. India too conveyed its displeasure by responding similarly to Australian Government's actions. Since then bilateral relations have been on hold. General elections were held in Australia on 3rd October and the ruling Liberal Party of PM John Howard was returned to power, though with a reduced margin and formed a Coalition Government with the National Party.

Economic and trade relations between Australia and India, continued to expand. Two-way bilateral trade in 1997-98 stood at US $ 1.58 billion (an increase of 23% over the last year). With a sustained export effort, Indian exports to Australia in 1997-98 increased by 19% over the previous year reaching US $ 427 million. Australian companies are now taking an active interest in investments in India, in areas like mining, power, oil and natural gas and coal.

During the period, the Chief of Airstaff, Air Chief Marshall S K Sareen visited Australia (March 30-April 3) to attend the 1998 RAF Air-Power Conference before nuclear tests and a 7 member Australian Young Leaders Delegation comprising young Australians of different political and corporate backgrounds visited India (29 November-6 December) to initiate a programme of youth exchanges between Australia and India.

Former Australian FM Mr Gareth Evans paid a private visit (14-16 December) to India which was undertaken with full encouragement and support of the Australian Government.

The Australian Senate's Foreign Affairs, Defence and Trade References Committee held a public hearing on India and Pakistani nuclear tests on December 4, 1998. The officials of the Department of Foreign Affairs and Trade gave evidence to the Committee at the hearing for the second time - their previous appearance being in July 1998. Our High Commission has been told that the Government of Australia, in a review of measures adopted in response to the nuclear tests, has decided to relax suspension of Ministerial and senior officials visits. However, suspension of non-humanitarian aid and bilateral defence relations with India and Pakistan will remain in force.

New Zealand

New Zealand Government reacted strongly to India's nuclear tests. It announced a temporary recall of its High Commissioner from New Delhi for consultations. Its Foreign Ministry summoned the Indian High Commissioner S Kipgen twice to its Foreign Office to lodge New Zealand's protest against India even before our High Commissioner had presented his credentials. New Zealand also declined to accept the accreditation of our Defence Attache from Canberra. Since the Pokhran tests bilateral relations have been somewhat lukewarm. But efforts are being made by the New Zealand Government to improve trade relations with India. New Zealand's Minister for International Trade Dr Lockwood Smith visited India (10-15 October) to attend the 8th JBC Meeting in New Delhi on 12th October. A 30-member delegation comprising MPs and Speakers of State Legislatures led by Lok Sabha Speaker GMC Balayogi attended the 44th Commonwealth Parliamentary Conference in Wellington, New Zealand (17-23 October).

Bilateral trade between India and New Zealand has moved up at a satisfactory pace though in overall terms, it has remained on a modest scale with the balance of trade being in New Zealand's favour. India's exports to New Zealand for the year 1997-98 were Rs. 2,534 million/ US $ 63 million and imports Rs. 3,031 million/ US $ 76 million.

Papua New Guinea

Bilateral relations between India and Papua New Guinea have been friendly and cordial since the opening of our resident Mission in April 1996 in Port Moresby. PNG deplored India's nuclear tests of May 1998 but it was more or less, a proforma protest, as they had earlier also condemned similar tests by France and China. The leadership showed understanding and India's security concerns.

About 250 Indian professionals continued to be employed in Papua New Guinea. India awarded 12 scholarships for PNG nominees for short term training courses under ITEC/Colombo Plan. PNG utilised all the 12 slots awarded to them.

Two PNG artists from National Museum and Art Gallery attended the Workshop and Exhibition of Contemporary Folk & Tribal Artist of India and South

East Asia in Bhopal from 27th May to 5th June. M/s UBS Publishers and Distributors, New Delhi signed a Memorandum of Understanding with the PNG Writers and Artists Association in October under which the books written by the Members of the Association will be published by the Indian firm.

PNG continued to support India's candidatures to the UN bodies, including those of Shri V K Shunglu, Comptroller and Auditor General of India for election to the UN Board of Auditors and India's candidature to the Executive Board of the International Coffee Organisation.

One of the Islands of Papua New Guinea was devastated by the onslaught of strong tidal waves on July 17 causing large scale destruction of property and loss of many lives. Medicines worth Rs. 5 lakhs have been gifted to the Government of Papua New Guinea as relief assistance.

Bilateral trade between India and PNG gained momentum. According to available indications, India's direct exports as well as exports through third countries to PNG, continued to increase during the period.

Fiji

India and Fiji enjoyed, close, cordial relations in the past. The new constitution of Fiji came into effect from July 27, 1998 and according to it, the country is now known as "The Republic of Fiji-Islands" and its nationals as "Fiji-Islanders". Trade relations between two countries resumed with the lifting of trade embargo by the Ministry of Commerce. Government of India communicated its acceptance in principle and on June 9, Cabinet accorded approval to the re-opening of the Indian High Commission in Suva (Fiji).

This decision of the Government was conveyed to the Government of Fiji and the host Government's approval was received on June 25th. A three-member delegation from Ministry of External Affairs visited Fiji (1-3 November) to assess government property and to finalise pending issues to facilitate re-opening of Indian High Commission in Suva. Joint Secretary (South) also visited Fiji (11-14 November) to meet with various important dignitaries / Govt. officials. This was the first high level official visit to Suva after the closure of Indian Mission nearly a decade ago. Fijian PM Rabuka announced that general elections would be held on 24 April, 1999 under the newly amended constitution.

Bilateral relations with Pacific-Islands have been cordial and friendly though there have been minimal contacts. The Pacific Islands mildly condemned our nuclear tests. President of Nauru H.E. Mr Kinza Godfrey Cloduman visited India to attend the Global Environment Facility (GEF) assembly (1-3 April, 1998).

4

East Asia

China

We seek good relations with all our neighbours including China. We believe that the Five Principals of Peaceful Coexistence, jointly enunciated by India and China, are of continuing relevance to the development of our relations. We seek a relationship in which both sides are responsive to each other's concerns. We remain committed to the process of dialogue to resolve outstanding differences and to the development of friendly, cooperative, good neighbourly and mutually beneficial relationship with China.

The India-China border has remained generally peaceful. Both sides have reiterated their commitment to the maintenance of peace and tranquillity in accordance with the Agreement on Border Peace and Tranquillity (1993) and Agreement on Confidence Building Measures in the Military Field along the Line of Actual Control in the India-China Border Areas (1996).

The Joint Working Group (JWG) on the boundary question was set up by a decision of the Prime Ministers of the two countries in 1988, to seek a fair, reasonable and mutually acceptable settlement of the boundary question. The JWG has met ten times so far. The Eleventh meeting of the JWG, scheduled to be held in Beijing in

1998, was not convened by the Chinese side. Foreign Office Consultations, in the framework of the Protocol on this subject concluded in August 1997, were held in Beijing on 25-26 February, 1999.

Exchanges at the governmental, parliamentary, nongovernmental, people-to-people and other levels continued during the year. Functional exchanges in trade & commerce; environment; railways; industries; agriculture; energy; non-conventional energy; education; civil services and public administration; space; science & technology; remote sensing; aeronautics; medicines; engineering; academics; culture 'and sports continued. Chief of General Staff of Chinese People's Liberation Army (PLA), General Fu Quanyou, visited India from April 26-May 1, 1998 - the first-ever visit by a PLA Chief of General Staff. The 6th meeting of the India-China Expert Group of diplomatic and military officials, a sub-group of the JWG, was held in Beijing on June 8-9,1998. Deputy Chairman, Planning Commission met the Chinese Foreign Minister during the ASEAN Regional Forum - Post Ministerial Conference (ARF -PMC) Meeting in Manila on July 27,1998. The Vice Chairman of China's National People's Congress (NPC) met our Speaker during the International Parliamentary Union (IPU) Conference in Moscow on 11 September, 1998. A delegation of Parliamentarians visited China in October to participate in the 6th General Assembly of the Asia-pacific Parliamentarians' Conference on Environment and Development. Bilateral party-level exchanges during this period included visits of a delegation of the Chinese Communist Party to India in September to attend the CPI party congress in Chennai and in October in Calcutta for the CPM party congress. A 3-member delegation from the Janata Party visited China in October 1998. At the NGO level, the first ever gathering of academics of the neighbouring regions of North-Eastern

India and South-Western China deliberated on "Regional Development in India and China", in New Delhi, on November 19-20, 1998. Another delegation of Chinese scholars participated in the "Sino-India Track 11 Dialogue" organised by the Centre for Policy Research from 25-28 January, 1999 in New Delhi.

India-China trade relations have continued to grow. Bilateral trade during 1998 reached US$ 1.922 billion, marking an increase of 5.02% over 1997. India-China border trade conducted through Lipulekh Pass (Uttar Pradesh) and Shipki La Pass (HP) amounted to Rs. 51.7 lakhs in 1998.

Japan

We remain committed to friendly co-operative, mutually beneficial relations with Japan with whom we have shared cultural links and values of human freedoms, commitment to peace, stability and economic development of the people in Asia and the world.

In the immediate aftermath of our nuclear tests in May 1998, Japan took several measures including a freeze on Yen loans and grant assistance for new projects and calling off a series of scheduled meetings and visits. Bilateral dialogue, encompassing issues covering our multifaceted relationship, resumed in January 1999. This includes Foreign Secretary level talks, Trade Talks and MEA-MITI dialogue. Other meetings are being scheduled.

High level exchanges during the year include the meeting between:

- Our two Speakers in Tokyo (26 October, 1998)
- Shri I K Gujral, Chairman of the Standing Committee on External Affairs and Prime Minister, Foreign Minister and Finance Minister of Japan (October 1998)

- Shri Sikander Bakht, Industry Minister and the Japanese Minister for International Trade and Industry (November 1998)

Visits from Japan include :

- A six-member Japanese Parliamentary Delegation led by Deputy Speaker Mr Kozo Watanabe(November 1998)
- Dr Taro Nakayama, President of the Japan-India Parliamentary Friendship League (April 1998)
- Ms Akiko Yanamaka Member of House of Representatives of Japan (April 1998) and
- Mr Shin Sakurai, Chairman of the Asian Forum of Parliamentarians on population and development (April 1998)

Our Minister of Industry participated in the FICCI sponsored seminar "Destination India" in Japan (1-6 November, 1998) organised by FICCI. The 29th meeting of the India-Japan Business Cooperation Committee was held in Delhi (30 November-1 December, 1998)

India's exports to Japan amounted to Rs. 69072 million in 199798 and India's imports from Japan Rs. 79117 million. According to the Sectt. of Industrial Approvals, proposals approved for Japan's investment in India, till July 1998 amounted to Rs 72,103 million.

Exchanges of scientists, engineers and research scholars continued. Eminent Buddhist scholars and monks participated in the Buddha Mahotsava (5-8 November, 1998).

Republic of Korea (ROK)

Relations with the Republic of Korea (ROK) continue to be marked with cordiality and understanding.

Smt Vasundhara Raje, MOS (EA) visited Seoul (January 21-24) for bilateral consultations. She met the ROK PM, the FM and the MOS for Trade in the Ministry of Foreign Affairs and Trade. MOS (EA) extended an invitation to the ROK PM to visit India.

The ROK PM, Mr Kim Jong Pil, visited India (February 10-11). Alongwith the Vice President he inaugurated the CII sponsored India Engineering Trade Fair (IETF'99) where ROK participated as a Partner Country. More than 140 Korean companies participated in the IETF. A week long festival of cultural events from Korea was organised to coincide with the IETF.

High level exchanges during the year include

- Meeting between Shri I K Gujral, Chairman of the Standing Committee on External Affairs and President Kim Dae-Jung in Seoul (October 1998)
- Visit of a 31-member Korea Chamber of Commerce and Industry delegation for the 15th meeting of the India-ROK joint Business Council (JBC) in New Delhi (29 October, 1998)
- Visit of Dr M Thambi Durai, Union Minister of Surface Transport to ROK (October 1998) for the 5th World Congress on Intelligent Transport Systems.

The two-way trade between India and ROK in 1997-98 amounted to Rs. 48,615 million, India's exports to ROK being Rs. 1,53,00 million and imports from ROK Rs. 33,315 million. Investment approvals till July 1998 amounted to Rs. 59,051 million.

Buddhist leaders and scholars from ROK participated in the Buddha Mahotsava (November 1998). Exchanges of cultural delegations, students and research scholars continued.

The Government of ROK opened an Honorary Consulate General in Calcutta in November 1998.

Democratic People's Republic of Korea (DPRK)

India's relations with the Democratic People's Republic of Korea(DPRK) continue to be friendly and cordial. Consultations between the Foreign Offices of the two countries were held in Pyongyang (14-18 February, 1998). During the occasion, a protocol of co-operation between the Foreign Ministries of India and DPRK was also signed.

According to Foreign Trade Statistics of India, trade between India and DPRK during 1997-98 amounted to Rs. 6,982 million, India's export to DPRK being Rs. 3,164 million and imports from DPRK Rs. 3,817 million.

Shri Mukhtar Abbas Naqvi, Union Minister of State for Information & Broadcasting visited Pyongyang (22-26 September, 1998) to participate in the Sixth Pyongyang Film Festival for Non Aligned and Developing countries.

India continued its humanitarian assistance to DPRK which has been experiencing food shortage for some time. India sent 50-meteric tonnes of baby food and 1000 metric tonnes of rice during the year.

5

Central Asia

Both bonds of history and geo-strategic location of the Central Asian States (CAS) in an extended neighbourhood make India's relations with them a matter of priority. The region has profound strategic and economic importance for us. Since independence of these countries seven years ago, conscious efforts have been made to strengthen and diversify relations and to bring a contemporary focus to our age-old ties.

India and the CAS share common values of democracy, secularism and opposition to fundamentalism and terrorism. There is also the mutual recognition that national security concerns of Central Asia and India are closely inter-linked. Bilateral political relations with these countries are marked by close understanding.

In the economic sphere, abundant natural resources of Central Asia and India's technological and scientific capabilities provide the rationale for collaboration, notwithstanding the current problems of transitional economies in these states. Efforts are being made to overcome these temporary difficulties.

Cultural and people-to-people relations are excellent and consciously nurtured by us.

Azerbaijan

Initiatives to develop all round bilateral relations with

Azerbaijan were continued. Smt Vasundhara Raje, Minister of State of External Affairs visited Baku in June 1998 which coincided with an exclusive Indian trade exhibition organised by ITPOùHINDEXOPO 98. Minister of Petroleum and Natural Gas, Shri V K Ramamurthy visited in June 1998 to attend the Baku International Oil and Gas Conference. It has been decided to open a resident mission in Baku which is likely to start functioning in March 1999.

Kazakhstan

Indo-Kazakh relations progressed smoothly during the year under report. Foreign Minister Tokaev met Minister of State for External Affairs Smt. Vasundhara Raje in September, 1998 at the UNGA. The second session of the Indo-Kazakh Joint Science and Technology Committee was held in Almaty in October 1998. A Kazakh parliamentary delegation is likely to visit in the first quarter of 1999. Indian Airlines and Air Kazakhstan signed a code sharing agreement in September 1998 and the latter is in the process of starting their flights to India in the near future. India participated in the 7th Asia Pacific International Trade Fair (ASPAT '98) in Almaty in October 1998 under the aegis of India Trade Promotion Organisation (ITPO). Punjab National Bank opened its representative office in Almaty in October, 1998.

The next meeting of Indo-Kazakh Joint Commission is likely to be held in the second half of March 1999 and Dr. Umirzak Sultangazin, Director Space Research Institute of Kazakhstan and Co-Chairman of Indo-Kazakh Joint Committee on Science and Technology is likely to visit India in March 1999 for a series of lectures.

Kyrgyzstan

Traditional relations with Kyrgyzstan progressed well. Foreign Office consultations were held in July 1998 when Deputy Foreign Minister of Kyrgyzstan H.E. Mr Erian

Abdildayav visited New Delhi. Our Minister of State for Tourism Shri Omak Apang visited Kyrgyzstan in October 1998. We gifted a 'mini dairy plant' to Kyrgyzstan under the ITEC programme. Mr B T Shamshiev, Director of State Agency for Tourism and Sport, visited India along with a delegation of tour operators in December 1998.

H.E. Mr Bolot T Shamshiev, Chairman of the State Agency for Tourism and Sports (Ministerial status) visited from 14-18 December, 1998 on the invitation of Shri Omank Apang, Minister of State for Tourism.

Days of Kyrgyz Culture in India are scheduled to be held from 6-14 March, 1999. Kyrgyz Defence Minister visited India from 2027 February, 1999 on the invitation of the Defence Minister, Shri George Fernandes.

Tajikistan

Official level consultations with Tajikistan on bilateral matters as well as situation in Afghanistan were held in Dushanbe in August 1998. Two consignments of humanitarian assistance were sent. Tajikistan participated in short term training courses under the ITEC programme. Smt Vasundhara Raje, MOS for External Affairs met Tajik Minister of Foreign Affairs Mr Nazarov in September 1998 at UNGA.

Tajik President Mr Emamali Rakhmonov paid a working visit to New Delhi on 22 January, 1999 and had a luncheon meeting with PM. Both the sides agreed to step up economic and commercial cooperation between the two countries.

Turkey

India-Turkey relations witnessed significant forward movement with high level political exchanges and important initiatives in the commercial, economic and cultural fields. The high points of the year was the state visit of President Shri K R Narayanan in September 1998, followed by the visit of Vice-President Shri Krishan Kant in October 1998 to participate in the 75th Anniversary of founding of the Turkish Republic. During President's visit, Agreements on Prevention of Traffic in Narcotic Drugs, and Bilateral Investment Promotion and Protection, besides an MOU on scientific and technological cooperation and a Protocol on exchange of trade information were signed. Foreign Office consultations were held in Ankara in April 1998 for which Secretary (East) Shri Nareshwar Dayal visited Turkey. Shri G M C Balayogi, Speaker of Lok Sabha, along with a Parliamentary delegation visited Turkey in July 1998. India participated in the Izmir International Trade Fair in August 1998 as 'Guest Country'. The third meeting of the Indo-Turkish Joint Business Council was held on that occasion. A defence industry delegation from India visited Turkey in May 1998 and a team from National Defence College (NDC) in June 1998. On the cultural and educational front, an Indian food festival was organised in Izmir in August, 1998 when an ICCR sponsored cultural troupe also visited. A delegation of University Grants Commission (UGC) headed by its Chairman visited in May 1998. Turkish Minister of Transport and Communications, Mr Ahmet DenizonIgun visited India to participate in the Management Policy Seminar of Transport Ministers. During the visit, he called on Minister of Railways Shri Nitish Kumar, Minister of State of Communications Shri Kabindra Purkayastha and Minister of Civil Aviation Shri Ananth Kumar,

Turkmenistan

An Indian scientific delegation representing Central Electronics Ltd. (CEL) and Council for Scientific and Industrial Research(CSIR) visited Turkmenistan in June 1998 to study the possibilities of cooperation in the solar energy sector. A delegation from Indian Oil

Corporation(IOC) visited Turkmenistan and had useful discussions with the Deputy Minister of Oil and Gas Industry of Turkmenistan. A three-member delegation from Punjab Agri-Export Corporation visited Turkmenistan in November, 1998 with a proposal to set up joint commercial farming for which a Protocol of Intent was signed. The Indo-Turkmen joint venture - 'Ajanta Pharma Turkmenderman' was inaugurated by President Mr Niyazov in Ashgabat on 11th December, 1998 in the presence of Shri Som Pal, Minister of State for Agriculture.

Uzbekistan

Relations with Uzbekistan remained active. Shri V K Ramamurthy, Minister for Petroleum and Natural Gas, at the head of a delegation, visited Uzbekistan in October 1998. A delegation of science and technology experts from Ministry of Science and Technology visited Uzbekistan in May 1998 with a view to exploring further possibilities of cooperation in S&T. Shri Jasjit Singh, Director, Institute of Defence Studies and Analysis visited Uzbekistan in June 1998 to establish institutional linkages between IDSA and the Institute of Strategic and Regional Research of Uzbekistan. Two rounds of Foreign Office consultations were held, in May, 1998 when Secretary (East) Shri Nareshwar Dayal visited Tashkent and in December 1998 when Mr I Ergashev, Deputy Minister of Foreign Affairs visited Delhi. In the economic and commercial sphere, a delegation of manufacturers of auto components and another of consultancy firms visited Uzbekistan in May and June 1998 respectively. The fourth session of IndoùUzbek Joint Commission is likely to be held in the first quarter of 1999.

Mr I Ergashev, Deputy Foreign Minister of Uzbekistan visited India from 9-12 December, 1998 for Foreign Office Consultation.

The 4th Session of the Indo-Uzbek Joint Commission was held in New Delhi from 17-20 February, 1999. The Uzbek Deputy Prime Minister, Mr M Z Usmanov visited New Delhi for the purpose.

6

The Gulf, West Asia and North Africa

Gulf/Haj division

Dating back to historical times, India's ties with all countries of the Gulf are cordial, substantial and mutually beneficial. Given India's geographical proximity, cultural affinity and economic complementarities with the Gulf countries, India's multifaceted relations with the countries of this region have continued to flourish. While about 3.5 million Indians -workers and professionals - are engaged in the economic development of the Gulf countries, the region is also the primary source of India's energy needs and one of India's most important economic partners in the areas of trade, investments and joint ventures. With a view to continually strengthening and diversifying relations between India and the Gulf, interactions take place regularly, particularly through high-level visits. Important developments and events which took place in 1998-99 in India's relations with the Gulf countries are summarised in the following paragraphs.

Bahrain

The warm, cordial and friendly relations between India and Bahrain received an impetus with the meeting of the Joint Committee on Technical and Economic Cooperation in New Delhi on 12-13 November, 1998, after a gap of nearly seven years. Noting that a vast potential existed for the expansion of the two-way trade, both sides agreed to find ways and means for stepping up bilateral trade not only in the existing fields, which included oil and other downstream products but also in the services sector such as off-shore banking and tourism. Both sides expressed keenness to enhance industrial and technical cooperation for setting up joint ventures in the small and medium-scale sectors, as well as cooperation in fields of health, education, agriculture, youth & sports and information and culture. They also agreed to expedite finalisation of the pending bilateral Agreements.

Secretary (East) and Joint Secretary (Gulf) visited Bahrain in June 1998 to explain India's position on the nuclear tests. Bahrain Ispat Limited Company, a joint venture with a large Indian steel company, made considerable progress in setting up a US $ 290 million sponge-iron project in Bahrain. Prime Minister sent an invitation to the Bahraini Prime Minister to visit India.

Iraq

India's relations with Iraq, which have traditionally been close, received a boost with the revival of the India-Iraq joint Commission for Economic and Technical Cooperation. A 7 member Iraqi delegation, led by H.E. Mr Amir Mohammed Rashid, Minister of Oil, visited New Delhi for joint Commission Meeting from 31 August to 2 September, 1998. A Memorandum of Understanding on cooperation in the field of oil and a Cultural Exchange Programme for the period 1998-2001 were signed between the two countries during the visit. Several areas of cooperation in the hydro-carbon and oil related sectors were identified. Indian companies offered bids for the exploration and development of Iraqi oil fields. As part of the Cultural Exchange Programme, both sides agreed to exchange visits of researchers, professors and academicians, sports and cultural troupes, journalists, etc.

India continued to reiterate its position calling for compliance by Iraq with the UN Security Council Resolutions on Iraq while reiterating that use of force against Iraq would serve no useful purpose but would only aggravate the sufferings of the Iraqi people. The appointment of the Indian diplomat Shri Prakash Shah, as Special Envoy of the UN Secretary-General, was welcomed by Iraq. The Indian Ambassador in Iraq Presented life-saving drugs to the Iraqi Ministry of Health and 700 scientific text-books to the Iraqi Ministry of Higher Education and Scientific Research, as also five container loads of educational material, including geometry boxes, school bags, calculators, and exercise books for use of the children of Iraq.

Dr Sadoun Hamadi, special envoy of the President of Iraq, visited India from 25-29 May, 19,98. He called on the President, Vice President, Prime Minister and Speaker (Lok Sabha). An 11 member Parliamentary delegation, led by the Hon'ble Speaker, Shri G M C Balyogi, visited Iraq from 20-26 August, 1998. The Speaker called on President Saddam Husein. Shri Som Pal, Minister of State for Agriculture visited Iraq from 8-10 October, 1998; he called on the Iraqi Minister of Agriculture and Minister of Industries. A 2 member delegation from the ONGC (Videsh) Ltd. visited Baghdad to hold technical discussions with the Ministry of Oil regarding their offer for exploring Iraqi oil fields in the western desert of Iraq. Twenty four Indian organisations participated in the Baghdad International Fair held in Baghdad from 1 to 10 November 1998. The Indian pavilion was awarded the extra-ordinary gold medal. A 20 member Iraqi Football Team also visited India to participate in the Rajiv Gandhi Football Cup Tournament.

Kuwait

Friendly relations with Kuwait were strengthened by high-level visits which included a Parliamentary delegation, led by H E Mr Talal Mubarak Al-Ayyar, the Deputy Speaker of the Kuwaiti National Assembly, to New Delhi from 27 September to 1 October, 1998, on the first leg of its visit to some Asian countries. The delegation called on the President. Secretary (East) and joint Secretary (Gulf) visited Kuwait on 10-11 June, 1998, and had detailed discussions with the Kuwaiti Foreign Secretary H E Mr Sulaiman Majid Al-Shaheen; they also met Deputy Prime Minister and Foreign Minister of Kuwait, Mr Sheikh Sabah Al-Ahmed Al-Sabah, and explained India's position on the nuclear tests to the Kuwaiti leader. Two Indian naval ships paid a goodwill visit to Kuwait on 1-4 June, 1998. Following Government of India's approval to the setting up of the Orissa Oil Refinery, an Indo-Kuwait joint venture, Indian Oil Corporation opened a Representative office in Kuwait in June. Smt Sonia Gandhi, Congress Party President, visited Kuwait on 29 August, 1998 and had separate meetings with the Amir and the Crown Prince and Prime Minister of Kuwait. Prime Minister issued an invitation to the Crown Prince and Prime Minister to visit India.

Oman

Since the visit of the former President Dr. Shanker Dayal Sharma to Oman in October 1996 and that of H. M. Sultan Qaboos bin Said to India in April 1997, relations between India and Oman have scaled new heights. The Prime Minister, Shri A B Vajpayee, accompanied by a high-level delegation which included Shri K Ramamurthy, Minister of Petroleum and Natural Gas and Shri S S Barnala, Minister of Chemicals and Fertilisers, visited Salalah on 29-30 August, 1998. The Prime Minister and Sultan Qaboos had substantial discussions on bilateral, regional and international issues, and committed the two countries to promote ties in political and economic fields. The Omani Minister of Commerce and Industry, Mr Maqbool Bin Ali bin Sultan, visited India from 30 April to 2 May, 1998 in connection with "OMAN WEEK", which was inaugurated by the Vice President on 1 May, 1998. Mr Maqbool Sultan also met the Petroleum, Industry and Fertiliser Ministers and Minister of State for External Affairs. He addressed Indian business leaders under the auspices of the Confederation of Indian Industry (CII). Secretary (East) and joint Secretary (Gulf) visited Oman on 31 May to 2 June, 1998. They called on the Minister responsible for Foreign Affairs as well as Minister of National Economy to brief them on India's nuclear tests. In June 1998. Bharat Heavy Electricals Limited (BHEL) commissioned a 30-MW Gas turbine-based power plant turnkey project at a cost of Rs. 560 million. A flotilla of three naval ships paid a goodwill visit to Oman from 30 May to 4 June, 1998 and undertook joint exercises with the Royal Oman Navy. The formalities for setting up two multi-million dollar joint venture projects, namely the India-Oman Fertiliser Project and the Bharat-Oman Fertiliser Project and the Bharat-Oman Refinery Project, proceeded satisfactorily. An Indian ocean (IOR) Exhibition was organised by the Federation of Indian Chambers of Commerce and Industry (FICCI) at Muscat from 10-14 October, 1998, in which 56 Indian organisations participated. Meetings of the India-Oman joint Economic Committee and the Annual Political Consultations will take place in New Delhi and Muscat respectively in early 1999.

Qatar

India's traditionally warm and friendly relations with Qatar continued to grow during the year Mr Abdullah Bin Hamad, Al-Attiyah, Minister of Energy and Industry, visited Indian in July 1998 and called on the Prime

Minister and handed over a letter from the Amir of Qatar to the PM. The Visiting dignitary also called on his counterpart, the Minister of Petroleum and Natural Gas, Shri K Ramamurthy, on 8 July 1998. The Qatari Minister was accompanied by a 6 member delegation from the Qatar General Petroleum Corporation. A 22 member delegation from Qatar, led by assistant Under Secretary in the Ministry of Energy and Industry, visited India on 6-8 May, 1998, and participated in two Seminars on "Indo-Qatar Trade Relations" organised by the Confederation of Indian Industry (CII) in New Delhi and Mumbai. Secretary (East) and joint Secretary (Gulf) in the Ministry of External Affairs visited Qatar on 3 June, 1998. They called on the Qatari Minister of State for External Affairs and held discussions on bilateral relations. They also explained India's position on the nuclear tests conducted in May 1998. Qatar has been selected for holding negotiations for supply of 7.5 million tonnes of LNG per year to India on a long-term basis.

The Minister of State for External Affairs, Smt Vasundhara Raje, accompanied by Secretary (East) and joint Secretary (Gulf), visited Qatar from 26-29 October, 1998. She handed over a letter from the Prime Minister to H.H. Sheikh Hamad Bin Khalifa Al-Thani, Amir of Qatar. She had a meeting with H.E. Sheikh Hamad Bin Jassem Bin Jabor Al-Thani, Foreign Minister of Qatar. The MOS also laid the foundation stone of the Indian chancery building in Doha, capital of Qatar. Shri E A Nayanar, Chief Minister of Kerala, visited Qatar from 26-28 September, 1998. He called on Mr Abdullah Bin Hamad Al-Attiyah, Minister of Energy and Industry. A Bilateral Investment Promotion and Protection Agreement (BIPPA) was initialled between India and Qatar in Doha on 30 November, 1998. The meeting of the India-Qatar joint Commission will take place in New Delhi on 8-9 March, 1999.

At the invitation of our Minister of Petroleum and Natural Gas, H. E. Mr Yousef Hussain Kamal, Minister of Finance, Economy and Commerce of the State of Qatar, visited India from 13-15 December, 1998. The visit was in connection with the purchase of 7.5 million tonnes of natural gas per year by India from Qatar on long-term basis. The visiting dignitary called on Shri Yashwant Sinha, Minister of Finance, and Smt Vasundhara Raje, Minister of State for External Affairs.

Saudi Arabia

India's traditional relations with the Kingdom of Saudi Arabia are marked by cordiality and friendship. The bilateral trade between India and Saudi Arabia amounts to about US $ 3.5 billion. The Kingdom is host to around 1.3 million Indians. Secretary (East) and joint Secretary (Gulf) in the Ministry of External Affairs visited Saudi Arabia between 17-20 July, 1998 to explain the rationale of the nuclear tests conducted by India in May 1998. An Indian team visited Saudi Arabia on 24-25 November, 1998 to hold negotiations for finalising the text of the Bilateral Investment Promotion and Protection Agreement between the two countries.

With a view to stepping up defence cooperation, an invitation was extended for a goodwill visit of a Saudi defence delegation to India. The battle ships-INS Rajput and INS Varuna-called at the Jubail Port on 6 June, 1998 on a goodwill visit, the first time in ten years that Indian Naval ships have made a friendly port call in the Kingdom. The Saudi Minister of justice, H.E. Dr Abdulla Ibn Muhammed Ibn Ibrahim Al Sheikh, visited India to participate in the 37th session of Asian-African Legal Consultative Committee which was held in New Delhi from 13-18 April, 1998.

A total of 95,119 Indian pilgrims performed Haj in March 1998, of whom 63,583 pilgrims had gone through the Haj Committee, Mumbai, and the rest through Private Tour Operators (PTOs) or privately on international passports. To look after the welfare of the pilgrims 398 deputationists (223 doctors and para-medical staff and 175 administrative staff) were deputed to Saudi Arabia; 88 Haj volunteers were also sent by 13 State Haj Committees. A 28 member Haj Goodwill delegation visited Saudi Arabia during the Haj. While, on the whole, the Haj was very well-organised, there was one untoward incident a stampede at Mina in which 32 Indian pilgrims lost their lives.

To safeguard the interest of the pilgrims who perform Haj through PTOs and to regulate the working of the latter, the Ministry invited applications from companies organising Haj/Umrah pilgrimages. After detailed scrutiny, a number of PTOs have been recommended for registration with the Saudi Missions in New Delhi and Mumbai.

Haj 99 will take place in the last week of March 1999, and arrangements relating to accommodation in Makkah and Madinah and the Haj charter flights have been finalised satisfactorily. A team of three Members of Parliament from the Parliamentary Standing Committee on External Affairs visited Saudi Arabia in February 1999 to review the arrangements made for Indian pilgrims.

UAE

The age-old multidimensional relations between India and the United Arab Emirates (UAE) were further strengthened and diversified during the year. With a view to promoting investment, the Bilateral Investment Protection and Promotion Agreement between the two countries was initialled in June 1998. In order to promote investment in Maharashtra, a delegation, led by Shri R V Patil, Minister of Culture and Water Conservation, Government of Maharashtra, visited the UAE on 15

September 1998. A delegation led by the CII President, Shri R V Shah, visited the UAE on 1 August, 1998 and held discussions with Indian businessmen, the Dubai Chamber of Commerce and Industry and the Abu Dhabi Chamber of Commerce and Industry to promote greater economic cooperation and joint ventures. The UAE-based Non-Resident Indian (NRIs) contributed US $ 1.26 billion to the Resurgent Indian Bonds (RIBs) which was around 30% of the total global collection of the RIBs. Secretary (East) and Joint Secretary (Gulf/Haj) in the Ministry of External Affairs visited Abu Dhabi on 2 June, 1998 and met the UAE Minister of Information and Culture, Mr Sheikh Abdullah Bin Zahid, and Acting Secretary of the UAE Foreign Office, Mr Saif Saeed Bin Saad and discussed ways to strengthening bilateral relations. They also explained the rational for the nuclear tests conducted by Indian in May 1998. The Vice-President of India, Shri Krishan Kant, made a stopover in Dubai en route to India and was received by the UAE Minister for Cabinet Affairs, Mr Saeed Al Ghaith. The UAE Minister for Petroleum and Mineral Resources, Mr Obeid bin Saif Al-Nasiri, visited India on February 22-24,1999 to discuss cooperation in the energy sector.

A delegation of the Abu Dhabi Chamber of Commerce and Industry, including some private businessmen, visited India during April 1998 and met various industrial bodies, organisations and businessmen. The Sharjah Chamber of Commerce and Industry sent a delegation, led by its Chairman, Mr Ahmed Al Medfa, for a six-day presentation in India from 20 April 1998 which aimed at exploring business and investment opportunities both in India and Sharjah.

Yemen

Indo-Yemen relations are characterised by mutual goodwill, cordiality an friendship. The foreign policies of the two countries have much in common as both are committed to Non-alignment and support for Arab issues. Again, both India and Yemen are members of the Indian Ocean Rim-Association for Regional Cooperation (IOR-ARC) and engage in continuous interaction cooperating in the various projects identified for benefit of the people of the member-countries of the IOR-ARC. The annual Foreign Office Consultations were institutionalized with Yemen in 1993; the next session of the Foreign Office Consultations is scheduled to be held in New Delhi during February 1999. The third session of the Indo-Yemen Joint Committee for Economic, Scientific and Technical Cooperation is expected to be held in Sanaa during March 1999. With a view to further strengthening relations between the parliamentarians of the two countries an invitation was extended to the Speaker of Yemeni National Assembly to visit India. Steps have been taken for making institutional arrangements with Yemen for close cooperation in curbing the menace of drug trafficking, combat terrorism and organised crimes; negotiations are under way for concluding these agreements, including extradition treaty. An Indian film festival and a photographic exhibition were inaugurated on 3 August 1998 in Sanaa by the Yemen Minister for Culture, Mr Abdul Al Mansoor.

Special Kuwait cell

The Special Kuwait Cell has been working since 1991. Its main task is obtaining and distributing compensation for the Indian nationals and organizations who were adversely affected by the Gulf War of 1990-91. After a considerable time, funds are now being transferred by the United Nations Compensation Commission (UNCC), Geneva. Transfer of funds is taking place roughly once every six months for partial settlement of category A & C claims @ $ 2500 per claim.

Disbursement of the compensation money to successful claimants is being done by four designated nationalised Banks. The four Banks, with the active cooperation and guidance of the Special Kuwait Cell, are carrying out the task of locating the successful claimants (many of whom have shifted residences or gone abroad), and paying their claim amounts.

In September 1998, UNCC transferred $ 93,542,500 for partial settlement of 37,417 claims approved in the 4th instalment of category A. UNCC has also transferred $ 14,255,510.61 for partial settlement of 5,869 claims in the 4th instalment of category C.

UNCC has also finalized the list of approved claims for the 6th instalment of category C. This covers 8,621 Indian claims, of a total value of over $ 101 million. UNCC is in the process of finalising the list for the 7th (and the last) instalment of category C. They have also started sending lists of approved claims in category D, i.e., claims exceeding $100,000.

In the 29th UNCC Governing Council Meeting (Geneva, 28-30 September, 1998), 23 Indian claims in category D have been approved for a total value of $ 522574.

In April 1998, a UNCC team of loss-adjustors and legal experts visited India for an on-site appraisal of documents pertaining to the Government of India claim in category F. Special Kuwait Cell made effective arrangements for a successful appraisal operation. As a result, the India's Govt. claim was processed expeditiously, although it was initially classified as "unusually large and complex". It has been approved for $ 92,621,397 in the 29th UNCC Governing Council Meeting. The actual transfer of the amount may, however, take some time. It would depend on the availability of funds from Iraq and payment prioritization between different claim categories, decided upon by the UNCC. India was among the few countries who made official statement at the 29th Governing Council Meeting. The thrust of India's statement was that some degree of priority should be given to the small claims under categories A & C, after the first-part payments are completed.

It is the exclusive responsibility of the UNCC to evaluate and scrutinize the claims, evolve a payment procedure and deliver the awarded compensation to eligible claimants for payment through national Governments.

Up to 31 December, 1998 the Special Kuwait Cell had been instrumental in the disbursement of the following amounts, in cooperation with the four designated Banks:

Category	*Amount disbursed (US $)*	*No. of claimants Covered*
A	85022500.00	30201
B	617000.00	163
C	12141782.49	4890
Total	97781282.49	35254

Towards end-March 1999, we expect to receive from UNCC, further funds for installments V of categories A & C (depending on the financial situation on UNCC).

As important meeting of the UNCC Governing Council is also expected to take place in March. Among other things, this Meeting is expected to take a view on the payment priorities, after the first phase of payments for categories A & C gets completed. In the Governing Council Meeting of September '98, India made an official statement which, inter alia, stated that in the second phase of payments, a degree of priority should be given to completion of payments for categories A & C."

WANA region

India maintained its support for the Arab and Palestinian causes as well as the Middle East Peace Process. Developments in the region and lack of progress in the Middle East Peace Process gave rise to growing concern. India had welcomed the Wye River Memorandum signed between Israel and Palestine Liberation Organisation on 23 October, 1998 and had maintained that the signed agreements and accords should be honoured and implemented without any pre-conditions. India's multi-faceted relations with countries in West Asia and North Africa were further strengthened through exchange of visits and conclusion of functional Cooperation Agreements. Our trade with the region witnessed a steady growth. Work continued apace on the Indian joint venture in Morocco and this project is likely to come on stream by the middle of 1999. India's gesture of humanitarian assistance to Sudan and the human resource development under the ITEC Programme were a manifestation of our commitment to South Cooperation.

Algeria

Relations with Algeria continued to be marked by warmth and closeness. On the margins of the G-15 Summit held in Cairo in May 1998, Vice-President Shri Krishan Kant met President Mr Liamine Zeroual of Algeria. Again on the sidelines of the NAM Summit at Durban and the UNGA at New York, Algerian Foreign Minister Mr Ahmed Attaf called on Prime Minister Shri Atal Behari Vajpayee and exchanged views on important global, regional and bilateral issues. Additional Secretary(UN) and Joint Secretary (WANA) in the Ministry visited Algiers in August 1998 for pre-NAM consultations. President of the Algerian Constitutional

Council Justice Said Bouchair, alongwith members of the Constitutional Council, visited India from 6-12 September, 1998 at the invitation of Chief Justice of India. During their visit, "New Dell-d Declaration" was issued. This Declaration provides for exchange of information, documents and setting up of a forum of the judges, lawyers and professors of law. A delegation from the national oil company of Algeria - SONATRACH - visited India between 21-24 June, 1998 and held discussions with officials of ONGC-VL and IOC on the possibilities for cooperation in the areas of drilling, oil field equipment, joint ventures in third countries, joint research and development, human resource development, etc.

Egypt

Bilateral ties of friendship, mutual understanding and cooperation with Egypt were strengthened. Vice-President Shri Krishna Kant led the Indian delegation to the G-15 Summit in Cairo from 11-13 May, 1998. The other members of the Indian delegation to the G-15 Summit included Commerce Minister Shri Ramakrishna Hegde and Minister of State for External Affairs Smt Vasundhara Raje. On the sidelines of the Summit, the Vice-President met President Mr Hosni Mubarak and exchanged views on important issues. The meetings between the Prime Minister and Foreign Minister Mr Amre Moussa during the NAM Summit in Durban, UNGA in New York and Minister of State for External Affairs Smt Vasundhara Raje and Foreign Minister Mr Amre Moussa during the G-15 Summit in Cairo and NAM Ministerial Meeting in Cartagena sustained the high level dialogue between the two countries. Minister of State for Health & Family Welfare Shri Dalit Ezhilmalai visited Cairo to attend the 4th Annual Board Meeting of 'Partners in Population & Development' from 7-11 November, 1998. A delegation led by Minister of Environment Shri Suresh P Prabhu visited Cairo from 16-

24 November, 1998 to attend the meeting of the Parties to the Montreal Protocol. Minister of Textiles Shri Kashi Ram Rana visited Egypt from 19-22 August, 1998 to preside over the Valedictory Reception for the 5th exclusive Indian Jewellery Exhibition organised by the HHEC from 13-19 August, 1998 in Cairo. The Minister met Egyptian Minister for Trade and Supply Dr. Ahmed al-Goweili and a group of Egyptian businessmen. Chief of Army Staff Gen V P Malik transited through Cairo on 14 December, 1998 on a private visit. During his stay in Cairo, Gen. Malik called on Chief of Egyptian Armed Forces Lt Gen Mogdy Hatata. Chief Election Commissioner of India Dr M S Gill paid an official visit to Egypt from 26 April - 2 May, 1998. Additional Secretary (UN) and Joint Secretary (WANA) in the Ministry visited Egypt in August 1998 for pre-NAM consultations. Indian delegation was received by Foreign Minister Mr Amre Moussa. A Memorandum of Understanding between India and Egypt for Co-operation in the Development of Small Scale Enterprises Sector in Egypt was signed in Cairo on 9.5.98 by Minister of State for External Affairs Smt Vasundhara Raje and Foreign Minister Mr Amre Moussa. President of the Court of Cassation in Egypt Justice Mehdat El-Maraghi visited India from 11-18 April, 1998 at the invitation of Chief Justice of India. The first exclusive "Made in India" Exhibition held in Cairo from 15-19 April, 1998, was inaugurated by Prime Minister of Egypt Dr Kamal el Ganzouri. Other dignitaries present at the inauguration were Egyptian Foreign Minister Mr Amre Moussa and Minister for Industry and Mineral Wealth Dr Soliman Reda Ali Soliman. Minister of Industry and Social Welfare of Kerala Smt Susheela Gopalan led the Indian delegation to the Exhibition. A Round Table Conference on Indo-Egyptian Relations was held in New Delhi on 16 December, 1998. Deputy Editor of Egyptian Arabic

language newspaper' AlûAhram' Mr Mahmoud Mourad participated in this Conference. A high-powered media delegation led by the Chairman and Chief Editor of Arabic language daily 'Al-Ahram' Ibrahim Nafie to India from 24-29 June, 1998. The delegation called on the Prime Minister Shri Atal Behari Vajpayee, Minister of Defence Shri George Fernandes, Minister of Finance Shri Yashwant Sinha, Deputy Chairperson of Rajya Sabha Dr (Mrs) Najma Heptullah, External Affairs Minister (then Deputy Chairman of Planning Commission) Shri Jaswant Singh and Minister of State for External Affairs Smt Vasundhara Raje. The first round of Annual Indo-Egyptian Foreign Office Consultations are scheduled to be held in New Delhi on 22-23 February, 1999.

Israel

Cooperation with Israel in the areas of trade and agriculture continued to develop satisfactorily. The Deputy Director General in Israel's Foreign Office Mr Yitzhak Shelev visited India for the Fourth round of Foreign Office Consultations held in New Delhi on 21 January, 1999. The Indian delegation was led by Secretary (East) Shri Nareshwar Dayal. The Second Meeting of Indo-Israeli Joint Trade & Economic Committee was held in New Delhi on 27 October, 1998 and was co-chaired by the Commerce Secretary and Director General in Israel's Ministry of Industry, Dov Mishor. The joint Trade & Economic Committee Meeting was co-chaired by Commerce Secretary Shri P P Prabhu and Director General, Israel's Ministry of Industry Mr Dov Mishor. The Attorney General for India Shri Soli J Sorabjee visited Israel from 20-24 December, 1998 at the invitation of his counterpart in Israel. Minister of State for Health & Family Welfare Shri Dalit Ezhilmalai went to Israel on a private visit from 11-13 November, 1998. Minister of State for Rural Areas & Employment, Shri Babagouda Patil visited Israel from 30.10.98 to 5.11.98 at the invitation of

Israel's Minister for Agriculture and Deputy Prime Minister Mr Rafael Eitan. Minister of Urban Affairs and Employment Shri Ram Jethamalani visited Israel from 7-11 September, 1998 at the invitation of Israel's Minister of Infrastructure Mr Ariel Sharon. Agreement on Co-operation in the field of Telecommunications and Posts between India and Israel, signed on 29 November, 1994, was ratified by India on 24 September, 1998.

Jordan

Bilateral relations with Jordan retained their positive trends of increasing understanding and co-operation. Vice President Shri Krishan Kant represented India at the funeral of King Hussein in Amman on 8 February, 1999. Both Houses of Parliament adopted an Obituary Reference to King Hussein on the opening day of the Budget Session of Parliament. Additional Secretary (UN) and Joint Secretary (WANA) in the Ministry visited Amman in August 1998 for pre-NAM consultations. The delegation was received by Crown Prince Hassan. Speaker of Lok Sabha, Minister of State for Agriculture and Chief Election Commissioner transited through Jordan.

Lebanon

India's relations with Lebanon continued to be warm and friendly. India maintained its support for the immediate and unconditional implementation of the UN Security Council Resolution No. 425 which calls for withdrawal of Israeli forces from Lebanon's occupied territories forthwith. At the request of the United Nations, India sent an Indian Army contingent as part of the UN Interim Force in Lebanon (UNIFIL). Secretary (East) in the Ministry Shri Nareshwar Dayal visited Lebanon from 15-17 July, 1998 for Foreign Office consultations. He was received by Prime Minister Mr Rafik AI-Hariri and Foreign Minister Mr Fares Bouez.

Libya

India's relations with Libya continued to be marked by understanding and co-operation. India has consistently believed and worked for a just and equitable solution to the Lockerbie issue. Under Secretary for Asian Affairs in Libyan Foreign Office Mr Saad Mustafa Mujber visited India from 23-25 April, 1998 for Foreign Office consultations. During his stay in New Delhi, Under Secretary Mujber called on Minister of State for External Affairs Smt Vasundhara Raje and delivered a letter addressed to Prime Minister Shri Atal Behari Vajpayee from Libya's Foreign Minister. He also called on Minister of Petroleum & Natural Gas Shri V K Ramamurthy, Minister of State for Information & Broadcasting, Shri Mukhtar Naqvi and Secretary (Industry) Shri T R Prasad.

Morocco

Relations with Morocco witnessed qualitative enhancement. Prime Minister Shri Atal Behari Vajpayee visited Morocco on 13-14 February, 1999. He had a tete-eûtete with Prime Minister Abderrahmane El Youssoufi, followed by delegation-level talks. Prime Minister also called King Hassan II. The King honoured the Prime Minister by conferring on him "Grand Cordon of the Alawy Wissam". During Prime Minister's visit, Bilateral Investment Protection Agreement, Tourism Co-operation Agreement and Agreement between Press Trust of India (PTI) and Maghreb Arab Presse (MAP) for mutual professional co-operation were signed. Foreign Minister of Morocco Abdellatif Filali called on Prime Minister Shri Atal Behari Vajpayee on the margins of the NAM Summit in Durban in August 1998 and Minister of External Affairs (then Deputy Chairman of Planning Commission) Shri Jaswant Singh met Morocco's Prime Minister Abderrahmane El Youssoufi in New York on the sidelines of the Special Session of the UN on Narcotics and Drugs held in New York from 8-10 June, 1998.

Minister of State for External Affairs Smt Vasundhara Raje, accompanied by Secretary (East) Shri Nareshwar Dayal, visited Morocco from 25-27 June, 1998. Besides holding discussions with her counterpart State Secretary in the Ministry of Foreign Affairs for International Cooperation Mme Aicha Belarbi, MOS also called on Prime Minister Mr Abderrahmane El Youssoufi, Foreign Minister Abdellatif Filali and Finance Minister Mr Fthallah Oualalou. She signed a Memorandum of Understanding between India and Morocco on Foreign Office Consultations. Speaker of Lok Sabha Hon'ble Shri G M C Balayogi led a Parliamentary delegation to Morocco from 7-12 October, 1998. The Hon'ble Speaker was invited to the inauguration of the Moroccan Parliament by the President of the Majlis An-Nuwab (House of Representatives) Mr Abdelwahed Radi. The Hon'ble Speaker was received by King Hassan II of Morocco and honoured with the title of "Officer Wissam Alaoui". The Hon'ble Speaker also called on Morocco's Prime Minister Mr Abderrahmane El Youssoufi. During the visit of Indian Parliamentary delegation, it was decided to establish an Indo-Moroccan Parliamentary Friendship Group. Minister of State for Finance (RB & 1) Shri K M R Janardhanan visited Morocco from 28-30 October, 1998 to sign the Convention on Avoidance of Double Taxation between India and Morocco. Amongst others, he called on the Prime Minister of Morocco. General Manager of the Moroccan National Railways Office (ONCF) Mr Mohammed El Als visited India on 7-12 December, 1998. During his visit, he held discussions with RITES and IRCON. Ambassador of the King of Morocco Mr Hassan Abouyoub visited India from 6-7 November, 1998. He called on Hon'ble Speaker of Lok Sabha, Minister of Commerce, Principal Secretary to the Prime Minister and Secretary (East) in the Ministry of External Affairs.

Palestine

India continued to extend political, material and technical support to Palestine. India repeatedly expressed its concern at the stalling of the Middle East Peace Process. India welcomed the Wye River Memorandum signed between Israel and PLO on 23 October, 1998. India believes that this Memorandum will improve the quality of life of the Palestinian people and pave the way to commence, Final Status Negotiations so that a just, comprehensive and lasting peace could be achieved in the region on the basis of the Principle of "Land for Peace" and the relevant UN Resolutions. India calls upon the parties concerned to faithfully implement this Memorandum and eschew unilateral measures which are not in conformity with this Memorandum and other understandings and agreements. India's traditional friendly relations with Palestine were enhanced by several exchanges. Additional Secretary (UN) and Joint Secretary (WANA) visited Palestine Authority territory in August 1998 for pre-NAM consultations. The Indian delegation was received by President Arafat. Additional Secretary (FA) and Joint Secretary (WANA) in the Ministry visited Gaza in June, 1998 to sign two MOUs and Agreed Minutes for the implementation of two Indian-aided projects, namely, construction of a Library at Al Azhar University and construction of a Library-cum-Activity Centre at Palestinian Technical College at Deir El Balah. Joint Secretary (WANA) was received by President Mr Yasser Arafat, Minister for International Co-operation Dr Nabil Sha'ath and PLO Executive Secretary Dr Mahmoud Abbas (Abu Mazen). Grand Mufti of Jerusalem and Islamic Holy Sites in Palestine Sheikh Ikrima Sabri visited India from 10-16 December, 1998 on a goodwill mission. He was received by the Vice-President, Prime Minister and the Minister of Industry. He also visited Hyderabad and Bangalore. Member of the Executive Committee of Al-Fateh, In-charge of Foreign Relations and Member of Palestine National Council Mr Hani Al-Hasan visited India as a representative of PLO to attend the 17th Congress of CPI from 18-20 September, 1998 held in m Chennai. During his visit, he called on Minister of State for External Affairs. The Palestine Authority's Minister of Housing & Energy Mr Abdel Rehman T Hamad visited India to attend the Seminar organised by the Council of Arab Ambassadors. During his stay in New Delhi, the Palestinian Minister called on Minister of Petroleum & Natural Gas Shri V K Ramamurthy and Minister of State for External Affairs Smt Vasundhara Raje. India offered more than 50 training slots to the Palestinian personnel for specialised training courses during the current financial year 199899. At the International Donors Conference was held in Washington DC on 30 November, 1998 to help the Palestinian people, India pledged an amount of US $ 1 million. The utilisation of this amount will be decided on consultation with the Palestinian authorities.

India supported the UN efforts on Western Sahara. India has contributed 10 Police personnel to the civilian contingent under the MINURSO. In Somalia, India supports UN efforts to restore peace and normalcy. The President of Djibouti Hassan Gouled Aptidou transited through Chennai on 1-2 August, 1998.

Sudan

Relations with Sudan were strengthened through expansion and diversification of bilateral economic co-operation. India reiterated its support for Sudan's territorial integrity and sovereignty. Minister of Transport of the Government of the Republic of the Sudan Dr Lam Akol and the Secretary General of the Ministry of Transport Mr Mudawi Eltiraifi visited India to attend the

Seminar on "National Transport Policy - Environmental and Energy Issues" held in New Delhi from 9-11 December, 1998, at the invitation of the Chairman of the Railway Board. While in New Delhi, the Sudanese Minister called on the Minister of Railways. A 3-member Sudanese Parliamentary delegation led by the Deputy Chairman, Federal Relations Committee, Sudanese National Assembly Dr Salah Eldin Mirghani M A Gaili visited India in the first week of October 1998 to get acquainted with the functioning of the federal system in India. During their visit, the Sudanese delegation called on the Minister of Parliamentary Affairs & Tourism Shri Madan Lal Khurana and Lt Governor of Delhi. 'Sudan's Minister of Animal Wealth Mr Joseph Malawal came to India on a private visit in June, 1998 and amongst others, called on the Minister of State for Agriculture Shri Som Pal. The Government of India sent relief supplies consisting of baby milk powder and medicines to Sudan to help the flood victims.

Syria

Bonds of understanding and co-operation with Syria were strengthened. Chief of Army Staff Gen V P Malik visited Syria from 10-14 December, 1998 at the invitation of Syria's Chief of Army & Armed Forces Lt Gen Ali Asslan. Gen Malik was also received by Syria's Defence Minister First Lt Gen Mustafa Tlass and Foreign Minister Mr Farouq al-Shara. Secretary (East) in the Ministry Shri Nareshwar Dayal visited Syria on 13-15 July, 1998 for Foreign Office Consultations. Secretary (East) was received by Foreign Minister Mr Farouk Al-Shara. The Director General of the Atomic Energy Commission of Syria Dr I Othman visited India for the IAEA Meeting from 12-16 October, 1998 held at BARC, Mumbai.

Tunisia

Bilateral relations with Tunisia continued to develop

satisfactorily. Tunisia's Minister for Environment and Land Use Planning Mohamed Mr Mehdi Mlika visited India from 1-3 April, 1998. to attend the meeting of Global Environment Facility at New Delhi. During his stay in India, the Tunisian Minister called on Minister of Environment and Forests Shri Suresh Prabhu and Minister of State for External Affairs Smt Vasundhara Raje.

India maintained cordial relations and co-operation with the regional organisations, namely, League of Arab States (LAS) and Union of Arab Maghreb.

7

Europe

Eastern Europe

India's traditionally warm, friendly and cooperative relations with the Russian Federation and the countries of East and Central Europe continued to develop steadily during the year. There is a consensus on maintaining good relations with most of these countries in India, where there is considerable goodwill for these countries, and vice versa. With the consolidation of democracy and democratic institutions in East and Central Europe, our friendship with the countries in this region has acquired an added dimension, based on shared values and aspirations. India's multi-faceted cooperation with them in all spheres including trade and commerce, science and technology, culture, etc. has been progressing satisfactorily.

The tradition of high level bilateral exchanges with these countries continued during the year and contributed to strengthening our bilateral cooperation. Sustained efforts were made to further strengthen our political understanding with them. Exchanges of visits by Parliamentary delegations helped to revitalise contacts with the legislatures of these countries. We also sought to build upon our existing business and institutional linkages with them, so as to benefit from the parallel processes of economic change and development in India and East/Central Europe. Efforts were made to consolidate and expand our cultural ties. turn, these countries acknowledged the importance of their traditional ties with India.

Close and friendly ties between India and Russia, based on continuity, trust and mutual understanding, constitute an important foreign policy priority for both countries. Our multi-faceted relations have been developing apace in different areas of cooperation. The tradition of high level bilateral exchanges with Russia, which has contributed to strengthening our bilateral, cooperation in a wide range of areas, was maintained during the year, culminating in the visit of Prime Minister Mr Y M Primakov to India in December, 1998. There is a consensus in both countries on maintenance of good bilateral relations. Recognition of the strategic dimension to Indo-Russian relations has grown. India and Russia share similar perceptions on many international issues.

Prime Minister inaugurated the 7 RCR-Kremlin Hot-line with a telephonic conversation with President Yeltsin on 13 April 1998, the 51st anniversary of the establishment of diplomatic relations between India and Russia.

Defence Secretary visited Russia from 15-19 June 1998 and held discussions with First Deputy Defence Minister Mr N V Mikhailov, and met Defence Minister Mr Igor Sergeev, Economy Minister Mr Yakov Urinson and other Russian dignitaries. During the visit, an Inter-Governmental Agreement on the long-term Programme of Military and Technical Cooperation for the period upto the year 2010 was initialed.

Russian Minister for Atomic Energy Mr Yevgeny Adamov visited India from 19-22 June, 1998. He signed with Dr R Chidambaram, Secretary, Department of Atomic Energy, a Supplement to the 1988 Indo-Soviet Inter-Governmental Agreement on the construction of a 2x1000 MW Nuclear Power Station in Kudankulam, Tamil Nadu.

Governor of the Voronezh region of the Russian Federation, Mr I M Shabanov visited India from 9-11 July, 1998. During his stay in India, he met the Chief Minister of Delhi Shri Sahib Singh and Secretary (West), MEA, and visited Calcutta.

Chief Minister of Delhi Shri Sahib Singh visited Russia from 13-15 July, 1998 to attend the International Youth Games. During his stay in Russia, he met the Mayor of Moscow Mr Yuri Luzhkov, and visited the Voronezh region of the Russian Federation.

A contract on the preparation of the Detailed Project Report for the construction of a 2x1000 MW Nuclear Power Station in Kudankulam was signed in Moscow on 20 July, 1998.

Chief of Naval Staff Admiral Vishnu Bhagwat visited Russia from 24-31 July, 1998. During the visit, he called on the Russian Defence Minister Mr Igor Sergeev and had talks with the Commander-in-Chief of the Russian Navy Admiral Vladimir Kuroyedov. He also visited St. Petersburg and Severomorsk.

Deputy Chairman of the Planning Commission Shri Jaswant Singh met the Russian Foreign Minister Mr Yevgeny Primakov in Manila on 28 July, 1998, during the 5th meeting of the ASEAN Regional Forum.

Mr Yevgeny Primakov, Russian Foreign Minister, met Prime Minister Shri Atal Bihari Vajpayee during the 53rd Session of UN General Assembly UNGA in September 1998 in New York.

Lok Sabha Speaker, Shri G M C Balayogi, led a multi-party Indian Parliamentary delegation to the IPU Conference in Moscow from 6-13 September, 1998. An Agreement on Indo-Russia Inter-Parliamentary Commission was also signed during that visit.

The Chairman of the Russian State Duma Committee for International Relations, Mr V P Lukin, accompanied by a mutli-party Russian Parliamentary delegation visited India from 13û16 September, 1998, during which he held detailed discussions with the Parliamentary Standing Committee on External Affairs. He, also called on PM, Vice President and other Indian dignitaries.

Foreign Secretary visited Moscow on 11 September, 1998 for Foreign Office Consultations.

Vice Mayor and First Deputy Prime Minister of the Moscow Government, Mr Valeri P Shantsev, visited India from 23û26 September, 1998 and on 23 September, 1998, inaugurated the "Days of Moscow in Delhi" jointly with Home Minister.

Petroleum Minister, Shri V K Ramamurthy, visited Russia from 21-23 October, 1998, during which a meeting of the Indo-Russian, Joint Working Group on Oil was also convened.

Russian Deputy Foreign Minister Mr G B Karasin visited from 1-3 November, 1998. He held discussions with Foreign Secretary and called on Home Minister and Principal Secretary to PM.

Defence Secretary visited Russia from 10-12 November, 1998 for the Joint Working Group meeting on military-technical cooperation.

Lok Sabha Speaker led a multi-party Indian parliamentary delegation to Russia from 12-17 November,

1998. In addition to having discussions with his Russian counterpart, he addressed the Russian State Duma and called on Prime Minister Mr Y Primakov.

President Mr M S Shaimiev of the Republic of Tatarstan (Russian Federation) visited India from 22-26 November, 1998 at the invitation of Commerce Minister. During the visit, he also called on Vice President.

Finance Minister led an Indian delegation to Moscow from 2628 November 1, 1998 for the 5th session of Indo-Russian Inter-Governmental Commission as its co-chairman. Besides meeting his counterpart and Russia's First Deputy Prime Minister Mr Yuri Maslyukov, Finance Minister called on Russian Prime Minister Mr Y Primakov, Finance Minister Mr M M Zadornov and Deputy PM Mrs V I Matvienko.

Russian Prime Minister Mr Yevgeny Primakov paid an official visit to India from 20-22 December, 1998. During the visit, he called on President, Vice President and PM, and met Lok Sabha Speaker and EAM besides other high Indian dignitaries. Discussions took place in the warm and friendly atmosphere traditional to Indo-Russian interaction. There was a coincidence of views on practically all issues discussed, and both sides expressed satisfaction that bilateral cooperation was proceeding well. Both sides reiterated their commitment to close and stable relations in a long-term perspective. During the visit seven bilateral documents were signed in the presence of the two Prime Ministers. Mr Primakov also attended a business seminar organised by CII.

Chairman of the Federation Council of the Federal Assembly of the Russian Federation, Mr Y S Stroev, accompanied a high-level parliamentary delegation including eight regional governors visited India from 8-10 February, 1999. During the visit Mr Stroev and the delegation called on the President, Vice-President, Lok Sabha Speaker and Home Minister.

Russian Defence Minister Mr Sergeev is expected to visit India from 11-15 March, 1999.

India's relations with other countries of the CIS - Armenia, Belarus, Georgia, Moldova, Ukraine - continued to develop satisfactorily.

Smt Vasundhara. Raje, Minister of State for External Affairs met Mr Ivan Antonovich, the Foreign Minister of Belarus in New York on September 29,1998 during the 53rd Session of UNGA.

Belarusian Foreign Minister, Mr Ivan Antonovich, paid an official visit to India from 13-17 October, 1998, during which he held talks with MOS for External Affairs. He also called on Prime Minister, the Vice President, and Industry Minister. An IndoûBelarus ITEC Agreement was signed during the visit.

Industry Minister, Shri Sikander Bakht, led the Indian delegation to Minsk from 25-28 October, 1998 at the 1st session of the Indo-Belarus Inter-Governmental Commission. He co-chaired the session with the Belarusian Industry Minister. During the visit, he called on the Belarusian President, Prime Minister and Minister of Foreign Economic Relations.

Minister of State for Coal, Shri Dilip Ray, accompanied by officials from Coal India Ltd. visited Minsk from 10-12 January, 1999. During the visit Coal Minister called on the Prime Minister Mr Sergei Ling and also held discussions with the Belarus Minister for Industry, Mr A D Kharlap.

India's relations with the countries of Central/East Europe and the three Baltic Republics, i.e., Lithuania, Latvia and Estoniaùcontinued to be close and productive. High level visits were exchanged with several of these countries during the course of the year, which confirmed the importance and priority that these countries attach to their relations with India.

Bosnia and Herzegovina opened its resident Mission in New Delhi in 1998.

Bulgarian Deputy Minister of Trade and Tourism, Mr Hristo Mihailovski visited India from 27-30 April, 1998, accompanied by a group of officials and businessmen. He called on the Commerce Minister, MOS for Agriculture and Commerce Secretary.

The 12th Session of Indo-Bulgarian joint Commission was held in Sofia from 22-25 September, 1998. MOS for Agriculture, Shri Sompal, led the Indian side and met Bulgarian PM Kostov, Speaker Sokolov, and the Ministers of Trade, Transport and Agriculture.

President Petar Stoyanov paid a state visit to India from 25-28 October, 1998 accompanied by his wife and a high-level official delegation. He had separate meetings with the President, the Vice-President and the Prime Minister. The Indo-Bulgarian BIPA, an Agreement on Mutual Cooperation between ITPO and the International Fair Inc. Plovdiv, an MOU between the National Centre for Trade Information (NCTI) and the Bulgarian Export Promotion Centre, and an MOU between the CII and the Bulgarian Industrial Association were signed. President Stoyanov visited Agra, Udaipur and Mumbai. The 10th meeting of the IndoûBulgarian Joint Business Council was convened in New Delhi on 27 October, 1998 coinciding with the visit to India of the Bulgarian President.

Bulgurian Deputy Minister of Transport, Mr IIko Miloushev, visited India from 8-10 December, 1998 to take part in a seminar organised by the ministry of Railways. He met Railway Minister Shri Nitish Kumar, Minister for Surface Transport Shri Thambi Durai, MOS for Agriculture Shri Som Pal and senior officials of the Ministry of Civil Aviation, RITES, Cimmco Birla and Konkan Railways.

Mr George Ganchev, MP and Chairman of the Bulgarian Parliamentary Group for "Friendship with India" visited India from 21-26 February, 1999. He called on Shri Krishna Kant, Vice President of India and Shri G M C Balayogi, Lok Sabha Speaker. He also met Shri P R Kumaramangalam, Parliamentary Affairs Minister, Shri R K Hegde, Commerce Minister, Smt Vasundhara Raje, MOS (External Affairs), and Shri Som Pal, MOS for Agriculture, and attended a lunch hosted by FICCI in his honour.

Croatian Minister for Economy Mr Nenad Porges led the Croatian delegation to the Fourth session of the Indo-Croatian joint Committee on Trade and Economic Cooperation which took place on 16-18 November, 1998 in New Delhi. He met Minister of Commerce Shri R K Hegde, Minister of Surface Transport, Shri M Thambidurai, Minister of Petroleum and Natural Gas Shri K Ramamurthy.

Croatian Minister for Culture Mr Bozo Bispkupic is expected to visit India on 4-6 March, 1999.

The President of Croatian Parliament Dr Vlatko Pavletic will be leading a Parliamentary delegation to India from 28 March to April, 1999.

Minister of State for Coal, Shri Dilip Ray, visited Prague 11 May 1998, and held detailed discussions with the Czech Trade and Industry Minister, Mr Kuhnl.

The Indo-Czech Agreement on Avoidance of Double Taxation was signed in Prague on 1 October, 1998 by the Indian Ambassador and Czech Finance Minister, Mr Ivo Svoboda.

The Third session of the joint Committee took place in Prague on 5 & 6 October, 1998. The Indian delegation was led by Shri P Prabhu, Commerce Secretary, and the Czech delegation was led by First Deputy Minister of Industry and Trade, Mr Vaclav Petricek. Commerce Secretary also met the Minister of Industry and Trade, Mr Miroslav Gregr, and Deputy Finance Minister, Miloslav Fiedler. The 2nd meeting of the Indo-Czech joint Business Council was held simultaneously with the meeting of the joint Committee in Prague on 5 & 6 October, 1998, which was attended by Indian businessmen.

A Czech Parliamentary delegation led by the President of the Chamber of the Deputies of the Czech Parliament, Mr Vaclav Klaus, is expected to visit India from 8-14 March, 1999. Mr Klaus will be accompanied by his wife, six Members of Parliament and government officials.

The President of the Republic of Estonia, Mr Lennart Mery, paid a State visit to India 3-10 February, 1999. During the visit, President Mery had separate meetings in New Delhi with the President, the Vice President and the Prime Minister of India as well as other Indian dignitaries. An Indo-Estonian Agreement on Co-operation in the field of Science and Technology and an MOU on co-operation between FICCI and the Estonian Chamber of Commerce was signed during this visit. Besides New Delhi, President Lennart Mery also visited Agra, Jaipur and Mumbai.

Foreign Minister of FRY, Mr Jovadin Jovanovic, met Smt Vasundhara Raje, Minister of State for External Affairs in New York on 29 September, 1998 during the 53rd session of the UNGA. Discussions were held on the need to intensify and renew bilateral cooperation in all fields.

The FRY Minister for Agriculture Mr Nedelijko Sipovac, visited India on 2-7 November, 1998. He met Shri Som Pal, Minister of State for Agriculture, Shri R K Hegde, Minister of Commerce, Shri P A Sangma, Member of Parliament, and called on the Vice

President of India. He also visited Maharashtra and met the Chief Minister, Shri Manohar Joshi, and the Minister of Agriculture of Maharashtra, Shri Harsh Vardan Patil.

Dr Murli Manohar Joshi, Minister for Human Resource Development, visited Hungary on 26-28 November, 1998 in connection with the Golden jubilee of the establishment of diplomatic relations between India and Hungary. He inaugurated a symposium on "Hungary, India and the European Union" on 26th November, 1998. Dr Joshi called on Hungarian President Dr Arpad Goncz and held discussions with Prof Janos Hamori, Minister for National Cultural Heritage, Dr Janos Martonyi, Minister for Foreign Affairs and Dr Zoltan Pokornyi, Minister of Education. The Cultural Exchange Programme for 1999-2000 was also signed during the visit.

To commemorate the 50th Anniversary of the establishment of diplomatic relations between India and Hungary, an International Round Table Conference on "India and Hungary: Perspectives on the Changing World Order" was held at the School of International Studies, Jawaharlal Nehru University, New Delhi from 17 - 18 November, 1998, with the participation of distinguished academics and experts from India and Hungary.

A Hungarian Parliamentary delegation led by Dr Janos Ader, Speaker of the Hungarian Parliament is expected to visit India on 7-13 March, 1999.

Latvian Under Secretary of State Mr Janis Karklins, visited India from 7-12 December, 1998. He held discussions at MEA, besides visiting the 5 Latvian pilots detained in Calcutta in connection with the Purulia Arms Dropping Case. During the visit, he and Joint Secretary (East Europe) initialed the text of the Agreement on the establishment of an Indo-Latvian joint Commission.

The Chief of General Staff of the Polish Armed Forces Lt Gen H Szumski visited India on 30 March - 3 April, 1998, and called on Raksha Mantri, COAS, CAS, Defence Secretary and Secretary (West).

Indo-Polish Working Consultations on Trade and Economic Related Issues were held in Warsaw on 22 & 23 June, 1998.

The Indo-Polish Working Group on Coal under the Indo-Polish joint Commission for Economic, Trade, Scientific and Technical Cooperation met in Warsaw on 14 October, 1998. The Indian delegation was led by Mr S S Boparai, Secretary (Coal) who held discussions with the Deputy Minister of Economy, Mr Jan Szlazak and called on Mr Janusz Steinhoff, the Minister of Economy.

Mr Czeslaw Bielecki, Chairman of the Foreign Relations Committee of the Polish Parliament (Sejm) visited India on 14-16 February, 1999 to participate in the "Global Conference on Democracy" jointly organised by CPR and CII in New Delhi. He met Smt Vasundhara Raje, MOS (External Affairs) and Shri I K Gujral, Chairman, Standing Committee on External Affairs of the Indian Parliament.

The Deputy Defence Minister of Poland Mr Romuald Szeremietiew, is expected to visit India from March 22, 1999.

The 13th session of the Indo-Romanian joint Commission was held on 15-16 December, 1998.

Commerce Minister, Shri R K Hegde, visited Bucharest. He met PM Radu Vasile, Foreign Minister Andrei Plescu and the Romanian Ministers of Health, Finance, Industry and Commerce. Commerce Minister also led the Indian delegation as Co-Chairman of the Indo-Romanian joint Commission. The Romanian side was led by Industry Minister, Mr Radu Berceanu. A Protocol was signed between the two governments on Economic, Scientific and Technical cooperation.

Shri Suresh Prabhu, Minister of Environment and Forests, visited the Slovak Republic from 3-6 May, 1998 to attend the Ministerial Round Table of the 4th Meeting of the Conference of Parties to the Convention of Biological Diversity.

The third session of Indo-Slovak joint Committee took place on 7-8 October, 1998 at Bratislava. The Indian delegation was led by the Additional Secretary in the Ministry of Commerce, who is also the co-chairman on the Indian side. The Slovak delegation was led by Mr Dusan Gutan, Vice-Minister, Ministry of Economy. The delegation was received by the Minister of Economy, Mr Milan Cagala, State Secretary in the Ministry of Finance, Mr Peter Stanec, and by the Director General in the Ministry of Foreign Affairs, Mr Anton Pitner. A meeting of the Indo-Slovak joint Business Council took place at Bratislava on 7 & 8 October, 1998, concurrently with the Joint Committee meeting.

Smt Vasundhara Raje, Minister of State for External Affairs met Dr Ernest Petric, State Secretary, Ministry of Foreign Affairs of Slovenia on September 1, 1998 during the meeting of the Nonaligned Movement held in Durban.

Dr Ernest Petric, State Secretary, Ministry of Foreign Affairs of Slovenia, visited New Delhi on 2-6 February,

1999 for the fourth round of Indo-Slovene Foreign Office Consultations. During the visit, he held discussions with Secretary (West). He met Shri Nripendra Mishra, Additional Secretary, Ministry of Commerce, and called on Smt Vasundhara Raje, Minister of State (External Affairs), and Smt Maneka. Gandhi, Minister of State, Ministry Welfare.

Western Europe

West Europe is a region of considerable political and economic significance to India. The European Union (EU), of which 15 countries of the region are members, is India's largest trading partner and the second largest source of approved foreign investment. The adoption of the Euro by 11 of its member states and the evolution of a Common Foreign and Security Policy are significant pointers to the emergence of an "European identity", which would have an increasingly important role in international affairs.

Normal dialogue and interaction has continued in 1998-99 with the countries of West Europe, as also with the EU. A number of high level visits have been exchanged with West Europe. The President visited Germany, Portugal and Luxembourg, in September 1998. The Prime Minister visited France in Sept-Oct 1998. We have also received the visits of the President of Switzerland, and the Crown Prince of Belgium and the Prime Minister of Luxembourg. The 11th Round of the India-EU Troika Ministerial Meeting was held in New Delhi on November 13,1998. There has also been an exchange of several other Ministerial visits with various other countries. High level official consultations have been conducted with France, the UK and Germany.

During this period, India's trade with the countries of the region has grown and there has been a further strengthening of the investment and technology cooperation ties between India and Europe. The diversification and deepening of the economic linkages and continuing political dialogue between the two sides reflects a shared desire to pursue a closer relationship for mutual benefit.

While most of the countries in West Europe and the EU expressed concern at the nuclear tests conducted by India in May 1998, the specific reactions by different countries were far from uniform. A few countries like the Netherlands, Switzerland, Norway, Sweden and Denmark imposed unilateral economic measures (primarily curtailing development assistance and banning arms sales) with the others being opposed to such action.

Austria held the Presidency of the EU during the second half of 1998. In this capacity the Austrian Minister of State for Foreign Affairs, Dr (Mrs) Benita Ferrero Waldner led the EU Troika delegation at the 11th India-EU Troika Ministerial Meeting held in New Delhi on November 13,1998.

Our bilateral relationship with Belgium has progressed well. Belgium is the 7th largest trading partner for India. Bilateral trade, dominated by trade in diamonds, was over US $ 4 billion in 1997. The total approved Belgian investment in India from 1991 to Aug. 1998 has been around US $ 1 billion, making Belgium the 9th largest investor in India in terms of approval figures. There are around 140 Indo-Belgium joint ventures in operation.

H.R.H. Crown Prince Philippe of Belgium, accompanied by the Deputy Prime Minister and Minister for Economy and Telecommunications, in-charge of Foreign Trade, Mr Elio Di Rupo, led a large high level business delegation to India from 22-29 November, 1998 at the invitation of the Vice President. The delegation included nearly 80 senior representatives of professional organisations, top Belgian companies and financial institutions. The 9th Session of Indo-Belgium-Luxembourg Economic Joint Commission was held in Brussels on 29 June 1998. Commerce Secretary led the Indian delegation and the Secretary-General, Ministry of Foreign Affairs, External Trade and Development Cooperation of Belgium led the Belgium-Luxembourg side.

The 3rd Session of the Indo-Cyprus Joint Economic Committee was held in Nicosia in September, 1998. A Protocol was signed at the end of the meeting by the heads of the two delegations. An MOU between the National Centre for Trade Information (NCTI) of India and the Cyprus Chamber of Commerce and Industry for exchange of information on electronic media, country and product profile, trade statistics, import tariffs, import/export policy was also finalised on this occasion.

Indo-French relations have continued to progress in a satisfactory manner. There has been an intense high level substantive political dialogue between the two sides. Bilateral economic relations with France have also progressed satisfactorily. The Prime Minister visited France on 29 & 30 September, 1998. He held discussions with President Chirac, Prime Minister Jospin and Defence Minister Richard. His visit helped consolidate the progress in bilateral relations subsequent to President Chirac's visit to India in January 1998. Raksha Mantri visited France from 11-13 January, 1999 and held detailed discussions with his French counterpart. The Minister of Railways visited France from 19-20 January, 1999. Principal Secretary to PM visited France from 1-2 June, 1998 as Special Envoy of the Prime Minister and from 18-19 January, 1998.

The Indo-French Forum (IFF), a high level non-governmental group of eminent personalities from both sides, set up in January 1998 to advise on ways of diversifying and enriching the bilateral relations, held its first meeting in Paris on 2 & 3 July, 1998. Dr Karan Singh and Mr Jean Francois-Poncet are the two Co-Chairman of the Forum. The second meeting of the Forum was held in New Delhi from 16-17 February, 1999.

The French Minister of State for Trade and Commerce, Mr Jacques Dondoux led the French delegation for the ninth meeting, of the Indo- French joint Committee for Economic and Technical Cooperation held in New Delhi in November 1998. On 24 November, 1998, officials of the Ministries of Industries of India and France, signed a 'Protocol of Intent' for cooperation. Mr Laurent Fabius, former Prime Minister of France and the present President of the French National Assembly led a Parliamentary Delegation to India from 15- 17 September, 1998. Mrs. Segolene Royal, the French Minister of State for Education visited India from 28 Nov-1 Dec, 1998. She inaugurated the French Education Fair in New Delhi during the visit.

Indo-German relations have grown closer in recent years Germany is India's largest trading partner in Europe and the second, largest overall. The two-way trade is of the order of DM 9 billion (over US $ 6 billion). Approved German investment in India in 1997 was worth Rs 21.5 billion million and the figure for the period 1991-August 1998 is over Rs. 64 billion. Germany is also an important source of technology and has cooperated in various development projects in India.

The President visited Germany from 6-10 September 1998. This was the first Head of State/Government visit from either side in four years. The President held discussions with the German President, Chancellor and

Foreign Minister. A Memorandum of Understanding on bilateral Cooperation in the field of Environment was signed by two sides during the visit.

Mr Guenther Verheugen, one of the two new Ministers of State for Foreign Affairs in Germany, visited India on 13 November 1998 for the 11th India-EU Troika Ministerial Meeting. A high level business delegation, led by Dr Walter Doering, Minister for Economic Affairs in the state of Baden Wuerttemberg, visited India from 22-28 March, 1998. Dr Franz-Josef Feiter, State Secretary and Deputy Federal Minister for Food, Agriculture and Forestry led an economic delegation to India during the same period. Mr Rudolf Kraus, State Secretary in the Federal Ministry of Labour, visited India from 13-19 April, 1998.

The 13th session of the Indo-German Joint Commission on Industrial and Economic cooperation was held in New Delhi from 8-10 January, 1998. The then Finance Minister of India and the then Minister of Economics of Germany, Mr Guenter Rexrodt jointly chaired the meeting. The seventh annual meeting of the high-powered Indo German Consultative Group was held in Dresden on 29 & 30 August, 1998. Bilateral Foreign Office Consultations, at the level of Foreign Secretary, were held in Bonn on 13 July, 1998. The Instruments of Ratification of the Agreement for Bilateral Investment Promotion and Protection were exchanged by the two sides during the visit.

Indo-Greek relations made significant progress. The Greek National Minister for Defence, Mr Apostolos Athanasios Tsohatzopoulos visited India from 5-8 December, 1998. His visit coincided with Aero India '98, to which he was invited by Raksha Mantri. An MoU on Defence Cooperation between India and Greece was signed during the visit. The Greek Defence Minister called on the Prime Minister and had detailed meetings with Raksha Mantri and the three Service Chiefs. Foreign Office Consultations were held with Greece on November 30 & December 1, 1998.

The 13th Session of the Indo-Italian joint Commission on Economic Cooperation was held in Rome from 17-18 December, 1998. The Indian delegation was led by our Commerce Minister while the Italian side was led by the Italian Minister for Foreign Trade, Piero Fassino. Both sides reviewed bilateral industrial cooperation projects and renewed their commitment to maintaining and strengthening the multilateral trade system. The fourth session of the Indo-Italian joint Committee on S&T Cooperation was held in New Delhi/ Calcutta on 9 & 10 November, 1998. The Indian delegation was led by Secretary, Dept. of S&T, Ministry of S&T while the Italian delegation was led by H. E. Mr Gaetano Zucconi, Ambassador of Italy in India. Both sides agreed to promote joint activities in-S&T areas of mutual interest. Foreign Office consultations will be held in Rome shortly, the first since October 1996.

There has also been an intensification of our linkages with Luxembourg. The President visited the Grand Duchy of Luxembourg from 14-16 September, 1998 at the invitation of the Grand Duke Jean. This was the first major high level political visit from either side in the last 25 years. The President held discussions with the Grand Duke, Prime Minister Jean-Claude Juncker, Deputy Prime Minister and Minister of Foreign Affairs Jacques Poos and the President of the Chamber of Deputies Jean Spautz. The Prime Minister of Luxembourg visited India from 11-13 January, 1999. This was the first visit by a Prime Minister of Luxembourg to India. The Instruments of Ratification of the bilateral agreement on cooperation in the fields of art and culture, education, mass media and sports were exchanged during the visit.

India's relations with the Netherlands have a strong economic content, with a growing bilateral trade of the order of US $ 1.5 billion and total approved Dutch investment of over Rs. 37 billion (1991-July 1998). The Netherlands is our sixth largest trading partner in Europe. The Netherlands ranks 8th in terms of overall approved investment in India since 1991. The Netherlands was among the few countries to have imposed economic measures -restrictions on the sale of arms and on certain categories of government-to-government credit and project assistance against India in the wake of the nuclear tests. Commerce Minister visited the Netherlands in October 1998.

The Nordic countries were critical of India's nuclear tests. While Sweden, Norway and Denmark stopped their development assistance programmes to India, Finland and Ireland did not impose any economic measures.

The Danish Minister for Development Cooperation, Mr Poul Nielson visited India from April 1-4, 1998 at the head of their delegation to the Assembly of the Global Environment Facility.

The Ethics Committee of Rajya Sabha, led by Shri S B Chavan, visited Finland in May, 1998. A Finnish Parliamentary delegation led by the Deputy Speaker of Finnish Parliament, Mr Mikko Pesala returned the visit and was in India from 13-19 November, 1998. Earlier, in June, 1998, the Minister of State for Communications visited Finland to attend the Inter-Governmental Conference on Emergency Telecommunications.

The Secretary-General to the Icelandic President, Ambassador Kornelius Sigmundsson visited India from 29 August - 2 September, 1998.

The Deputy Foreign Minister of Norway, Mr Leiv Lunde visited India from 31 March - 4 April, 1998 at the head of the Norwegian delegation to the Assembly of the Global Environment Facility. Two consular agreements; an "Agreement on the Transfer of Convicted Offenders" and a Treaty for "Mutual Legal Assistance in Criminal Matters" were initialled by both the sides in May 1998.

Our relations with Portugal received an impetus with a series of high level visits. The President visited Portugal from 10-14 September, 1998. He held discussions with Mr Jorge Sampaio, the Portuguese President and Mr Antonio Guterres, the Portuguese Prime Minister. He also visited the EXPO '98 Exhibition in Lisbon. A Double Taxation Avoidance Agreement between Portugal and India was signed during this visit. A nine member parliamentary delegation from Portugal visited India from 15-22 December, 1998. The delegation was led by Dr Antonio De Almeida Santos, President of the National Assembly. This was the first visit to India by a parliamentary delegation from Portugal to India. The Third Session of the Indo-Portuguese joint Business Council was held in New Delhi on 5 & 6 January, 1999. The Portuguese Secretary of State for Economy, Prof. Fernando Pacheco visited India from 6-9 January, 1999 for the CII Partnership Summit in Jaipur.

Normal interaction continued with Spain. Bilateral Foreign Office Consultations were held in Madrid on 3 & 4 December, 1998. The Indo-Spanish joint Commission and joint Business Council was held in Delhi from 15-16 February, 1999.

The President of Switzerland, Mr Flavio Cotti, was in India o, a State Visit from 20-25 November, 1998. This was the first ever visit to India by a Swiss President. He was accompanied by a ten member business delegation. He called on President, Vice President and held discussions with PM. He also visited the cities of Mumbai and Bangalore and interacted with the business communities.

Our relations with UK are important with a tangible and modem economic content, apart from the historical dimension, India's annual trade with the UK is of the order of Pounds Stg 3.3 billion. The UK is also the largest cumulative investor in India with a figure of Pounds Stg 3 billion. The presence of a large community of Indian origin, which has done well economically, strengthens the traditional links between the two countries.

The UK in its individual capacity and as the then EU Presidency had been initially critical of the nuclear tests conducted by India Since then bilateral consultations at a high level have helped to place relations on a firmer footing. The Principal Secretary to PM visited UK on 4 & 5 June, 1998, as the Special Envoy of the Prime Minister and on 20 & 21 January, 1999. The visit of Mr Derek Fatchett, Minister of State for Foreign Affairs and Commonwealth to India in November 1998 was also beneficial. The External Affairs Minister visited UK from 2-7 February, 1999. During this visit, discussions were held on a wide range of issues, including, inter alia, bilateral cooperation, regional developments, nuclear disarmament and non-proliferation. These have proved to be useful in promoting greater mutual understanding.

Chief Emeka Anyaoku, the Commonwealth Secretary General (CSG), visited India from 13-18 February, 1999. The visit was part of the traditional round of consultations that the CSG undertakes with member countries before a Commonwealth Heads of Governments Meeting, the next one being held in South Africa in November 1999. During the visit, the CSG called on the President, the Prime Minister and the Minister of External Affairs. The CSG's visit to India coincided with the Asia Trade and Investment Forum organised by the Commonwealth Business Council and the Confederation of Indian Industry, from 14-16 February, 1999.

Developments with far reaching impact are presently taking place at the EU level. The finalisation of the Economic and Monetary Union with the adoption of a single currency Euro by 11 member states of the EU from January 1999 has significance for the international financial system as also implications for the attempts to forge a "European identity" in international affairs. The EU is working on plans for an eastward expansion and there is a serious discussion on the need for its internal financial reforms. There have been moves towards initiating a discussion on NATO's nuclear doctrine and the scope and mandate of its activities, even as it prepares to accept three new members from 1999, its 50th anniversary year. The forthcoming NATO Summit to be held in Washington in April 1999 is expected to consider a New Strategic Concept for the organization which may go beyond the defence of the territories of member countries. These developments impact on the evolving security architecture in Europe and have implications for the security around that region.

The EU, with its fifteen member countries is the largest economic entity in the world today. It is India's largest trade partner with an annual bilateral trade of over US $ 21 billion in 1997. It is also India's second largest source of approved foreign investment (over Rs 300 billion during 1991-August 1998) and an important partner in technology cooperation.

The 11th Round of annual India-EU Ministerial level talks was held in New Delhi on 13 November, 1998. MOS (EA) led the Indian delegation at the talks. The delegations from the EU side consisted of the then

Presidency (Austria), European Commission, Germany (next incumbent) and the UK (past incumbent). These were led by Dr (Mrs) Benita Ferrero-Waldner, Minister of State for Foreign Affairs of Austria, Mr Manuel Marin, Vice President of, the EC, Mr Guenther Verheugen, Minister of State for Foreign Affairs of Germany and Mr Derek Fatchett, Minister of State, FCO, UK respectively. The discussion covered India-EU relations, new initiatives in this regard, regional developments, disarmament and non-proliferation, reform of the UN, international terrorism and other subjects of mutual interest. The first India-EU Senior Officials Meeting had earlier been held in London on 21 April, 1998. The first meeting of officials of the two sides dealing with Policy Planning was held in April 1998 in New Delhi.

8

The Americas

USA

Relations with the United States during the year can be seen broadly in two phases. In the early part of the year, there was continuation of a broad based dialogue which both countries had agreed upon. In that context, US Permanent Representative to UN, Bill Richardson headed a delegation to India from April 14-15,1998. The Indian and the US side had useful exchanges of views on a number of important international, bilateral and regional issues.

Following India's nuclear tests, the US reaction was extremely critical and negative. The reaction was made up of several elements including what the United States saw as a challenge to the nonproliferation regime which the United States and other nuclear-weapon states have south to put in place to preserve their monopoly of nuclear weapons. It also contained elements of frustration at US inability to detect the tests in advance. India look every opportunity to respond to such statements wherever necessary.

The US also took the initiative in meetings of the P-5 and G-8 to orchestrate condemnation of the nuclear tests. Many of these countries, however, did not go along with attempts to multilateralise the imposition of restrictive economic measures against India.

Since then, the reaction has toned down and, to some extent, moderated, This has been reflected in more balanced coverage in the US media. There have been a number of articles and statements, from eminent US political personalities and strategic analysts which reflect a better understanding of India's security concerns. There has also been considerable debate in the United States regarding. the effectiveness of the coercive economic measures called "sanctions".

Despite development of the strains in the bilateral relationship the visits of prominent US political representative continued. US Senators Sam Brownback and Charles Robb, visited India from June 26-30. On their return to the US, these Senators introduced an Amendment to provide authority to the President to waive for up to one year some of the, economic measures under Glenn Amendment. In July 1998, US Congress passed an amendment, which was called "Agriculture Export Relief Act of 1998" which exempted finance and credit guarantees for agricultural commodities, medicine and fertilisers from the purview of 1994.

After the nuclear tests and the apprehensions expressed in several countries, it was decided to have a more intensive dialogue with the United States. Shri Jaswant Singh, then Deputy Chairman, Planning Commission and Mr Strobe Talbott, Deputy Secretary of State have been designated as Representatives to conduct this dialogue.

The talks are being conducted on the basis of the comprehensive proposals that India has put forward on disarmament and nonproliferation matters, our unilateral moratorium on explosive nuclear tests, willingness to discuss converting this moratorium into a de jure obligation, our offer to enter into constructive negotiations on the FMCT and reaffirming our policies on stringent control on export of sensitive technologies.

The talks have focussed on issues related to disarmament and non-proliferation. Both sides have agreed that these issues should be kept distinct from regional issues.

After six rounds of discussions the talks have narrowed down four issues. These are the CTBT, the FMCT, Export Controls and Defence Posture.

On Export Control Issues an expert level meeting was also held in New Delhi on 9-10 November, 1998. The meeting was deemed helpful by both India and the US to the prospects of continuing cooperation in this area.

Both sides have agreed to meet in 2nd half of January 1999 in New Delhi to carry forward this dialogue.

The US has recently announced a partial lifting of the restrictive measures imposed against India. These relate to EXIM, OPIC, TDA Financing and Military Training. The US has stated that these measures are being lifted in recognition of the progress made in the bilateral dialogue. It is however noted that non-basic human needs financing from multilateral financial institutions is still subject to US restrictions. India regards these coercive and restrictive measures as unjustified and counter-productive which should be lifted.

The US has also issued a list of Indian Government Organisations, Research Institutions, PSUs and Private Companies, which will be subject to export restrictions. This step is with clearly punitive intent. India has made it clear to the US that such measures will be regarded as adverse developments in our relations and will not be conducive to the ongoing dialogue. These aspects were reiterated strongly at the last round of discussions held on 19-20 November, 1998. So far there has been no change in the US position. India will continue to take up this matter in bilateral discussions and is also examining the feasibility of multilateral options, such as consistency with WTO provisions.

US Deputy Secretary of State, Strobe Talbott visited India from January 29 to February 1, 1999 with an 8-member delegation including the Vice-Chairman of the US Joint Chiefs of Staff General Joseph Ralston for the 8th round of Indo-US talks. Discussions between the Indian and US delegations were held on January 29, 30 and 31. The Indian side was led by Shri Jaswant Singh, External Affairs Minister.

During the talks, the security perspectives of the two sides were further elaborated and clarified and proposals for harmonising these perspectives were explored. Both delegations were satisfied with the outcome of these talks and believed that progress was made in some of the subjects under discussions.

Both sides are determined to create a positive atmosphere for advancing the bilateral relations. Indian and US expert level teams will meet in March for follow-up talks on export controls. The two sides have agreed to remain in close contact.

The next round of the dialogue is envisioned towards the middle of the year, the dates and the venue of the same would be determined in consultations between the two sides.

Canada

The Governor General of Canada, Romeo LeBlanc and Mrs LeBlanc, accompanied by Canadian Revenue Minister, Herb Dhaliwal, paid a State visit to India from March 26 to April 1, 1998. It was the first ever visit by a Governor General of Canada to India specifically undertaken in the context of the 50th Anniversary celebrations of India's independence.

Canada reacted very adversely to India's nuclear tests in May 1998, and unilaterally restricted government contact. The Canadian position contained a number of elements which were totally unacceptable to India. Canada also placed restrictions on assistance under CIDA. Subsequently, Canada informed that all ongoing projects would continue to receive funding and that new projects of a basic needs nature could be taken up.

The Canadian Leader of the Opposition, Mr Preston Manning visited India in July-August, 1998. He observed that although Canada did not agree with India's nuclear tests, that was no reason for lack of dialogue, and that India and Canada should be able to talk over differences as friends. There is little change in the official Canadian position so far. Government of India will conduct its relations with Canada in a reciprocal basis. Finance Minister visited Canada in September 1998, for the Commonwealth Finance Minister's meeting.

Trade between India and Canada continued to flourish. Last year, Indian exports to Canada registered an increase of nearly 23% . This year, during the period January-July, the Indian exports have reached C$ 536.569 from 424.532 during the same period last year marking a growth of 26.38%. On the other hand, Indian imports from Canada during this period have declined to C$ 182.614 from 287.695 showing a decrease of 36.52%.

Mr Jonathan T Fried, Assistant Deputy Minister for Trade and Economic Policy of Canada visited India from January 25-27,1999. He had meetings with the Ministries of Commerce, External Affairs and Finance. The discussions related to international trade, WTO, foreign investment in India. India's trade and economic relations with SAARC, ASEAN etc. The Speaker of Lok Sabha, Shri G M C Balayogi visited Canada from January 5-9 to participate in the meeting of the Standing Committee of Commonwealth Speakers held in Ottawa.

Latin America and the Caribbean

India's relations with the countries of the Caribbean, Central, 11 America and South America have been traditionally warm and friendly. Presently India maintains 13 Resident Missions and 1 post in the region. India's interaction and collaboration with these countries is close both in the bilateral context and in multilateral fora. 11 countries from the region maintain Resident Diplomatic Missions in New Delhi, Uruguay being the latest to open their Mission in November 1998. Guyana is also considering opening of a Resident Mission in New Delhi.

Interaction with the countries of the region is conducted through bilateral consultative mechanisms. Presently we have such agreements with 9 countries. High level visits complemented by bilateral and official visits have further cemented our relations with the region. In the economic field, realising the potential of the region a concerted effort has been made to diversify and enhance bilateral cooperation. Similar economic reforms in most of the countries in the region have facilitated mutually beneficial cooperation. There have been an increased number of visits of official and private business delegations to and from the region. India has trade and economic agreements with 7 countries of the region and set up Joint Business Councils with some other countries. In continuation of the FOCUS LAC Programme, exclusive Indian exhibitions have helped the dissemination of information on the opportunities available for mutual beneficial economic interaction. Due to concerted efforts trade between India and the LAC region in 1997-98 has grown to over US $ 1.3 billion.

In the field of culture India enjoys considerable goodwill in the LAC region. Some of the countries like Guyana, Surinam and Trinidad & Tobago have a substantial percentage of people of Indian origin. The region also has also more than 500 institutions, schools, libraries and streets named after Indian leaders. At the institutional level there are cultural agreements and Cultural Exchange Programmes with governments that provide the framework for meaningful interactions between artistes, academicians and scholars. In addition, India gives technical assistance under the ITEC programme to several countries of the region.

India also has been able to establish institutional relations with the regional organisations like the Organisation of American States (OAS), Association of Caribbean States (ACS) and the Andean Community where we have Observer Status. India participated in the meetings of the regional organisations, in our capacity as Observers. A mechanism for dialogue with the Rio Group and MERCOSUR has also been established.

After the nuclear tests on 11 & 13 May, 1998, Brazil cancelled the Agreement with India on Cooperation in Peaceful Uses of Nuclear Energy. The OAS General Assembly held in Caracas, 1-3 June, 1998 through a resolution condemned Indian and Pakistani nuclear tests and urged them to refrain from further testing, missile deployment and weaponisation.

The President of India Shri K R Narayanan paid a State visit to Peru from 29 April - 3 May, 1998 and held discussions with President Fujimori. Two bilateral documents - (i) MoU on Cooperation in Space Technology between ISRO of India and its counterpart Peruvian agency CONIDA and (ii) A Work Plan for Cooperation in the field of Agriculture - were signed during the visit. The President had wide ranging discussions with President Fujimori on issues of mutual interest. Peru is the first country in Latin America with which India has signed a MOU for cooperation in space.

President Shri K R Narayanan also paid a State visit to Brazil from 3-8 May, 1998. During the visit, President had fruitful discussions with President Cardoso of Brazil in the presence of the two delegations. The Brazilian delegation included the Ministers of Foreign Affairs, Health, Science & Technology and Agriculture. The President of India was assisted by the Minister of Civil Aviation. An Implementing Arrangement for cooperation in the field of Health and Medicine under the Agreement on Cooperation in Science & Technology was signed for cooperation in areas like biotechnology, epidemology, Public Health Systems, Traditional Medicine, Pharmacology and Pharmaceuticals, Infectious Diseases, Maternal and Child Health care and Tropical Medicine. A MoU on Cooperation between Foreign Service Institute of India and the Rio Branco Institute of Brazil was also signed during the visit. A Festival of India was held in Brazil on the occasion of the President's visit. The Festival was inaugurated in Brasilia by the two Presidents. Subsequent cultural events were held in Sao Paulo, Rio de Janeiro and other major cities in Brazil.

The Minister of State for External Affairs Smt Vasundhara Raje led the Indian delegation to the Ministerial Meeting of the NAM Coordinating Bureau in Cartagena, Colombia 18-20 May, 1998. During the visit, the Minister interacted with her counterparts and briefed them on our foreign policy priorities and the context in which India undertook the nuclear tests. The Minister also called on the President of Colombia.

Utilising the opportunity provided at the 53rd Session of the UNGA, Prime Minister had a meeting with the President of Honduras and Minister of State for External Affairs met the Foreign Minister of Uruguay.

During the XII NAM Summit at Durban, the Minister of State for External Affairs had bilateral meetings with the Foreign Ministers of Cuba, Grenada, Guyana, Jamaica and Surinam and discussed matters of bilateral and multilateral interest.

At the invitation of the Cuban Minister of Agriculture, Mr Alfredo Jordan Morales, the Minister of State for Agriculture Shri Som Pal visited Cuba 27-30 September, 1998. During the visit, areas of cooperation in agriculture and animal husbandry were identified.

The Minister of Power Shri R Kumarmanglam paid an official visit to Venezuela 17-20 September, 1998. He was accompanied by a group of select businessmen interested in the power sector. During his stay in Venezuela, the Minister called on President Caldera. and held discussions with the Venezuelan Ministers for Energy and External Relations on matters of mutual interests. The visit was essentially to study and assess the commercial viability of the fuel ORIMULSION, a Venezuelan product which has been included by Government of India in the list of approved fuels for power generation.

Invited by the Rural Society of Argentina, the Minister of State for Agriculture, Shri Som Pal visited Buenos Aires 8-10 August, 1998 to attend the inauguration of Argentina's most important trade fair - 112th Agriculture Trade Fair.

Shri Nareshwar Dayal, Secretary in the Ministry of External Affairs visited Jamaica, Surinam and Venezuela for consultations in the context of the NAM Summit. Shri Kamlesh Sharma, India's Permanent Representative to the United Nations, visited Havana from 13-16 August, 1998 for discussions with his counterparts ii Cuba.

Shri K M Chandershekher, Joint Secretary, Ministry of Commerce visited Cuba from 9-14 August, 1998 and held discussions with Cuban authorities on the question of revival trade between India and Cuba.

Shri Ramiah Rajagopalan presented his credentials on September, 1998 as the Ambassador of India to Cuba to the Vice-President of the Council of State of Cuba Mr Juan Almeida Bosque, in the presence of the Cuban Foreign Minister.

The first ever exclusive India Products Fair was held in Mexico City from 3-9 March, 1998. Simultaneously with the Fair, an Indian Food Festival and Cultural Festival were also held which received tremendous response well as general public.

India received a tremendous response and cooperation from the countries of the LAC region for the celebrations of the 50th Anniversary of India's independence.

A 2-member Venezuelan Parliamentary delegation consisting of Deputy Julio Castillo, Vice Chairman of the Chamber of Deputies and Deputy Gustavo Tarre Briceno, Chairman of the Permanent Commission on Finance of the Chamber of Deputies visited India from 5 to 12 July, 1998, at the invitation of the Lok Sabha. They had useful interactions with Members of Parliament in India.

General elections were held in Belize on 27 August, 1998. The Opposition Peoples United Party (PUP) won a landslide victory capturing 26 out of total 29 seats. PUP leader Said Musa will be the next Prime Minister of Belize.

Mr Raul Cubas Grau was sworn in as President of Paraguay on 15 August, 1998.

Mr Jamil Mahuad witt was elected as the new President of Ecuador on 12 July, 1998 and was sworn in on 10 August, 1998.

Mr Andres Pastrana Arango, of the Conservative Party was declared President-elect of Colombia in the final round of elections on 21 June, 1998. He took over office on 8 August 1998.

A new Government with H.E. Mrs Sussy Camelia Romer of National Party (PNP) as Prime Minister assumed office in Netherlands Antilles. Though the general elections took place in December 1997 till now there was only an interim Government in power due to lack of agreement between the various parties.

Sir James Fitz-Allen Mitchell was re-elected as the Prime Minister of St. Vincent & the Grenadines after his New Democratic Party won 8 of the 15 seats in Parliament in the general elections held on 15 June, 1998. This is his fourth consecutive term as PM of St. Vincent & the Grenadines.

H.E. Mr Miguel Angel Rodriguez E assumed charge as President of the Republic of Costa Rica on 8 May, 1998.

On 26 October, 1998 Peru and Ecuador signed a Peace Agreement at Brasilia ending a border dispute which started in 1942 and led to a number of border clashes, the last one in 1995. This was the last explosive border dispute in Latin America.

The impact of Asian currency crisis and the Russian crisis affected most of the Latin American economies, forcing the respective governments to adopt stringent austerity measures. Brazil was the worst affected. In view of the turbulent economic situation in the region, it is anticipated that trade between India and Latin America would receive a setback in the coming months.

In Guyana, where there is a significant presence of people of Indian origin, tension prevailed following violence between the Indo-Guyanese and Afro-Guyanese, especially after the disputed Presidential elections held in

9

Africa (South of Sahara)

As in the past, the period under review saw a continuation of the high-level of interaction with the countries of the African continent. The special priority attached to the region, with whom our ties have been both long-standing and time-tested, was underlined by the visit of Prime Minister Shri Atal Behari Vajpayee to Namibia, South Africa and Mauritius in August-September, 1998. It is significant that this visit to Africa was the first foreign visit by the Prime Minister outside the sub-continent.

In addition to a series of high-level exchanges with most countries of the region, the year also saw the visit to India of both Prime Minister Dr Navinchandra Ramgoolam and Vice-President Mr A V Chettiar of Mauritius. India's ties with Mauritius are one of kinship, and these high-level visits further cemented the already close ties between the two countries.

A significant element of India's relationship with sub-Saharan Africa was the growing level of economic interaction. The overall volume of trade with the region exceeded Rs.10,000 crores. Endeavours in the area of economic cooperation were particularly significant for the growing appreciation across the African region of India's prowess - and its special relevance to Africa - in the fields of small and medium-scale industrial enterprises, and agriculture. The already well-established respect for India's expertise in the human development sector was reinforced. A wide-ranging political dialogue with several key countries in the region displayed a considerable degree of understanding of India's security interests.

Bilateral

India's relations with the countries of East Africa are marked by friendship and cordiality. The relations between India and Mauritius continued to grow during the period. Prime Minister Shri A B Vajpayee paid an official visit to Mauritius on 3-4 September, 1998. During the visit a Protocol on Cooperation in the field of Meteorology and a Bilateral Investment Promotion and Protection Agreement was signed. Prime Minister Dr Navinchandra Ramgoolam paid a state visit to India on 13-19 October, 1998. The Vice President of Mauritius Mr A V Chettiar visited India on 26 December, 1998 to 8 January, 1999. Ms Marie Claude Arouff-Parfait, the Mauritian Minister for Youth and Sports visited India in January-February, 1999. During the visit a Protocol each on Cooperation in the field of Sports and Youth Affairs were signed. Cooperation in the sectors of education, science and technology, information technology, trade and industry was further intensified.

Shri Suresh P Prabhu, Minister for Environment and Forests visited Kenya to attend the Special Session of the Governing Council of the United Nations and Environment Programme at Nairobi in May 1998. General DRC Tonje, Chief of General Staff, Kenyan Armed Forces visited India on 20-28 March, 1998. General V P Malik, Chief of Army Staff of India visited Kenya in July 1998. The High Commission of India organised a seminar on "India-Kenya Relations: Vision - 2000" in Nairobi on July 14,1998. Two prominent Kenyan

Ministers i.e. Dr Bonaya Godana, Minister for Foreign Affairs and Hon. S Nyachae, Minister for Finance delivered keynote addresses at the Seminar. Shri A N Ram, former Secretary, MEA, Shri Amit Mitra, Secretary General, FICCI and Shri Pavan K Varma, JS, MEA attended the Seminar. The scope for Kenya to learn from India's development experience was under-scored, as was the potential for enhancing the level of interaction in Indo-Kenyan cooperation in all fields. India organised "India-Tech 98" on 1-4 September, 1998 at Nairobi. More than 60 companies from India displayed their goods and technology at the show. The show received considerable attention from the Government and the business community of Kenya. The exposition show-cased India's capabilities, the comparative and cost effective quality of its technologies and their appropriateness to local needs. The exposition was inaugurated by Shri Som Pal, Minister for State for Agriculture. He also discussed matters of mutual concern with a number of Kenyan Ministers. Hon. J J Kamotho, Kenyan Minister for Trade accompanied by a trade delegation visited India on November 11-13, 1998. Apart from his meetings with Shri R K Hegde, Minister of Commerce, he also led the Kenyan side at the Joint Trade Committee Meeting held during the visit. Shri S T Devare, Secretary(ER) visited Nairobi on 20-25 November, 1998 and held discussions with his Kenyan counterpart on various matters of mutual concern.

India's growing relations with Uganda were further strengthened during the period under review. Ugandan President Mr Y Museveni made a transit halt at Mumbai in April 1998. The first Deputy Prime Minister and Foreign Minister Mr Eriya Kategaya. paid a private visit to India from 28 April to June 1, 1998. An exhibition by Building Materials Technology Promotion Council of India on low-cost housing was held in Kampala from 3-

10 April, 1998. This was the biggest ever exhibition/fair in Uganda organised by India. It generated considerable interest in Uganda. During the year, Indian Council of Agricultural Research and National Agricultural Research Organisation of Uganda signed an Agreement on Cooperation in the field of Agricultural Research. Ugandan Minister for Higher Education, Dr. Abil Rwendeire led a delegation to India on 1-7 November, 1998. The Indo-Ugandan Joint Committee met in Kampala on 23-24 November, 1998. Shri S T Devare, Secretary (ER), led the Indian delegation. The Joint Committee deliberations identified several areas of mutually beneficial cooperation between the two countries including the establishment of a small-scale industrial estate at Jinja, cooperation in commercial farming, human resource development, the identification of new areas such as information technology etc. Dr P Byarauhanga, Ugandan Minister of State for Health visited India in December 1998.

The Minister of Education of Rwanda visited India from May 18-21, 1998. During the visit, an Agreement between the Ministry of Education of Rwanda and Educational Consultants India Limited was signed. Under this Agreement EDCIL is to facilitate admission of over 430 Rwandese students in various Indian universities/ institutions. On a specific request by Rwandan Government a specialised training course for one month for 5 Rwandan dairy farmers was arranged at National Dairy Research Institute, Karnal.

During the year, several delegations from Ethiopia visited India seeking to gain from India's development strategy and experience. These included a 20-member Ethiopian dairy farmers delegation, an 8-member veterinary delegation, a 10-member delegation of the Ministry of Finance, Industry and Trade and a 3-member pharmaceuticals delegation. A delegation from Ethiopia also came to study income-generating employment strategies for women in India. Ethiopia continued to recruit Indian professors and experts for its universities and technical training institutions. In May 1998, a Bilateral Cultural Exchange Programme (1998-2000) was signed with Ethiopia. India and Seychelles signed a Bilateral Trade Agreement at Mahe on 18 September, 1998. The agreement provides for most favourable nation facilities to imports from each other. The agreement also envisages the setting-up of a joint Trade Council to review trade and commercial relations.

The ties of friendship and cooperation between India and Madagascar continued to expand further during the year. The President Mr Didier Ratsiraka met Prime Minister Shri A B Vajpayee, at Durban on the margins of the NAM Summit. The National Mineral Development Corporation signed an MOU on 11 September, 1998 with the Malagasy organisation for exploration of gold, and, Telecommunications Consultants India Limited bagged a contract worth US $ 9 million in Madagascar.

After a gap of nearly 20 years, India participated at the Dar-esûSalaam International Trade Fair in Tanzania and won the first prize in the foreign participation category.

India's relations with the countries in southern Africa made significant progress during the year. The traditionally close and friendly relations between India and South Africa were sustained through exchanges of visits and bilateral consultations at all levels. Shri Brijesh Mishra, Principal Secretary to the Prime Minister, visited South Africa as a Special Envoy of the Prime Minister in July 1998 for bilateral consultations. General V P Malik, Chief of Army Staff of India visited South Africa in July

1998. The Deputy Minister in the South African Deputy President's Office, Dr Essop Pahad, visited India on 2-10 October, 1998. Mr Mac Maharaj, the, South African Minister of Transport visited India on 2-12 October 1998. The 3rd meeting of the Indo-South Africa Joint Commission took place in Pretoria on 4-5 December, 1998. The meeting was chaired by Smt Vasundhra Raje, Minister of State for External Affairs and Mr Aziz Pahad, the South African Deputy Foreign Minister. The joint Commission reviewed the progress c cooperation in the entire gamut of bilateral relations and identified areas where progress could be accelerated. An Agreement on Air Services was also signed during the meeting. These high level bilateral contracts served to reinforce and expand the existing areas of bilateral cooperation while at the same time opening new areas of cooperation. Other high level exchanges included the visits t South Africa of the Minister of Petroleum and Natural Gas, the Minister of Mines, and the Minister of State for Rural Development and the visits to India by Mr Jay Naidoo, the Minister of Posts, Telecommunications and Broadcasting and Dr A M "Dullah" Omar, the Minister of Justice, Mr Ismail Mohamed, the Chief Justice of Supreme Court and Mr Narend Singh, the Minister for Agriculture of Kwazulu Natal served to provide further focus to bilateral cooperation in these areas.

The relations between India and Namibia were marked by the, traditional sense of closeness and understanding. Prime Minister Shri Atal Behari Vajpayee paid an official visit to Namibia on August 30-31, 1998 at the invitation of President Sam Nujoma. During the visit, extensive talks were held on issues of bilateral interests, and subjects of multilateral concern. A prominent street in Windhoek was named after Mahatma Gandhi in the presence of India's PM. Four important bilateral agreements in the areas of Technical Cooperation,

Agricultural Research, Technology Demonstration and Foreign Office Consultations were signed. An Agreement facilitating exchange of information between Press Trust of India and Namibia Press Agency was also exchanged. President Laurent Kabila of the Democratic Republic of Congo met Prime Minister Shri A B Vajpayee in Windhoek in August 1998.

The Hon'ble Speaker of the Lok Sabha, Shri G M C Balayogi accompanied by 5 members of Parliament attended the 99th IPU meeting held in Windhoek in April 1998. Mr H Palichta, the Namibian Minister of Works, Transport and Communications visited India in August 1998. During the visit he held extensive talks on possibilities of cooperation between the two countries in the field of railways.

The relations between India and Zimbabwe continued to be warm and friendly. Shri Dilip Lahiri, Additional Secretary (UN), Ministry of External Affairs held consultations with his counterparts in the Zimbabwean Ministry of Foreign Affairs in May 1998. The first Indo-Zimbabwean joint Trade Committee meeting was held in Harare from 17-19 August, 1998. The Indian delegation was led by Shri P P Prabhu, Commerce Secretary. TCIL of India won a major contract worth US $35 million in Zimbabwe during the year.

The relations between India and Zambia continued to grow during the period of the report. The India-Zambia joint Trade Committee meeting was held in Lusaka on 6-7 January, 1999. The Indian delegation was led by Shri P P Prabhu, Commerce Secretary. The Conference of India's Commercial Representatives in the Region was also held at Lusaka on 8 January, 1999.

The Deputy Commander of the Botswana Defence Force, Major General T H C Masire visited India from 24-30 January, 1999.

The relations between India and the countries in West Africa continued to expand in all fields. Nigeria is an important trading partner of India in Africa with the volume of bilateral trade reaching Rs 3000 crores; in 1998-99. General Olusegun Obasanjo, former Head of State of Nigeria paid a private visit to India in September 1998. In October 1998, the Chief of the Naval Staff Rear Admiral Jubrilia Ayinia paid an official visit to India. Nigeria is in lead up to national elections scheduled for February 1999. As a gesture of support for this transformative process, India has gifted indelible ink worth Rs 74.65 lakh for use during the elections.

Shri S S Barnala, Minister of Chemicals & Fertilizers and Consumer Affairs visited Dakar, Senegal on 7-10 November 1998 to attend the foundation laying ceremony as Chief Guest of the project of Industries Chimique Du Senegal in which IFFCO is an equity partner.

H.E. Mr Salifou Diallo, Minister of State for Environment and Water of Burkina Faso visited India over 12 & 13 October, 1998 to exchange views on the ongoing aspects of bilateral cooperation.

India's relations with Cote d'Ivoire have been improving steadily. A delegation organised by the EXIM Bank of India and the CII visited Cote d'Ivoire and also had discussions with the Abidjan based African Development Bank in May 1998.

Shri Kashiram Rana, the Minister of Textiles led a delegation of the Indian jute industry to Nigeria, Ghana and Cote d'Ivoire in August 1998 for promoting export of hydro-carbon free jute bags to the West African region.

India's assistance to African countries

The Prime Minister of Senegal Mr Habib Thiam received 100 Indian tractors in May 1998 as part of the

Agricultural Development Project being set up with India's assistance. India assisted Togo in rural development by gifting water pumps, sewing machines, corn grinding mills, and TATA mobile ambulances worth Rs 3.26 crores during the year. In Mali, a drilling rig gifted by India was installed and commissioned during the period of the report. Two TATA ambulances were handed over to President Sam Nujoma of Namibia on 17 November 1998 for use at a maternity clinic. Another gift of 10,000 litres of cooking oil and 5 tonnes of baby milk powder were formally handed over to President Sam Nujoma on 27 January 1999. A cheque for Rs. 10,00,000 was presented to President Mugabe by the Indian High Commissioner in support of the Jawaharlal Nehru-Robert Mugabe Trust Fund. As a gesture of solidarity and support; in the aftermath of the US bombing at Nairobi and Dares-Salaam. on 8 August 1998, India provided medical assistance worth Rs 10 lakh and Rs 5 lakh respectively to Kenya and Tanzania. A consignment of books on economics, management, computers and public administration was presented to the Institute of Public Administration and Management in Sierra Leone in July 1998.

Evacuation/repatriation assistance provided to affected Indian community in Africa

On the humanitarian front, India was prompt in providing assistance to the affected Indian community residing in African countries. Following the outbreak of hostilities between Ethiopia and Eritrea in June 1998,153 Indian nationals were evacuated from Asmara capital of Eritrea by chartering an aircraft in Djibouti and brought safely to India. During the political upheavals in Lesotho in September 1998, the Indian community crossed over the border into South Africa. They were provided all possible consular assistance by our mission in South Africa. Following demarches made by India, ten Indian soldiers serving in Angola with the MONUA (UN Observer Mission in Angola), held hostage by UNITA, were released on 6 December, 1998. Following the outbreak of armed revolt in Guinea Bissau in June 1998,49 Indians nationals were evacuated and repatriated to India. Assistance was also rendered to the Indian nationals affected by the rebels' attacks which took place in Sierra Leone in December 1998.

Multilateral

Prime Minister, Shri A B Vajpayee, led the Indian delegation to the NAM Summit in Durban in September 1998. Shri A B Vajpayee, Prime Minister addressed a Message to the OAU Summit (June 8-10, 1998) held at Ouagadougou, capital of Burkina Faso. It was handed over by Shri S T Devare, Secretary (ER) and was put on record as a document of the proceedings of the Summit. India also gifted seven heavy duty photocopiers to Burkina Faso for use during the Summit.

As part of the consultation preceding the NAM Summit at Durban, South Africa in September 1998, high level envoys visited several African capitals: Shri S T Devare, Secretary (ER) visited Dar-es-Salam, Harare, Lusaka and Shri A N Ram, Special Envoy visited Libreville, Lagos, Dakar, Freetown, Banjul and Accra.

Conclusion

Africa is in a phase of-transition, leaving behind the legacies o the past, and moving towards a many-splendoured future embracing democracy, economic reform and a constructive emergence of regional identities. India, with its unique developmental experience, and as the world's largest democracy undergoing significant economic reform, has a vital role to play in underpinning and moulding such an African future. The people of Indian origin who have made Africa their home in almost every corner of the continent are a natural bridge in re-enforcing our future ties with Africa. However, India's diplomatic vision extends beyond such natural ethnic affinities to embrace the interests of Africa as a whole, particularly in the priority area of economic progress and development. Such an economic congruence is facilitated by a broad agreement between India and the countries of Africa on their vision of a new world order characterised by peace, justice and equity, and fully responsive to the needs and interests of the developing world.

10

United Nations and International Organisations

The year 1998 continued to witness global changes in the political and economic spheres. The United Nations, which found itself in the midst of the change, was faced with the need for fundamental organisational reforms on the one hand and the desire to strengthen its role as the centre-piece of the international community on the other. In an era of globalisation and spread of democracy world wide, the United Nations, in its quest for being an effective instrument for the international community, was confronted with critical choices relating to its own revitalisation and reform. India, in keeping with its commitment to multilateralism and its perceptions of the role of the UN in a changed world reality, continued to participate actively and constructively in every sphere of UN activity. Of particular significance was India's contribution to the debate on UN reforms, expansion of UN Security Council, developmental issues, terrorism, disarmament and financial reforms.

India also actively participated in the XIIth Summit of the Movement of Non Aligned countries in Durban in September this year. India as a founder member of NAM stressed on the continued commitment of NAM to its basic principles which remain valid even in the post cold war era. India's vital concerns at the Summit included disarmament and security in the context of nuclear tests in South Asia, shaping of the global economic agenda and reinforcing the international community's condemnation of terrorism.

The 53rd Session of the UN General Assembly was held in the backdrop of India's nuclear tests. A major concern for India at the Session was to secure understanding for the rationale behind India's nuclear tests. Prime Minister Shri Atal Behari Vajpayee visited New York from September 23-28, 1998. The dominant themes of his address to the Plenary were disarmament, India's positive indications on CTBT, reiteration of India's candidature for permanent membership of UNSC, terrorism and other issues relating to globalisation. Denouncing terrorism as a scourge and a vicious crime against humanity, he noted that India had had to cope with terrorism, aided and abetted by a neighbouring country, for nearly two decades. He reiterated the call by the NAM Summit at Durban for an international conference in 1999 to launch the process of negotiations for an international convention to provide for collective action against states and organisations; which initiate or aid and abet terrorism. He also called for making the UN Security Council more representative, to reflect the interests of the developing world.

In the developed world, support for multilateralism continued to be lukewarm and selective. The funding of development through multilateral agencies continued to face difficulties, and the price for support was a demand that they reorient their work away from their traditional strengths in technical cooperation. In peacekeeping, there was an increasing tendency for powerful countries to supplant the UN, or to argue that the sanction of the Security Council was not needed, even for enforcement action. However, the financial crisis in East Asia forced attention to the urgent need for international and multilateral initiatives to address systemic faults, and the long-term needs for developing countries. Similarly India's nuclear tests attracted wide concern, but drew attention to the continuing failure of the international community to seriously address the need for nuclear disarmament.

Political issues in the UN

Restructuring of UN security council and reiteration of India's candidature for permanent membership

India actively participated in the Open Ended Working Group of the UN General Assembly on the Question of Equitable Representation on and an Increase in the Membership of the Security Council and other matters related to the Security Council which continued its consideration of a variety of complex issues during the year. The mandate of the Working Group was extended by one more year to enable it to submit its recommendations before the beginning of the 54th Session of UN General Assembly. On the question of expansion of UN Security Council, there appeared to be no general agreement as to the criteria, number of seats or time-frame. A group of countries led by Italy tabled a draft resolution on the question of voting threshold, seeking to ensure that the matter of Security Council reform was not subject to any time-frame and must be adopted by a two-thirds majority of UN membership. Another group of countries, comprising Germany, UK, France and Japan and led by Belgium countered the move and tabled amendments to the draft resolution. After protracted consultations instituted by the President of UN General Assembly, a compromise resolution was arrived at, which stated that the General Assembly would not adopt any decision on the question of expansion of the Security Council without the affirmative vote of at least two-thirds of UN membership.

The Prime Minister, in his address to the 53rd UNGA on September 24,1998, called for the Security Council to be made more representative, reflecting the interests of the developing world. He further reiterated that India was qualified, had the ability, and was prepared to accept the responsibilities of permanent membership.

Iraq

On December 16, the United States and UK launched an attack on Iraq, using cruise missiles followed by aerial bombardment. This action followed immediately on a report submitted to the Security Council through the Secretary General by the Chairman of UNSCOM, in which he alleged that Iraq had not cooperated with his Commission. However, the U S and UK acted without authorisation by the Security Council; even the other permanent members were not taken into confidence, and Russia and China were openly critical. Prime Minister made a statement in Parliament in New York deploring the military action against Iraq.

Peacekeeping

In keeping with its commitments to the maintenance of international peace and security and at the request of the United Nations, India decided to provide a military contingent for participation in the UN peace-keeping operation in LebanonûUNIFIL (United Nations Interim Force in Lebanon). UNIFIL was established in 1978 after Israel's occupation of Southern Lebanon. The Indian battalion of 618 ranks replaced the Norwegian force by end November 1998.

With the induction of an Indian infantry battalion in Southern Lebanon in November, India has emerged as the second largest troop contributor to UN Peace-Keeping Operations. Indian troops, military observers and civilian police personnel are currently serving in peace- keeping operations in every continent where UN peace-keepers are deployed. In Africa, Indian peace-keepers are deployed in Angola (MONUA) and Western Sahara (MINURSO); in Asia in Kuwait (UNIKOM) and Lebanon (UNIFIL); in Europe in Bosnia and Herzegovina (IPTF); and in Latin America in Haiti (MIPUNOH).

India has actively participated in the debates and decisions of the UN General Assembly relating to peace-keeping operations as also in the deliberations of the Special Committee on Peace-Keeping (C-34). India, along with other like-minded countries, was able to get the UN to agree to dispense with gratis personnel, including a large number in UNDPKO, by February 1999.

The International Criminal Court

The statute of the International Criminal Court was adopted on 17th July, 1998 at Rome. India abstained, along with 20 other countries. The US, China, Russia and Israel voted against the statute. The statute provides for automatic jurisdiction of the International Criminal Court over genocide and crimes against humanity. India's fundamental objections to the statute were pointed out in the explanation of vote after abstention. The most important of these were the provision of powers to the UN Security Council, inter-alia, to bind even those states who are not signatories to the ICC statute; the deliberate exclusion of the use of weapons of mass destruction, including nuclear weapons, from the list of war crimes and, similarly, the exclusion of terrorism as a crime against humanity.

Indian proposal for a comprehensive international convention on terrorism

India was successful in reviving its proposal on a comprehensive international convention against terrorism which had been circulated by it at the 51st UN General Assembly in 1996. A resolution on "Measures to

Eliminate International Terrorism" was adopted by consensus in the Sixth Committee, deciding that an Ad Hoc Committee would consider, on a priority basis, the elaboration of such a comprehensive convention. The need for a comprehensive convention has arisen in order to provide a special focus on cross-border terrorism and to adequately address the problem of state-sponsored terrorism.

Disarmament and International Security

1998 marked a watershed for Indian diplomacy in disarmament and international security affairs. After a unique voluntary restraint of 24 years, India conducted a limited series of underground nuclear tests on May 11 and 13. The tests did not violate any legal obligation and were undertaken in response to pressing security needs and a technological imperative. India declared itself a nuclear weapon state and key elements of its nuclear doctrine were announced in succeeding months.

Pakistan's decision to conduct nuclear tests within two weeks of the tests conducted by India showed what had been widely believed - that it had maintained a clandestine nuclear weapon programme. It highlighted the failure of the non-proliferation regime.

India has announced that the following would constitute its nuclear doctrine:

- India will maintain a minimum and credible nuclear deterrent;
- India has no intention of engaging in an open-ended programme or an arms race;
- India subscribes to a policy of no-first-use of nuclear weapons and by implication, non-use with regard to non-nuclear weapon states;
- A moratorium on nuclear testing was announced on May 13, 1998. India is now

engaged in discussions with key interlocutors on a range of issues, including the CTBT. It is prepared to bring these discussions to a successful conclusion so that the entry into force of the CTBT is not delayed beyond September 1999. India expects that other countries, as specified in Article XIV of the CTBT will adhere to the treaty without conditions;

- India is engaged in negotiations in the Conference on Disarmament on a treaty banning the production of fissile material for nuclear weapons or other nuclear explosive devices in good faith;
- India shall not transfer nuclear weapons or nuclear weapons material and technology and will maintain a stringent system of export controls to demonstrate her commitment to non-proliferation;
- India's nuclear arsenal is under civilian command and control;
- A National Security Council has been established and tasked to undertake a Strategic Defence Review.

Having harmonised its national imperatives and security obligations and desirous of continuing to co-operate with the international community, India is engaged in a dialogue with key interlocutors on a range of issues. The aim of these dialogues is to reconcile India's legitimate security concerns with international concerns on disarmament and non-proliferation and build a stronger basis for future cooperation. These discussions have led to a narrowing of gaps in perceptions on security matters. Also as part of the resumed composite dialogue process with Pakistan, India has offered a set of concrete proposals to build confidence between the two nations, including in the nuclear field. India has also offered security assurances to the nuclear weapon free zone in South East Asia and has stated that as a responsible nuclear weapon state, it would be responsive to the need for such assurances from other regions as well.

India's commitment to nuclear disarmament remains undiluted. In a major new initiative, the UN General Assembly adopted a resolution, proposed by India, on reducing the threat posed by hair-trigger alert of nuclear weapons. The NAM Summit at Durban in September 1998 endorsed India's call for an international conference in 1999 to arrive at an agreement on a time-bound programme to abolish all nuclear weapons.

An important focus of Post-Pokhran 11 diplomacy has been to put out timely and regularly updated information for use of India's missions abroad. Regular contact has been maintained with key international and non-governmental organisations active in the field of disarmament with a view to keeping them appropriately informed about the Indian perspectives on disarmament issues.

Disarmament issues in NAM

The Ministerial meeting of the Non Aligned Co-ordinating Bureau, held in Cartagena, May 18-20, 1998 took place in the aftermath of India's nuclear tests. Despite efforts by some member States to criticise India's decision, the final document made no reference to India's nuclear tests. The Non-Aligned Summit held at Durban, South Africa from September 2-3,1998 endorsed India's call for NAM to come out with fresh initiatives towards global nuclear disarmament on a universal and non-discriminatory basis, within a specified time-frame, including, in particular, an international conference preferably in 1999 to prepare a plan of action before the start of the new millennium for the complete elimination of nuclear weapons and the conclusion of a global Nuclear Weapons Convention. India ensured that collective decisions worked out at the Summit on disarmament and international security issues were in harmony with India's approach and that references to the nuclear tests were handled in a pragmatic manner without adverse or critical references, while retaining a continued focus on the priority aspects of global nuclear disarmament.

UN general assembly

India participated in the First Committee on Disarmament and related matters of the 53rd United Nations General Assembly held in New York from October 12-November 13,1998. India actively projected its national policy in the First Committee on Nuclear Disarmament, through a plenary statement delivered by Shri Sharad Pawar, MP and through other interventions and statements. India's traditional resolution on the 'Convention on the Prohibition of the Use of Nuclear Weapons' was adopted by the General Assembly by 111 votes in favour, 39 against and 7 abstentions. The resolution on the 'Role of Science and Technology in the context of International Security and Disarmament' was adopted by the General Assembly by 99 votes in favour, 45 against and 23 abstentions. In addition, a new resolution on 'Reducing Nuclear Danger' introduced by India this year, to highlight the dangers associated with hair-trigger alert of nuclear weapons leading to risks of accidental or unauthorised launch of nuclear weapons, was adopted by 108 votes in favour, 45 against and 17 abstentions by the General Assembly. Attempts were made to isolate India through a coercive and discriminatory resolution on "Nuclear testing", but India was able to effectively convey the rationale for its tests which found considerable understanding and support.

Conference on disarmament

During 1998, India continued to play an important role in the Conference on Disarmament (CD). India, along with other developing countries, emphasised the need for commencing negotiations on nuclear disarmament which remains the highest priority for the Conference. The CD President's consultations for an Ad Hoc Committee on Nuclear Disarmament remained inconclusive. Towards the end of the CD session, an Ad Hoc Committee under agenda item I entitled "Cessation of Nuclear Arms Race and Nuclear Disarmament" was established to negotiate on the basis of the Shannon Report and the mandate contained therein, "a non-discriminatory, multilateral and internationally and exchange of views as a first step towards substantive negotiations on a ban on production of fissile material for nuclear weapons or other nuclear explosive devices.

India also contributed positively to work in the Ad Hoc Committee on Negative Security Assurances (NSAs) by articulating our nuclear doctrine of 'no-first-use' of nuclear weapons as well as I no-use' of nuclear weapons against non-nuclear weapon states. India's nuclear tests of May 1998 were discussed at length in the CD. India's diplomatic efforts were directed towards explaining and projecting the rationale of the tests in the context of our national policy. India succeeded in avoiding specific or critical reference to the nuclear tests in the CD Annual Report.

Limited progress was achieved during the year by the six Special Co-ordinators dealing with the ban on transfer of anti-personnel landmines, prevention of an arms race in outer space, transparency in armaments, review of the CD agenda, improved and effective functioning of the CD and expansion of CD membership. India was actively engaged in the work of both the Ad Hoc Committees and all the Special Co-ordinators. "The CD reconvened on January 19, 1999 for the first part of its three-part Annual Session".

United Nations disarmament commission

India actively participated in the United Nations Disarmament Commission (UNDC) which held its substantive session in New York in April 1998. The UNDC deliberations dealt with the following:

- Establishment of nuclear-weapon-free-zones on the basis of arrangements freely arrived at among the States of the region concerned;
- Fourth Special Session of the UN General Assembly devoted to Disarmament;
- Guidelines on Conventional Arms Control/ Limitation and disarmament, with particular emphasis on consolidation of peace in the context of GA Resolution 51/45N.

The Working Group on convening the Fourth Special Session of the UN General Assembly devoted to disarmament failed to reach a consensus due to opposition by some Western nuclear weapon States on the issue of reaffirming the principles and priorities of the First Special Session on global nuclear disarmament.

Chemical weapons convention (CWC)

The increasing number of ratifications to the CWC, one of the most intrusive disarmament mechanisms to date, is an acknowledgment of the non-discriminatory and universal character of the Convention. In its second year since entry into force, the Convention has entered into a politically significant phase. Implementation of all obligations assumed by India as an original state party to the Convention and related activities have proceeded satisfactorily. Having served as the first Chairman of the Executive Council of the Organisation for the Prohibition of Chemical Weapons (OPCW) in the Hague, India was again elected to the Executive Council for a two year period. At the Third Conference of the States parties to the CWC in November 1998, India called for a balance between the transparency and confidentiality provisions of the Convention and a non-discriminatory application of the provisions of the Convention. National implementing legislations containing provisions which undermine the Convention hold out the prospect of leading to matching responses by other states parties thereby leading to an unnecessary dilution to the spirit of confidence reposed in the CWC by a great majority of countries party to the CWC. Similarly, the existence of technology denial regimes such as the Australia Group remains an aberration when seen against the large number ratifications the Convention has enjoyed so far.

Biological weapons convention

India is a party to the 1972 Biological and Toxic Weapons Convention (BTWC). India actively participated in the work of Ad Hoc Group of State Parties to the Convention in Geneva during 1998 to negotiate a Protocol to the Convention on the basis of the agreed mandate. The Indian delegation continued to support strengthening of BTWC through an effective Protocol for creating a non-discriminatory and transparent compliance regime including the unimpeded exchange and transfer of technology for peaceful purposes. The negotiations are entering a decisive phase. India has continued to maintain its stand that the compliance regime should be formulated and implemented in a manner designed to protect sensitive commercial proprietary information and legitimate national security needs. The verification measures should be nondiscriminatory and avoid any negative impact on scientific research, international co-operation and industrial development. India is committed to the decision of the Fourth BWC Review Conference that the negotiations should be concluded as soon as possible before the Fifth Review Conference in 2001 without recourse to artificial deadlines.

International Atomic Energy Agency (IAEA)

The nuclear tests carried out by India in May were discussed in the IAEA Board of Governors in June 1998 and again in September during the IAEA General Conference. In a press statement, the IAEA had indicated that India had done something it had always reserved its right to do and observed that there was no violation of any safeguards commitment to the Agency (IAEA). However, four countries called for inclusion of this item in the agenda of the June Board and later tabled a resolution on nuclear testing at the General Conference. India pointed out the inappropriateness of discussing this issue at the IAEA, her own security compulsions, and the double standards practised by nuclear weapon states in thwarting attempts to move towards global nuclear disarmament.

Director General, IAEA has written to the nuclear weapon states and those with facility specific agreements (including India) with the Agency asking which measures of the Model Additional Protocol adopted in May 1997 with a view to strengthening existing safeguards consistent with their safeguards commitments they would be prepared to accept. In 1998 the US, UK and France have concluded agreements with the Agency along these lines.

ASEAN regional forum

In line with the high priority given to a "look east" policy, India continued to participate in the meetings of this security dialogue forum that groups together nine

ASEAN countries and their dialogue partners including USA, Canada, EU, Japan, China, Russia since 1996. Delegations comprising of officers from Ministry of External Affairs and Ministry of Defence have participated in the meetings of the Inter-Sessional Group (ISG) on Confidence Building Measures (CBMs).

An Indian delegation led by Shri Jaswant Singh, Deputy Chairman (Planning Commission), participated in the 5th ASEAN Regional Forum meeting at Manila from July 24-29, 1998. From India's point of view, it was important to avoid condemnatory references to the tests in the Chairman's Statement and ensure that discussions were meaningful and not polemical or contentious. It was equally important to demonstrate India's engagement in the economic and political stability of the region and take the opportunity provided by the presence of ARF ministers to put forth our point of view and share perceptions on regional and international developments. ASEAN countries, specially Indonesia, Malaysia and Singapore supported India and refused to join in the condemnation of India by non-ASEAN members. ASEAN's acknowledgment of India's role as a balancing power in Asia-Pacific security is implicit in this. India assured the ASEAN countries that it fully respected the status of the Nuclear Weapon Free Zone in South East Asia and announced its readiness to convert this commitment into a legal obligation. The series of meetings that Shri Jaswant Singh had with his ARF ministerial colleagues in the margins of the ARF meeting marked a crucial step in the post-Pokhran II diplomacy. In particular, the meetings with the Foreign Ministers of China, Russia, the Minister of State for Foreign Affairs of Japan and the US Secretary of State were constructive and oriented towards the future.

Conventional weapons, landmines & small arms

India is committed to strengthening the norm of

transparency in armaments general and greater participation in the Register in particular. India has continued timely reporting to the UN Register of Conventional Arms on an annual basis (since 1994). The issue of proliferation of and illicit trafficking in small arms has moved up the agenda of the international community on disarmament issues. India is acutely aware of this problem and intends to participate actively in international search for effective solutions, including a proposed international conference to discuss the issue of illicit trafficking in small arms in all its aspects.

India is fully committed to the eventual elimination of anti-personnel landmines and achievement of the objective of a non-discriminatory and universal ban on APLS. This objective can be achieved in a meaningful way through a step-by-step approach, beginning with a ban on export and transfer of APLS, that would enjoy international consensus, and by addressing humanitarian concerns and legitimate defence requirements of states. India is presently in the process of ratifying amended Protocol If of the 1980 Inhumane Weapons Convention (CCW), which deals with anti-personnel landmines. Amended Protocol 11, which has been ratified by twenty states, is due to enter into force on 3 December, 1998. Protocol IV to the Convention banning blinding laser weapons entered into force on 30 July 1998.

Social human rights and humanitarian issues

India participated actively in the discussions on human rights issues in sessions of the UN Commission on Human Rights, the Economic and Social Council and the General Assembly. There was a special significance to the discussions of human rights issues as December 10, 1998 marked the 50th anniversary of the adoption of the Universal Declaration of Human Rights. Special commemorative sessions were held by the General

Assembly and several other UN bodies to mark the occasion. Special events were also organised in India, where a series of activities overseen by a National Committee under the chairmanship of Minister for Home Affairs was organised to mark the occasion. The year also marked the five-year-review of implementation of the Vienna Declaration and Programme of Action adopted at the conclusion of the World Conference on Human Rights held in 1993. The adoption of the Declaration on "Human Rights' Defenders" by the General Assembly at its 53rd session was a significant development.

In the discussions on human rights India called for a constructive, balanced and cooperative approach to human rights issues, emphasising the universality, indivisibility and inter-relatedness of all rights and the inter-dependence of democracy, human rights, development and international cooperation. It was necessary to depoliticise any consideration of human rights and pursue measures and approaches which can lead to concrete results in the promotion and protection of human rights everywhere. The discussions were also used to project India's stature as a democracy fully committed to the preservation and protection of human rights in the country.

India also critically examined the 'rights-based' approach in relation to human rights in general and the right to development in particular, as also shortfalls in the international community's response to the challenge to human rights posed by terrorism, extreme ideologies, and market forces in an era of globalisation and the implications of recent scientific advances for the right to life, etc. India pointed to the persistent neglect of economic, social and cultural rights that had led to a human rights paradigm that was partial and where even the recent interest in economic, social and cultural rights was modeled on civil and political rights. It was stressed that the 'legitimate concern' for human rights should also be reflected in efforts to eradicate poverty from a human rights perspective and in a sprit of solidarity and brotherhood.

The 54th session of the Commission on Human Rights was held in Geneva from March 16 to April 24, 1998. India participated actively in the Commission's deliberations. The resolution of tolerance and pluralism initiated by India was able to attract 58 cosponsors during the session, demonstrating the widespread support that the theme commanded among the members and observers of the Commission, and was adopted by consensus. The resolution on the Right to Development, where again India played an important part, was presented by the group of Non-Aligned countries in the Commission and was adopted without a vote in the Commission, though similar consensus did not prevail at the time of adoption of a resolution on the Right to Development in the 53rd session of the General Assembly. Following adoption of the resolution, the Chairman of the Commission has appointed Dr Arjun Sengupta, well-known Indian economist as the independent expert of the Commission on the Right to Development.

The election of Shri Soli Sorabjee during the 54th session of the Commission on Human Rights to the Special Commission on Prevention of Discrimination and Protection of Minorities was followed by the election in September of Justice P N Bhagwati, Human Rights Committee of the International Covenant on Civil and Political Rights. With these, eminent Indian continued to serve with distinction as members of important human rights bodies, including Smt Shanti Sadiq Ali as member of the Committee on Elimination of Racial Discrimination; Shri Abid Hussain as Special Rapporteur on the Freedom of Expression; Shri Kapil Sibal on the Working Group of Arbitrary Detention and Shri Soli Sorabjee as Special Rapporteur on Nigeria.

India hosted the Seventh Asia Pacific Workshop on Regional Cooperation for the Promotion and Protection of Human Rights from February 16-18, 1999 in New Delhi. The UN High Commissioner for Human Rights and former President of Ireland, Mrs Mary Robinson visited New Delhi and addressed the opening session of the workshop jointly with the Minister of External Affairs. The Workshop adopted a set of agreed conclusions and decided to enhance capacity-building by focusing on four areas of national plans of action, human rights education, national institutions and strategies for the realisation of the right to development and economic and social and cultural rights, agreed at the 1998 Tehran Workshop. Mrs. Robinson met with several Indian leaders and non-governmental. organisations active in the field of human rights, during her visit.

India maintained its position in support of the advancement, empowerment and human rights of women in the Commission on the Status of Women as well as the General Assembly, highlighting the initiatives taken by the Government in implementing the Beijing Platform of Action, particularly with regard to the girl child, mainstreaming the gender perspective in policies and programmes of the government, and increasing the participation of women in decision-making through continuing efforts to guarantee one-third of all seats in the national Parliament and state assemblies for women, by legislation. India co-sponsored a number of women-centred resolutions in the Commission on Human Rights and in the General Assembly, including a resolution first moved by the Netherlands in 1997, on 'Traditional and customary practices injurious to women's health'.

India played an active role in the 49th session of the Executive Committee of the Office of the UN High Commissioner for Refugees held in October, 1998. The importance of international solidarity and burden-sharing, the need to take into account the economic and social consequences of massive refugee flows into the developing countries and India's own policy towards refugees were highlighted during the session. India called for effective and durable solutions to refugee crises and stressed the need for involving developing countries in evolving such solutions as refugee problems affect the developing countries most. It also highlighted the imperative of international cooperation for dealing with refugee problems.

The 36th session of the Commission on Social Development was held in New York from February 10 to 20, 1998. India was represented by Member Secretary, Planning Commission. The priority theme of the session was "Promoting Social Integration and Participation of all People, including disadvantaged and vulnerable groups and persons". India participated actively in the deliberation as the theme was of special interest to India, and assisted in the negotiation of agreed conclusions adopted at the end of the session.

India actively participated in the first Humanitarian Affairs Segment of ECOSOC held in July 1998. The agreed conclusions adopted at the end of the Segment fully reflect our concerns, namely that assistance must be undertaken at the request of recipient countries, who should also play a major role in planning the delivery of humanitarian assistance; that scarce resources for development should not be diverted to humanitarian assistance and additional resources must be made available; the need to increase the procurement from the developing countries, which are often situated closer to the site of a disaster and can provide cost-effective solutions; and recognizes the importance of effectively addressing the humanitarian emergencies related to natural disasters. India also played a major role in the drafting of resolutions relating to humanitarian assistance during the General Assembly. The small drafting group which excluded India and which used to negotiate the resolution on Afghanistan, including Special Assistance to War Stricken Afghanistan, was disbanded this year.

Environment and sustainable development issues

The Sixth Session of the United Nations Commission on Sustainable Development was held in New York from April 20ûMay 1, 1998. The Indian delegation was led by Shri Suresh P Prabhu, Minister for Environment and Forests. The Indian delegation emphasised the importance of transfer of environmentally sound technologies on concessional and preferential terms as well as the provision of predictable and adequate financial resources in achieving the objectives of economic growth and sustainable development.

The Fourth Conference of Parties to the United Nations Framework Convention on Climate Change (UNFCCC) was held in Buenos Aires from November 2-13,1998. The Indian delegation was led by Minister of Environment and Forests, Shri Suresh P Prabhu. There was renewed pressure for developing countries to accept voluntary commitments on Green House Gas emissions but this was successfully resisted. India, as Coordinator on the Kyoto Protocol Mechanisms on behalf of the Group of 77 and China, played an active role in ensuring that the concerns of developing countries were adequately addressed. A Work Programme on

Mechanisms leading up to the sixth session of the Conference of Parties has been agreed upon.

The Second Conference of Parties to the UN Convention to Combat Desertification was held in Dakar, Senegal from November 30 to December 11, 1998. The Indian delegation emphasised the need for the full operationalisation of the Global Mechanism which is scheduled to be reviewed, as provided in the Convention, at the Third Conference of Parties. India's nominee has been included in the ad hoc panel on traditional knowledge set up by the Committee on Science and Technology.

UNEP and HABITAT

Dr Klaus Toepfer was appointed the Executive Director of the United Nations Environment Programme also made the Director General of the United Nations Offices in Nairobi. Dr Toepfer was given the concurrent charge of Head of Habitat. The thrust during the year was on the reform and revitalisation of UNEP. The UN Secretary General appointed a Task Force, headed by Dr Toepfer, to study the environment and human settlements issues throughout the UN system. The Task Force also had representation from India and the other developing countries. Its report is under discussion in the UNGA. India continued to play an active role in this process.

A Revitalisation Team, based on donor support, was set up and submitted three reports containing recommendations to revitalise Habitat. India played an active role in modifying and refining the Team's recommendations.

Development issues

On 17 & 18 September, 1998, the UN renewed the long stalemated North-South dialogue through a 2-day dialogue session with no negotiated outcome. The effort was to rebuild confidence and to renew the dialogue, so that more substantive concerns on globalisation and other macro-economic issues could be taken up in the continuous and systematic manner through this process. This year, the dialogue focussed on the economic and social aspects of globalisation. The Indian delegation was led by Dr Montek Singh Ahluwalia, member of the Planning Commission.

In December 1997 during its 52nd session, the UN General Assembly had adopted a resolution calling for the convening of an appropriate high level inter-governmental forum on financing for development to further the global partnership for development. This is the first time after the collapse of the North-South dialogue in the early 1980s that these important inter-related issues, which go to the heart of international cooperation for development, are to be discussed seriously in the UN, with the participation of OECD countries and the Bretton Woods institutions. This is something India has always advocated. The General Assembly at its 53rd Session set up, by means of the decision, an open-ended Ad Hoc Working Group in order to consider and make recommendations on a number of procedural questions as well as the scope and agenda of the meeting. These recommendations are to be submitted to the 54th Session of the General Assembly. India's Permanent Representative in New York was nominated by the President of the General Assembly to co-Chair the Open-Ended Ad Hoc Working Group on Finance for Development.

India also played a prominent part in the 1998 session of the NGO Committee which met formally over three weeks in May, June and December, 1998. Constructive interaction was maintained with the academic and NGO community associated with the

United Nations in New York on matters such as human rights, disarmament, greater NGO involvement in the work of the United Nations, including in areas in which they have not been so active hitherto such as disarmament.

Drug control, crime prevention and criminal justice

The 20th Special Session of the General Assembly on "Countering the World Drug Problem Together" was held in New York from 8-10 June, 1998. India's delegation was led by the Deputy Chairman, Planning Commission, Shri Jaswant Singh and included Smt. Maneka Gandhi, Minister of State for Social Justice and Empowerment. The Political Declaration issued at the end of the Session reflects the strong commitment of the governments of the world to address the drug problem. India's concerns are reflected in the Declaration, specially with regard to the nexus between trafficking in narcotics and global terrorist activities. Developed countries, which had earlier been opposing measures on demand in reduction to address the problem, agreed to a declaration on guiding principles of drug demand reduction. The Special Session also considered money-laundering related to drug-trafficking and proposed in its declaration a set of principles to assist Member States evolve legislations in this regard and an initiative for imposing limitations on bank secrecy for investigation into all transnational crimes including narcotic offences. India was Vice-Chairman and Rapporteur of the Preparatory Committee for the Session and had played an important role in this capacity in the drafting and negotiations of the documents adopted by the Session.

The 7th session of UN Commission on Crime Prevention and Criminal justice was held in Vienna between April 21-30, 1998. For the first time, India attended the session as a regular member of the

Commission and was elected as Vice-Chairman of the Commission. The Indian delegation successfully introduced a resolution on "Regulation of explosives for the purpose of crime prevention, public health and safety". The Commission has established an inter-governmental group of experts for elaborating a preliminary draft of a comprehensive international Convention against organized transitional crime, with specific proposals dealing with specific offences. India has been participating actively in this exercise.

Economic and social commission for Asia and the Pacific

The Annual Commission Sessions are the highest policy making forum of ESCAP. India's delegation to the Ministerial segment of the 54th Session in April 1998 was led by the Commerce Minister, Shri Rama Krishna Hegde, and to the Senior officials segment was led by Shri P P Prabhu, Commerce Secretary. This year's Session, mainly focussed on social development issues, with the theme topic being "Asia and Pacific into the 21st Century: Prospects for Social Development". Other important issues which occupied the attention of the Commission were the financial crisis currently being faced by some countries of the region and the ongoing process of ESCAP Reforms.

Administrative, budgetary and financial issues

Discussions relating to the financial situation of the United Nations were accorded high priority in the Fifth Committee of the UN General Assembly following statements made by the Secretary General that the organization is facing an unprecedented crisis with practically no usable reserves and overwhelming debts to member states. Unfortunately, the Open ended High Level Working Group on the financial situation achieved no result even after prolonged negotiations and, consequently, the Secretary General continued to resort to borrowing from the peace-keeping accounts to finance routine and regular operations of the UN. With further anticipated decrease of peace-keeping budget, the Secretary General will find it increasingly difficult to take recourse to this action in the coming years. In all the debates on this issue, India called upon Member States in arrears to pay their contributions in full, on time and without condition and emphasized the need to work on arrangements that will lead to the clearing of financial backlog thereby ensuring smooth flow of funds in the future.

The question of financing UN peace-keeping operations has been engaging the continuous attention of the world community. As a major troop contributing country, India is vitally interested in this matter. While India is receiving current payments for participation in peace-keeping operations, there has been a considerable delay in reimbursement of past dues particularly reimbursement relating to contingent owned equipment provided by us. India has intensified its efforts with the UN Secretariat to reach settlement of its claims. Following part payment of arrears by the Russian Federation and a few other countries, the UN paid India $ 7,861,391.60 during 1998.

The UN owes India approximately $ 45 million. The rate of reimbursement remains extremely slow and the hope of receiving payment is nearly non-existent unless the United States which owes the UN more than $ 1.3 billion pays its arrears both for the regular and peace-keeping budgets.

On the substantive issues on which the Fifth Committee focussed its attention include Secretary General's reform proposals. In the context of the budget consideration for 1998-99, India's stand has been generally positive towards various proposals to introduce reform in the current procurement and asset management policy and procedures and on strengthening the internal and external oversight mechanism. On administrative aspects and proposed structural adjustments, the Fifth Committee debated issues relating to redirecting non-programme cost to a development account, revolving credit funds and result based budgeting. However, decisions relating to important issues such as development account, utilisation of development dividend, net (result-based) budgeting and revolving credit fund were deferred for consideration at the first resumed session of the Fifth Committee.

India was re-elected to the Advisory Committee on Administrative and Budgetary Questions (ACABQ) for the term January 1, 1999 to December 31, 2001. The other two elected members from the Asian Group are Japan and Pakistan. China, which has been a member since early eighties lost ACABQ election.

In the election to the UN Board of Auditors, India, Philippines and Pakistan contested for one vacancy in the Asian Group. Philippines was declared elected for a period of three years from July 1, 1999 to June 30, 2002. India (seeking re-election for the third term) and Pakistan lost the election.

Operational activities of the UN system/funds and programmes

India continued to play a significant and constructive role in the work of the UN Funds and Programmes. India was elected in January 1998 as the Vice President of the Executive Boards of the UNDP and UNFPA. In this capacity, it furthered the agenda of the Asian Group and safeguarded its positions in the negotiations on Narrowing of the Focus on UNDP, funding strategies of UNDP and UNFPA and in the Successor Programming

Arrangements. India maintained its contribution in Dollar terms to the core resources of UNDP, which was publicly appreciated by the Administrator of UNDP on several occasions. UNDP also honoured Ms Fatima Bee with the UN Poverty Eradication Award for her work in the context of the South Asia Poverty Alleviation Project. An additional amount of US $ 950,000 was made available for this project in India from within the funds made available by Ted Turner (UN Fund for International Partnership).

Executive Director of UNFPA Dr Nafis Sadik visited India from 19-26 July, 1998 on an official visit, becoming the first high-ranking UN official to visit India after the nuclear tests conducted in May 1998. She also paid a transit visit in December 1998.

During the year, new representatives were appointed by all New York based UN Funds and Programmes, viz., UNDP, UNFPA and UNICEF, in India.

UNICEF Executive Board, in its September meeting, approved the Indian regular programme for 1999-2002 for US $ 300.02 million. This was the first assistance programme for India to be approved by the UN after the nuclear tests of May 1998.

India also played a major role in the negotiations on the resolution pertaining to the Triennial Policy Review of Operational Activities of the UN system.

Specialised agencies

ILO

During the International Labour Conference in June 1998, a Declaration on Fundamental Principles and Rights at Work was adopted by the ILO. The Indian delegation contributed extensively to the drafting of the Declaration, ensuring thereby its promotional character and incorporating safeguards precluding its misuse for trade and protectionist purposes. Along with other developing countries, India underlined the importance of a purely promotional Follow-up to the Declaration, with technical assistance as a cornerstone.

During the year, India also participated actively in the work of the Asia-Pacific Group of the ILO related to re-defining the role of the Organization in the new millennium. We were instrumental in ensuring that positions of the Asia-Pacific Group reflected the priorities of developing countries and a new development-oriented paradigm stressing the role of the ILO in employment generation and national capacity building in order to promote social justice and higher standards of living, including through technical cooperation. We also supported the strengthening of the ILO's capacity for independent analysis of labour trends.

UNIDO

UNIDO which had gone through a near-fatal crisis in 1997 with major donors withdrawing and severe budget cuts showed promising signs of recovery in 1998. The Business Plan approved by the General Conference in December 1997 was put into implementation. Severe budget controls and staff reductions as agreed were implemented. The new Director General Carlos Magarinos initiated a process of reform and streamlining.

WIPO

India joined the Paris Convention and the Patent Cooperation Treaty of WIPO with effect from December 7,1998. This will enable India to play a more significant role in international developments relating to intellectual property. It will also encourage scientific research, inventive and innovative activity in the country and provide better and more extensive protection for Indian inventors abroad.

UNESCO

Close inter-action between India and UNESCO in the fields of education, culture, science and communication has been mutually beneficial and enriching. India actively participated in the two international Conferences organized by the UNESCO during 1998 - the Inter-Governmental Conference on Cultural Policies for Development held in Stockholm and the World Conference on Higher Education held in Paris. Director General of UNESCO during his visit to India in January 1998 agreed to set-up four more UNESCO chairs in Indian Universities.

Elections and appointments

During the year, India was elected or nominated to the following bodies:

1. Shri Prakash Shah, former Permanent Representative of India to United Nations in New York, was appointed by the UN Secretary General as his Special Representative for Iraq on March 3, 1998;
2. Shri Soli Jehangir Sorabjee was elected to the Sub-Commission on the Prevention & Discrimination And Protection of Minorities of the Commission on Human Rights for the period 1999-2002;
3. Council of International Civil Aviation Organisation (ICAO), for the period 1999-2001;
4. Council of International Telecommunication Union (ITU) for the period 1999-2003;
5. Shri Rajat Saha was elected to the Advisory Committee on Administrative & Budgetary Questions (ACABQ) for the period 1999-2001;
6. Justice P N Bhagwati was elected to the UN

Human Rights Committee for the period 1999-2002;

7. Shri A Narayan was elected the Executive Director of Asia Pacific Telecommunity (APT) for the period February 1999 - February 2002;
8. Shri Narendra Sharma was elected the Chairman of APT Management Committee for the period February 1999 -February 2002;
9. UNDP Executive Board for the period 1999-2001;
10. Committee on NGOs, ECOSOC for the period 1999-2002;
11. Commission on Science & Technology for Development, ECOSOC, for the period May 1998 - December 2001;
12. Shri Biswnath B Sen was elected to the Governing Council of UNIDROIT for the period 1999-2003.

Non-aligned movement

The 23rd meeting of the NAM Health Ministers took place in Havana (Cuba) from 25-26 June, 1998. The Indian delegation was led by the Minister of State for Health and Family Welfare, Shri Dalit Ezhilmalai. India was elected as one of the Vice-Chairmen of the Bureau of the Conference. The Final Documents adopted reflect India's views, including those on the primacy of the State in the health sector; the necessity of an integrated approach including eradication of poverty, provision of food, housing; need for additional resources for the health sector and correction of global imbalances in health sector expenditures; and the need to promote South-South cooperation.

The Meeting of the Coordinating Bureau of the

NAM at the Ministerial level held in Cartagena (Colombia) from May 18-20, 1998 was in preparation for the XIIth NAM Summit scheduled at Durban in September 1998. The Minister of State, Smt Vasundhara Raje led the Indian delegation to the Conference. She met a significant number of her counterparts and briefed them on the policies of the Government, India's foreign policy priorities and the context in which India undertook the nuclear tests in May 1998. Although the Cartagena meeting took place in the immediate aftermath of the nuclear tests, there were no critical references to the tests in the Final Document of the Conference. India successfully contributed in reiterating traditional NAM positions on nuclear disarmament, including the call for the elimination of nuclear weapons within a specified time frame. India made a proposal for the Durban Summit to call for a special session of the UN General Assembly on Africa.

The XIIth Summit of the Movement of Non-Aligned countries (NAM) was held in Durban, South Africa on September 2-3,1998. The Indian delegation for the Summit was led by Prime Minister Shri Atal Behari Vajpayee.

In his address to the Summit on September 3, 1998, the Prime Minister underlined that disarmament continued to be a cornerstone of India's foreign policy and that India had undertaken several initiatives to establish a nuclear-weapon-free and nonviolent world order. Explaining India's nuclear tests in the context of a unique geo-political environment where India's security was threatened by overt and covert nuclearisation of its neighbourhood, he urged the established nuclear states to join NAM in negotiating a Nuclear Weapons Convention. Dismissing apprehensions over heightened tensions in South Asia, Shri Vajpayee reiterated that differences would be resolved peacefully through bilateral negotiations and that there was no place for any third party involvement in the process, howsoever well-intentioned. He categorically stated that J&K was an integral part of India and that the real problem in the region was that of cross-border terrorism. He called for concerted international efforts in the form of an international conference to discuss and agree on measures to combat and defeat the menace of terrorism through collective action. The Prime Minister called for expansion and reform of UNSC on the basis of global and non-discriminatory criteria and urged NAM to develop strength to translate its numbers into an effective voice in international affairs. He also called for revitalisation of the agenda for management of the international economy.

The Summit adopted the Final Document containing formal positions taken by NAM on global issues, analysis of the international situation, economic and social issues. The Durban Declaration reiterates the continued relevance and importance of NAM in the post-Cold War world and focuses on the concerns of the developing world in a more consolidated manner. Of considerable significance were references to disarmament, terrorism, UN reforms and UNSC restructuring and expansion. Agreed positions adopted by NAM enjoyed broad-based support. Indian position was reflected in positions adopted on issues of interest to us.

The 23rd meeting of the NAM Health Ministers took place in Havana (Cuba) from 25-26 June, 1998. The Indian delegation was led by the Minister of State for Health and Family Welfare, Shri Dalit Ezhilmalai. India was elected as one of the Vice-Chairmen of the Bureau of the Conference. The Final Documents adopted reflect

India's views, including those on the primacy of the State in the health sector; the necessity of an integrated approach including eradication of poverty, provision of food, housing; need for additional resources for the health sector and correction of global imbalances in health sector expenditures; and the need to promote South-South cooperation.

Commonwealth

India, the largest member of the Commonwealth, is represented in all its important controlling bodies of the Secretariat and organisations. It is the fourth largest contributor, a major source of expert assistance provided to other Commonwealth countries and a major destination for Commonwealth trainees. India's High Commissioner to UK, led the Indian delegation which participated in the Commonwealth Senior Officials Meeting [CSOM] in London, during 9-11, November, 1998. CSOM reviewed the developments and progress in implementation of decisions of the 1997 Commonwealth Heads of Government Meeting.

International law: development and activities

The work of the International Law Commission which was reviewed at the 52nd Session of the UNGA resulted in the Commission adopting in its first reading a set of draft articles on the Principle of Prevention of Trans-boundary Harm arising from hazardous activities. This is regarded as a marked achievement of the Commission on the topic of international liability which has been under consideration of the Commission for the last 20 years. Dr P S Rao, JS (L&T) was the Special Rapporteur on this topic the principle of prevention provides for the obligation of due diligence on the part of States and private entities responsible of such hazardous activities to minimise the risk and wherever possible prevent the risk of trans-boundary harm. The obligation involved is one of conduct. This could be achieved by organising suitable legislative, executive and judicial mechanisms and establishing appropriate monitoring systems. It also involves the requirement of prior authorization from the State for conducting such activities within its territory. Prior authorisation in turn would require the submission of an environmental impact assessment as well as other measures taken or proposed to be taken by the operator by way of precaution and other contingency planning to achieve the desired objectives of running a safe operation.

The regime of prevention proposed by the commission also involves a duty of notification to other concerned States followed by duty to consult and negotiate in case where an activity is likely to cause significant trans-boundary harm. Further, it also provides for some newer concepts like public participation in the assessment of the impact or the significant harm. The need is to balance various competing but sometimes conflicting interests viz. The necessity for providing information and notification not only to Government but to the public in general, treating of affected persons or persons likely to be affected on an equal footing in terms of remedies available whether they are nationals or foreigners. A system of settlement of disputes involving institution of fact finding as the only compulsory element was also proposed.

The regime of prevention thus drawn by the Commission was seen as a further continuation of the interlocked concepts. The first came into play in the context of the regime incorporated in the UN Convention on Non-Navigational Uses of International Watercourses (1997).

The debate in the UNGA on the regime of prevention applauded the work of which was done by the special Rapporteur and the Commission in this regard with speed and without compromising on the scholarship. Questions however, have been raised on the nature of the implementation mechanism for the duty of prevention, the linkage of duty of prevention to the duty of compensation in case of actual damage i.e. liability and on the possible form the recommendation of the ILC in this regard could take. Further work in this area is expected next year by the Commission.

The work of the Commission also indicated progress made on the topic of State Responsibility and reservation to Law of the Treaties. The Commission is also now working on 3 other topics namely, the law of diplomatic protection, the effect of unilateral acts and statements of States on the development of international law. On these aspects the Commission recorded the preliminary progress.

The Fifty Third session of the United Nations General Assembly at its Sixth Committee (Legal) considered the following agenda items: Status of the Protocols Additional to the Geneva Conventions of 1949 and relating to the protection of armed conflicts; Consideration of effective measures to enhance the protection, security and safety of diplomatic missions and representatives; Convention on jurisdictional immunities of States and their property; Draft guiding principles for international negotiations; Report of the International Law Commission on the work of its fiftieth session; Report of the United Nations Commission on international trade law; report of the Committee on relations with the Host Country; Establishment of international criminal court; Report of the Special Committee on the Charter of the United Nations and on the strengthening of the role of the Organization; and Measures to eliminate international terrorism.

Important highlights of the work of the Sixth Committee during the 53rd Session of UNGA include as follows:

i) Adoption of resolution requesting the Special Committee on the UN Charter, to continue at its session in 1999, consideration of all proposals concerning the question of the maintenance of international peace and security, sanctions, assistance to third States affected by the application of sanctions, peace keeping missions, peaceful settlement of disputes between States, Trusteeship Council, International Court of Justice, and identification of new subjects for discussion, with a View to revitalize the work of United Nations.

ii) Noted with appreciation the activities undertaken by the International Committee of the Red Cross in the field of international humanitarian law, including with regard to the protection of the environment in times of armed conflict. Took note of the events that will take place during the year 1999 to commemorate the centennial of the first International peace conference and the closing of the United Nations Decade of International Law.

iii) Decided to establish an open ended working group at its fifty fourth session to consider outstanding substantive issues related to the draft articles on jurisdictional immunities of states and their property adopted by the International Law Commission.

The General Assembly session also witnessed intense work on account of a draft convention to be concluded by the UN dealing with nuclear terrorism based on a

Russian proposal. While the draft convention was generally acceptable to most delegations, the question as to the status of use of nuclear weapons by personnel of a State met with opposing views. Mexico, Egypt and South Africa were in favour of dealing with this aspect and prohibiting the same within the scope of the convention. The Western and East European countries and USA are opposed to dealing with the matter. Further work is also required on some other points which delayed the finalising of the convention at this session. Accordingly, further work would be taken up next year.

After work is completed on the subject of nuclear terrorism the UN is also likely to deal with a French proposal elaborating a convention prohibiting financing of terrorists activities. Thereafter, the General Assembly is expected to give priority to the conclusion of a comprehensive convention on suppression of terrorism on the basis of a proposal made by India.

The 31st annual session of the United Nations Commission on International Trade Law (UNCITRAL) was held at New York, from 1-12 June, 1998. The Commission had Privately-Financed Infrastructure Projects. The Government of India nominated Shri R L Meena, Law Secretary to assist the Secretariat in preparation of future chapters of the legislative guide on Private-Finance Infrastructure Projects. The Expert Group for this purpose met at Vienna from 6-8 October, 1998.

The Commission also discussed the report of the Working Group on Electronic Commerce of its 32nd Session, Practices with the task of preparing a uniform law on Assignment in Receivable Financing.

During the current session, on 10 June, 1998, the Commission held the special commemorative "New York Convention Day" in order to celebrate the 40th anniversary of the Convention on the Recognition and Enforcement of Foreign Arbitral Awards (New York 10 June, 1998).

On 11 June, 1998 the Commission held the Uniform Commercial Law Information colloquium in which the representatives of state members of the Commission and observers and some 250 invited persons participated in the colloquium leading experts presented their insights and assessment on the legal issues relating to Electronic Commerce, Privately-Financed Infrastructure Projects, Receivable Financing and Cross-Border Insolvency.

India hosted the 37th Annual session of the Asian African Legal Consultative Committee (AALCC) at New Delhi from 13-18 April, 1998. It was attended by the Ministers and the legal advisers of 44 Governments of Asia and Africa. This meeting discussed recent developments in the field of international law with a view to evolve a common Asian-African approach. The AALCC is an inter-governmental organisation having a special Observer status with the United Nations.

The meeting was inaugurated by the Hon'ble Minister for Law, justice and Company Affairs, Shri Tambi Dorai on 13 April, 1998 at Vigyan Bhawan.

The discussion focused on the 'extra-territorial application of national legislation', the complex legal issues on various subjects including: Law of the Sea; Refugees; Trade law; Environment; Mutual Cooperation in Judicial Assistance; and Criminal Court.

India has allotted to the AALCC, a plot measuring 0.60 acres at Chanakyapuri Diplomatic Enclave for its permanent Headquarters and a financial grant of $ 1.5 million towards its construction and the construction of its Secretary-General's residence. Proposal to conclude Headquarters Agreement between India and AALCC governing the privileges and immunities has been forwarded to the Cabinet Secretariat to solicit the Cabinet approval. A formal foundation stone laying ceremony took place on 13 April at 5 p.m. by the Hon'ble Minister of State for External Affairs, Smt Vasundhara Raje.

The Division participated in the Preparatory Committee (PREPCOM) negotiations held at New York on the Establishment of International Criminal Court (ICC). The Division also participated in the UN Plenipotentiary Diplomatic Conference on the Establishment of ICC held at Rome from 15 June to 17 July, 1998. At the Diplomatic Conference India made a proposal for the inclusion of terrorism within the jurisdiction of the ICC. India also proposed the inclusion of the use of nuclear weapons and the weapons of mass destruction in the category of war crimes.

The Legal & Treaties Division participated in negotiations, held at Paris, France from 1-3 April, 1998, and at Sofia, Bulgaria from 12-14 October, 1998 for concluding extradition treaties, respectively with France and Bulgaria.

The Division also participated in negotiations with Norway, held at Delhi from 28-29 May, 1998', for the conclusion of agreements on mutual legal assistance in criminal matters and in civil matters. Draft texts of agreements were adopted in principle and initialled, are pending formal signing.

This Division examined various extradition requests and as well as foreign jurisdictions and rendered legal advice there to requests for mutual judicial assistance, received both from domes c in. Various requests prepared by CBI aimed to seek assistance from foreign countries in ongoing criminal investigations including those with which there exists no formal agreement in this area, were also examined by this Division. Legal advice was rendered in all extradition court cases pending in Indian and foreign courts.

Draft extradition treaties and mutual judicial assistance agreements were prepared for proposing them to foreign countries for their consideration for concluding treaties /agreements on the subject matters. Also examined draft treaties/agreements on these subjects proposed by foreign countries for the consideration of Indian authorities.

This Division also participated in an interministrial meeting convened by the Ministry of Defence at New Delhi on 17 June, 1998 for discussion on a proposal regarding the constitution of Maritime Tribunals.

At the Initiative of the Austrian Government, 'European Convention on the transfer of sentenced persons' was examined in this Division, with a view for India's becoming a party to the Convention. On examination, the matter found several merits. Nevertheless, further process of the proposal would have to await the enactment of suitable domestic enabling legislation.

The Division participated in the Meeting of Senior Officials of Law Ministries held at London from 26-29 May, 1998. Various subjects were discussed in the meeting like computer and computer related crime; 50 years of Universal Declaration of Human Rights; Promoting and Implementing Human Rights; Advancing the Right to Information; criminal justice in the elimination of violence against women and mutual judicial assistance. A joint Meeting of Commonwealth Finance and Law Officials on Money Laundering was held at London from 1-2 June, 1998, for discussions on special problems of parallel economies and coordination of efforts in combating money laundering at the national level, where in the Ministry was represented by this Division. Also the Division participated in the Expert Group Meeting to negotiate the text of the SAARC Convention on Preventing and Combating Trafficking in Women and Children for Prostitution, held at New Delhi from 18-19 June, 1998.

The Division participated in the meeting of experts convened to review the general problems concerning the Fourth Geneva Convention relative to the Protection of civilian Persons in time of War from 27-29 October, 1998 at Geneva. The Meeting discussed the ways of implementing the IV Geneva Convention during armed conflict with a special focus on occupied territories specially in the context of the changing character of international and non-international armed conflict situations.

11

Foreign Economic Relations

Economic division

In the year under review, India faced a challenging international economic scenario. Whereas the global economy had recorded a modest growth of 3% per annum during the period 1994-97, it became widely apparent in 1998 that world economy may be hurtling towards economic contraction and a phase of intense instability. The recent but persistent financial crisis, which first hit East and South East Asia in 1997 and later showed its contagion effect in Russia, Latin America and even US and Europe, had shaken the world out of complacency. Recessionary trends in Japan further compounded the depressing economic and business scenario prevailing in the world today. As the recession spread, the investors shied away from the emerging economies. Even relatively insulated economies such as India and China felt its adverse impact. These events only proved how the economies all over the globe had become inter-linked in an era of globalisation.

The direct impact of these developments on India had been somewhat limited last year. However, since the beginning of 1998, it became apparent that the crisis in these regions had been more deep-rooted than expected. Following four years of impressive performance, India's industrial and export growth started turning sluggish since 1997-98. Notwithstanding the increasing strains and dampening effect on India 's external trade sector, macro-economic fundamentals of Indian economy remained strong. Against this setting, ensuring India's economic security and maintaining the momentum gained in Indian export expansion, FDI and FII inflows, technology transfers and that the confidence in the Indian economy was not eroded, was the major challenge confronting the economic diplomacy of India.

A key role that the Economic Division has been entrusted with and which it has been playing vigorously is the promotion of India's economic and commercial interests. The Economic Division interacted intensively with various Ministries, apex chambers of commerce and industry, business organisations, trade promotion councils & agencies and the business community to evolve strategies and contribute to promotion of trade and investment. The Division was associated with a number of economic policy making bodies, both inter-ministerial and public sector undertaking and industry associations. In particular, Economic Division represented MEA on the boards of EXIM Bank, Indian Trade Promotion Organisation, Empowered Committee of Oil and Natural Gas Commission-Videsh Limited, Special Committee of the Reserve Bank of India on Indian Investments Abroad, RITES, WAPCOS, Overseas Construction Council of India, National Centre for Trade Information, etc. This enabled the Ministry to provide not only the political inputs and MEA's thinking on various subjects but also the regional and global perspectives on various policy issues which have a bearing on the economic interests of India. Having been closely associated with the policy making aspects of trade reforms and liberalisations, streamlining of procedures for promotion of Indian exports and Indian investments overseas, analytical inputs were provided to the nodal ministries.

Another key role that the Economic Division undertook was to provide a standard backstopping arrangements and a nodal point for addressing the concerns of Indian exporters and industry by providing and seeking timely inputs to and from our Missions. Keeping in view the crucial importance of information dissemination and providing value added information, the Economic Division continued to provide a backup support and information wherewithal to our Missions abroad to enable them to carry out their economic and commercial functions effectively. The Economic Division continued to update its information base on the Indian economy, evolution of trade, economic and investment policies, database of Indian exporters, opportunities for Indian exporters abroad and technology-related aspects by liaising with concerned Government departments and trade information networks in India. Thus the Division could respond effectively and in a timely manner to various economic and commercial queries from the exporters and our Missions abroad. The Indian Missions were also advised from time to time to upgrade their databases and establish connectivity to online databases, develop promotional strategies and undertake large scale information dissemination campaigns regularly so that India's economic policies and concomitant opportunities reached out to the largest cross-section of the local investors and business community. Missions were continuously. urged to improve upon their lead response time in addressing the concerns and interests of Indian business and exporting community. While impressing on the Missions to accord highest priority to economic and commercial work, greater emphasis was placed on effectively projecting India's image and building up a global India Brand Equity as a competitive economy as well as in a number of niche products, both traditional and nontraditional including financial services and

Information Technology sectors so that a major export thrust could be achieved.

Being the export-promotion cell of the Ministry, the Economic Division interacted and rendered inputs and assistance in trade promotion efforts of Government agencies and industry associations in order to evolve a pragmatic approach towards our export promotion efforts and further improvements in our trade promotion strategies. The Division assisted in the efforts of various organisations in promoting the participation of foreign business organisations in Indian trade fairs and Indian business in foreign trade fairs, sector-specific seminars, road shows, buyer-seller meets etc. The Division also provided assistance in facilitating contacts between Indian businessmen and their counterparts in major target countries and where required in match making and joint ventures, penetrating new markets, marketing and trade promotion activities etc. Economic Division was actively associated with the "Made in India" show in South Africa and FICCI/CII exhibition in Oman, which were specifically aimed at showcasing India's achievements, strengths and potential and promoting Indian brand image abroad. The Division facilitated through contact with foreign Missions in India and Indian Missions abroad and in collaboration with apex chambers the visits of business delegations to and from India. The Indian industry and business community was increasingly associated in various events of G-15, IOR-ARC, BIMST-EC so that eventually there are trade and investment spin offs for India. The Division circulated wide range of useful information from time to time to apex business chambers and our missions abroad. The Division also received a number of trade complaints both from Indian and foreign companies which were promptly attended to in consultation with our Missions and concerned agencies including DGFT.

The Economic Division was involved in processing more than 150 proposals for setting up joint ventures and wholly owned subsidiaries relating to Indian investments overseas involving over US $ 250 million. Similarly the information on foreign investment regulation from various countries were procured and analysed in order to advise other concerned ministries on the viability of incorporating relevant and competitive aspects in our own policies.

Another important work of the Economic Division was its increasing and active involvement in work relating WTO. The Division provided inputs on a large number of trade related subjects to influence and purse the issues of interest to India. The Economic Division was actively associated in providing inputs and international perspective as well as political economic assessments in deliberations of various joint business councils and joint commission/committees.

The Economic Division has been actively contributing to crisis management as well as damage containment and damage prevention on a number of market access and trade related problems and issues affecting India's exports and imports. Emerging patterns with regard to regional groupings, free trade areas, trade blocs, market access related issues and use of restrictive and protectionist policies by various countries which have an impact on the Indian exports were monitored closely and strategies devised to best cope with non-tariff and technical barriers of various kinds. For instance EU has emerged as the largest user of trade protection instruments during the last 2-3 years on imports from India. In particular Indian textiles, steel products, engineering goods and pharmaceuticals have been subjected to around 25 antidumping and anti-subsidy investigations. Some of the items like unbleached cotton fabric, bed-linen, synthetic fiber ropes had been repeatedly targeted. The defence of such actions called for elaborate steps and extensive lobbying efforts. The Economic Division actively participated in coordinating efforts of the concerned Ministries, Export Promotion Councils, Trade Associations, Indian Missions abroad to take up the issues at appropriate fora to safeguard the interests of Indian industry. As a result of this coordinated action, EU's anti-dumping case on imports of unbleached cotton fabric from India ended satisfactorily without imposition of any definitive duties. Economic Division was also actively involved in monitoring and analysing the impact of economic sanctions imposed by certain countries after the nuclear tests by India. With regard to child labour issue which is increasingly being used for protectionist purposes, the Economic Division continued in its efforts to project the problem in its right perspective and to dispel the misconceptions and skewed impressions propagated by various vested interests in our major export markets. In another case involving grant of patent by US Patent and Trade Mark Office to an American company on basmati rice, the Economic Division actively participated in an inter-organisational exercise to prevent misappropriation of indigenous biogenetic resources of India by other countries.

Apart from the economic and trade-related activities, the Economic Division also processed the Government of India's nominations for various courses and training programmes offered by Singapore under the Colombo Plan and Thailand and Indonesia under the Technical and Cooperation among Developing Countries.

Multilateral economic telations

The world found itself in a difficult and uncertain economic environment during the year. What had started off as a liquidity crisis in Thailand in mid-1997 snowballed in 1998 into a loss of investor confidence in emerging markets as a whole, and more specifically in the ASEAN countries, South Korea and in Russia. One country after another experienced a sharp downturn in its stock market and a depreciation of its currency owing to a decline of confidence in the viability of its banks and financial institutions. The vast foreign capital that had made possible the Asian miracle of the 80's and early 90's, began to drain out rapidly.

Although largely protected from similar capital outflows, the Indian economy suffered on account of declining demand for its goods and services in South-East and East Asia, Russia and in recession-struck Japan. But despite the uncertain market conditions, Indian exports sustained their growth in the US and other select developed markets, and that in the face of increasingly competition. India's resilience gives us the confidence that Indian industry will be well-positioned to take advantage of the global recovery when it begins.

Today, governments are being called upon to have a more active economic agenda. The World Development Report of 1997 says that development requires an effective State, one that plays a catalytic, facilitating role, encouraging and complementing the activities of private. Businesses and individuals. The reform agenda is hence not just one of liberalisation and a greater reliance on market forces. It is as importantly a redefinition of the government's economic role and responsibilities. Driven by globalisation, rapid diffusion of new technologies, and multilateral harmonisation of international economic activity, there are changes continuously taking place in global trade and investment, with both government and business having to respond.

The Ministry has accordingly made use of its

vantage position by its outreach with economic agencies both within and outside the country, and thus has been a conduit for the flow of information. Our work with economic ministries and state governments as well with trade and industry associations helped our embassies abroad to project the range of opportunities for foreign investors in India. We have tried to play the role of an informed and committed intermediary helping to interpret the expectations that India and the outside world have of each other.

Our effort has been to interpret change, identify opportunities and anticipate challenges for our industries and companies. Our objective has been to balance the country's self interest with obligations deriving from our participation in the larger international economic community. Our work, therefore, has been an integral part of India's collective endeavour for commercial and economic development and for a greater Indian presence in the world markets.

Multilateral economic relations division

In the light of these parameters, Multilateral Economic Relations (MER) Division has pursued promotion of India/s relations with international multilateral economic organisations and regional, sub-regional and supra-regional economic and trade groupings.

Given the emerging importance of the World Trade Organisation (WTO), the Ministry was actively involved in trade policy-making in GOI and in negotiations on various trade issues. WTO issues are an integral and intrinsic part Of international relations and impact on our overall economic and political relations with other WTO member countries. Accordingly, important multilateral developments which have a bearing on global trade and commerce, are regularly analysed and monitored. Inputs on various trade policy issues like

Investment, Competition Policy, Government Procurement, Intellectual Property Rights, etc. are duly conveyed to concerned GOI Ministries from time to time. Besides theoretical analysis, MEA was also represented at important events like the Second WTO Ministerial Conference at Geneva to ensure that it keeps abreast of the nuances involved in the WTO multilateral negotiations.

India's Dialogue Partnership with ASEAN saw many positive developments this year. The Second Meeting of the ASEAN-India Joint Cooperation Committee (AIJCC) was held at Singapore on April 28-29, 1998. India reaffirmed its solidarity with ASEAN in the wake of the financial crisis plaguing the region. Measures outlined by India in this context included Government-to-Government Credit, EXIM Bank credit for trade finance, facilities for counter trade, EXIM Bank credit finance for outward and inward investment to and from South-East Asia, feasibility study and consultancy financing by EXIM Bank for infrastructure projects, guarantees and counter guarantees for trade finance, and enhancement of Indian Technical and Economic Cooperation Programmes for ASEAN countries.

As part of the on-going India-ASEAN Cooperation in academic and People-to-People Contacts, the India-ASEAN Lecture Series was initiated in December 1996. As many as five lectures by eminent persons from ASEAN countries were organised between May and August 1998. These included Dr Thaksin Shinawatra, former Deputy Prime Minister of Thailand, Mr Kavi Chongkittavorn, Executive Editor of "The Nation" (Bangkok), Dr J Soedradjad Djiwandono, former Governor of Central Bank of Indonesia, and Prof Tommy Koh, Ambassador-at-Large, Ministry of Foreign Affairs of Singapore. From the Indian side, eminent Space scientist

Prof U R Rao delivered lectures in Malaysia and Dr R A Mashelkar, Director General of CSIR in Thailand.

A large contingent of scientists was deputed to participate in the Fifth ASEAN Science and Technology Week (FASTW) and Exhibition held at Hanoi, Vietnam from October 12-15,1998. Besides taking part in the deliberations, the scientists made focussed presentations on the scientific and technological strides made by India. India also put up a stall at the Exhibition where its strengths in Information Technology, Remote Sensing, Advanced Materials, Biotechnology and India's vision 2020 were highlighted.

An India-ASEAN Small and Medium Enterprises (SMEs) Partenariat was organised by FICCI from November 10-11, 1998. The Partenariat was designed to facilitate business linkages amongst Indian and ASEAN SMEs by providing them an opportunity to interact closely and to apprise themselves of mutual strengths and complementarities. In all, 27 SME companies from ASEAN and nearly 200 representatives from Indian companies, participated in this event.

The nascent regional grouping called Bangladesh-IndiaûMyanmar-Sri Lanka-Thailand Economic Cooperation (BIMST-EC), launched in June, 1997, registered commendable progress. India participated in the BIMST-EC Working Group meetings, to give shape to emerging initiatives for cooperation. The BIMST-EC Economic Ministers' Retreat held on 7 August 1998 at Bangkok. decided that lead countries would coordinate cooperation in the six priority sectors, viz., Trade and Investment (Bangladesh), Technology (India), Transport and Communications (Thailand), Energy (Myanmar), Tourism (Sri Lanka), and Fisheries (Sri Lanka).

With the Ministry's support and in collaboration with the Ministry of Tourism, the Confederation of

Indian Industry organised a BIMST-EC Tourism Summit at Calcutta from October 30-31, 1998 which was attended by the Tourism Ministers, senior Tourism Officials and travel trade representatives from BIMSTûEC countries. It adopted an Action Plan identifying short, medium and long term measures and policies covering areas such as infrastructure corridors, facilitation and promotion measures, declaration of the Year 2001 as 'Visit BIMST-EC Year', Buddhist Circuit and technical training.

India also participated in the Second BIMST-EC Ministerial Meeting held at Dhaka from December 17-19, 1998. The meeting emphasised the need to take practical initiatives to implement projects in agreed sectors of cooperation. It recommended establishment of multimodal transport linkages, regional cooperation in the energy sector, promotion of tourism and active participation by the private sector for intensifying existing linkages between members. The meeting approved admission of Nepal as an Observer besides evolving general guidelines for admission of new observers and guests. It also outlined future priorities including South-South cooperation, trade facilitation and development of a free trade arrangement enhancing regional complementarities and taking initiatives for making the international economic and trading system more favourable for developing countries.

As in the past, India adopted an active profile in the context of 'Group of 15' (G-15) activities during the year. It participated in the Eighth G-15 Summit held at Cairo from May 11-13,1998. The high-level Indian delegation to the Summit was led by the Hon'ble Vice-President. The Summit focussed on two major themes, viz., developments in international financial markets; and developments in the Multilateral Trading System and enhancement of intra-G-15 Cooperation in trade and investment. The Summit examined different perspectives and called for comprehensive and urgent action on preventing the spread of the financial turmoil in East and South East Asia. On the issue of the multilateral trading system, the Summit focussed on evolving common (developing) country positions on various matters to be taken up at the Second WTO Ministerial Conference at Geneva in May 1998 ' as well as on facilitating a positive agenda for developing countries.

Apart from providing an Indian perspective to the two main themes of the Summit, the Indian delegation also played a major role in focussing Summit discussions on issues like terrorism and bio-diversity. On WTO issues, India emphasized that the pursuit of liberalisation which has become WTO's raison d'etre, was not an end in itself and should meet the core objectives of rapid development, welfare gains and best returns for the extant and potential resources of developing countries. Towards this end, India submitted proposals outlining developing countries' concerns and possible ways of ensuring special and differential treatment to developing countries in all aspects of the WTO agenda and its implementation.

An MOU on Small Scale Industries Cooperation was concluded between India and Egypt under the framework of the SSI Cooperation Project. The business cooperation pursued in parallel with the Summit included the setting up of a G-15 Federation of Chambers of Commerce and Industry. A composite Indian business delegation from the apex Chambers participated in the business workshop. India also exhibited a cross-section of its products under the theme "Modem India" at the C-15 Business Exhibition.

In pursuance of its commitment at the Cairo Summit, India hosted a G-15 Symposium on 'Special and

Differential Provisions for Developing and Least Developed Countries in the Uruguay Round Agreements' in New Delhi from November 10-11, 1998. The Symposium reiterated that the commitments made in the Uruguay Round Agreements must be fulfilled. The deliberations revealed that there was a common approach with regard to strengthening of certain concessions inherent in the WTO Agreement in the areas of longer transition periods, larger threshold limits, reorientation of 'best endeavour' clauses, linking of S&D treatment to development parameters, improvement of market access for developing countries through S&D provisions, transfer of technology, technical assistance and cooperation.

India also participated in the Ninth G-15 Summit held at Montego Bay, Jamaica from 10-12 February 1999. Hon'ble Prime Minister led the Indian delegation to the Summit. The G-15 Summit Meetings deliberated extensively on issues of concern to developing countries. These included discussions on the current international economic situation including the need for an international consultative process in respect of capital flows, reaffirmation of the importance of a transparent, fair and equitable rules-based multilateral trading system under the World Trade Organisation, reform of the international financial architecture, South-South and intra G-15 cooperation and prospects of undertaking a G-15 - G-8 dialogue in these matters. All such priorities were duly reflected in the Joint Communiqu_ issued at the end of the Ninth Summit. In order to be able to cope with challenges posed by globalisation and economic liberalisation and the ongoing financial crisis, members agreed to promote convergence of viewpoints on these issues. They also called for enhanced regional and international cooperation to combat the menace of terrorism.

India's offer to host a C-15 meeting at an appropriate level in preparation for the Third WTO International Conference was welcomed by the participants at the Ninth G-15 Summit. They also endorsed India's proposal which suggested adoption of a strategic sectors approach towards South-South cooperation focussing on core areas like bio-technology, information technology and infrastructure development.

India also took active interest in the programmes of the Indian Ocean Rim Association for Regional Cooperation (IOR-ARC). It participated in a major Indian Ocean Rim Trade Exhibition organised in Oman (Muscat) from October 10-14,1998. India also participated in the First Meeting of Experts on Standards & Accreditation from November 9-11,1998 in Colombo. A high-level delegation was deputed to participate in the First IOR-ARC Senior Trade Policy Officials Meeting held at Perth (Australia) from December 7-8,1998.

The Second Ministerial Meeting of IOR-ARC is scheduled to take place in Maputo (Mozambique) in March 1999. A high-level Indian delegation is expected to participate in the meeting. A Seminar on Trade and Investment in IOR-ARC countries, which will be coordinated by the IOR-ARC Chair in the University of Mauritius, is planned to be held alongside the meeting.

India is an active member of the 'Group of 77' and participated in the Annual Ministerial Meeting held at New York on 25 September, 1998 which was held against the backdrop of a global financial crisis and prospects of an economic recession. India has taken initiatives on (a) sensitisation and consciousness raising on the gravity of problems and on the systemic crises that need to be highlighted besides highlighting opportunities presented by the situation for developing countries (b) getting developing countries to focus on key issues that they need to stress and negotiate with the developed countries in the financial, monetary and trading system, (c) drawing attention of the North to the key concept of international public good rather than just market forces being an important determinant of international economic policy and order, (d) bringing back the focus on concessional financial flows, more favourable and relatively unhindered transfer of technology and special and differential treatment in trade to developing countries as part of development cooperation agenda, and (e) establishing synergy and connectivity between this agenda and the new liberalisation and globalisation agenda.

As a symbol of its solidarity with Africa, India participated in the Second Tokyo International Conference on African Development (TICAD-II) which was held in Tokyo from October 19-21, 1998. About 80 countries and 40 international organisations and the UN Secretary General, participated in the event at which the developmental concerns and priorities of African countries received attention. The need to step up the level of developmental assistance and cooperation with African countries was duly recognised by developed countries. India's intervention highlighted its special relationship with Africa and commitment to deeper economic cooperation as well as ongoing technical assistance projects in Africa. It recommended adoption of triangular cooperation involving developed countries or international organisations along with the technical expertise of a developing country for projects in Africa.

In keeping with its commitment at the South-South Conference on Trade, Finance and Investment held in San Jose (Costa Rica) in January 1997, India hosted a "G-77 Trade Fair and Trade Conference" in New Delhi in November 1998. The objective was to enhance South-

South Cooperation by providing an opportunity for developing business contacts and networking amongst the G77 countries, and also to create greater awareness for enhancing business opportunities by utilising the vast trade, economic and business potential existing in the South. A New Delhi Declaration setting the agenda for Trade and Investment cooperation for G-77 was adopted.

With the developed world's think-tank and policy consultation body, Organisation for Economic Cooperation and Development (OECD), India continued to develop a policy dialogue relationship. It participated in OECD's outreach programmes for Dynamic Non-Member Economies (DNMEs) by deputing experts to attend the OECD Seminars /Workshops on Steel Trade Issues, Benefits of Trade and Investment Liberalisation, Practical Application of Tax Treaties, Agricultural Policies, etc.

Technical cooperation

The Technical Cooperation Division administers bilateral assistance on a Government to Government basis to 130 developing countries in Africa, Asia, Latin America and Eastern Europe. While most countries in the world either give or receive technical assistance, India is unique in both receiving and giving technical assistance in a major way, the latter through two programmes conducted by TC Division, the Indian Technical and Economic Cooperation (ITEC) and the Special Commonwealth African Assistance Plan (SCAAP) programme. In this Report, reference to ITEC will also include SCAAP as the two programmes are different only in the budget heads under which accounts are maintained.

The ITEC Programme has four major components:

(1) Training (both Civil and Military)

(2) Projects, including feasibility studies and consultancy services

(3) Depumtation of Experts and

(4) Study Tours for foreign decision-makers to India.

In regard to Civilian Training, 1485 slots were provided under ITEC during this year in 39 prestigious Training Institutions and Establishments (AppendixûXIII) of which 1326 slots were utilised (lists at Appendices-XIV-XV). These slots were for training in various types of courses such as Audit and Accounts, Banking, Diplomacy, Manpower Planning, Parliamentary Studies, Poultry, Rural Development, Small Scale Industries, Computers and Software, Maintenance of Biomedical Equipment, Food Processing Technology etc. During the year, a new subject "English Language for Professional Purposes" was introduced into the Programme and courses in various S&T fields were conducted for Vietnam and Cuba under special Agreements. A special training course was conducted for 25 Zimbabwean Police Officers in computer software. The wife of the Prime Minister of Senegal Mrs Silvie Aicha Loum was trained at the Fragrance and Flavour Development Centre, Kannauj and KVIC, New Delhi on production of Agarbatti and Dhoop Batti to enable her to organize Dhoop production centres for unemployed women in Senegal, using locally grown raw materials. Training slot offers to Iraqi nationals under sanction-affected Iraq were increased from 35 to 50 in the current financial year. These offers cover many fields such as agriculture, water management, desert cropping, genetic engineering, tyre industry, telecommunications and several others.

The assistance offered under ITEC is a fully self-contained package inclusive of international air passages, boarding, lodging and training costs etc. Currently, India bears an average cost of Rs.1.25 lakhs on each foreign participant under the ITEC Programme which has benefited over 10,000 nominees of foreign Governments since its inception in 1964. Demands for our training programmes are growing as during 1998-99, 1326 nominees were trained which is the highest number as compared to 1995-96 (970 nominees), 1996-97 (1001 nominees) and 1997-98 (1031 nominees).

Every year ITEC Day is celebrated by the Indian Missions abroad on 15th September. This year the event was also celebrated at Headquarters after a gap of 5 years. The event was attended by about 350 guests consisting of Heads of Diplomatic Missions/other Diplomats of more than 60 countries who are recipients of ITEC assistance, high-level Government officials, representatives of various Training Institutes, media personnel and about 100 trainees both civilian and military trainees who were at that time undergoing training at various Institutes located at New Delhi. The gathering was addressed by the Foreign Secretary who spoke about various activities being undertaken under ITEC Programme and its future orientation. This was followed by a cultural programme presented by candidates from Zimbabwe, Uzbekistan, Mauritius, Uganda.

On December 14-15, 1998, a Conference of the Training Institutes empanelled under ITEC was convened at New Delhi under the Chairmanship of Secretary (ER) Shri S T Devare and addressed by AS(FA) Shri B N Jha. The Conference was the first of its kind organized by the Ministry of External Affairs and was considered timely in view of the growing potential which training and capacity building activities for promoting India's bilateral relations with the developing countries. The Conference was also useful to discuss problems of coordination between our Diplomatic Missions, the Training Institutes and TC Division and many suggestions for procedural improvements emerged from it. There was a consensus that India can be more effectively projected through the ITEC programme as an important training destination for developing countries by streamlining the effectiveness of performance at these three levels. Training Institutes, appreciating the leverage which, having an international profile, can give them to generate important commercial spin-off benefits for themselves, and by extension for the country, were urged to improve their performance under ITEC accordingly.

Military Training is another important task undertaken under ITEC Programme. TC Division is a nodal point for organizing Military Training for nominees of friendly foreign Governments in some of the more prestigious Defence institutions of India such as Indian Military Academy, National Defence College, Defence Service Staff College etc. During this year approximately 198 slots for long and short term training courses were offered under ITEC and approximately 237 slots under Self-Financing Schemes. Some slots were also offered on a reciprocal basis. Appendices-XVI-XIX contain the lists of countries whose candidates were trained under ITEC Programme.

Another important aspect of the ITEC Programme is project cooperation with partner countries. Such cooperation, extended over many years since ITEC was established in 1964, has enhanced India's image as a country which is generous in sharing her experience and expertise acquired in the past fifty years of her independent existence, with other developing countries. In 199899 plans to establish a Plastic Technology Demonstration and Common Facility Centre in a backward region of Namibia by NSIC at a cost Rs. 3.40 crores were finalised, soon after a visit to that country by the Indian Prime Minister Shri Atal Behari Vajpayee. A major project to set up an Entrepreneur and Technical Development Centre (ETDC) at a cost of Rs. 13 crores in Dakar (Senegal) launched last year in fulfillment of a G-15 commitment, was executed in considerable measure by HMT (I) despite initial setbacks. The Mini Dairy Plant supplied last year to Kyrghyzstan at a cost of Rs-1.75 crores has gone into production of milk and butter. Plans to send six farmers from Punjab to Burkina Faso for three years to demonstrate Indian agricultural techniques especially for growing rice, were carried further.

In addition to project assistance, the TC Division supplied equipment for upgradation of the Upadhyay Training Centre in Mauritius, irrigation pumps to Uganda, Ambulances and Incubators to the Indira Gandhi Maternity Clinic in Namibia, diesel, pumps and sewing machines to Ivory Coast and textile machinery to Vietnam in 1998-99. A list of projects and project-related assistance extended this year to different countries may be seen at Appendix-XX.

As of now, there are 23 experts on long term deputation (from 2 to 3 years) to various countries as advisors in fields ranging from agriculture to medicine, marine engineering, water management, accountancy, fish toxicity, teaching, legislative drafting and in military fields (list is at Appendix-XXI). Seven short-term experts have also been sent to a few countries this year. Over the years, Indian experts have been acknowledged by many developing countries to have done commendable work in building institutional frameworks for self-reliant growth with limited means.

On the recommendations of Indian Heads of Missions, Study Visits by senior level officers and decision-makers are organized every year by the TC Division from various partner countries. Visits, generally in the areas of small scale industries, agriculture, health and education, trade and commerce etc. are an extremely popular method of introducing foreign visitors to different developmental sectors in the Indian economy and polity as they offer a first-hand exposure to Indian economic conditions. Nine study visits took place in the year under review. These include a visit by Prof Alberto Simao, Chairman, National Institute for Development of Local Industry, Mozambique to see the various industries and R&D centres engaged in improving the quality of products of the small-scale units under the supervision of the DCSSI. A four-member delegation from Nairobi University led by Prof D N Kariuku, Chairman, Department of Chemistry visited various Institutions and chemical industries to learn from Indian experience of the interface between academic training and commercial activity in the field of chemistry. Also invited was a three-member delegation from Vietnam headed by Director, Cuu Long Rice Research Institute, Dr Nguyen Van Luat to visit some Agricultural Universities and see some items of agricultural machinery which are manufactured in India. Two more agricultural delegations were invited in response to interest expressed by them in knowing about our Green Revolution - (i) a four-member delegation from Mongolia headed by Mr Y A Balgansuren, Director, Department of Policy Coordination, Ministry of Industry & Agriculture, and (ii) a three-member delegation from Kyrghyzstan headed by Mr Tolobek E Omuraliev, Advisor to the President of the Kyrgyz Republic and Head of the Department of Local Self Government and Agricultural Policy under the Presidential Administration. The visitors were taken to our Agricultural Research & Development Centres in Pusa, Karnal, Shimla, Ludhiana and for discussions with our authorities there. Mr A W Searle, Warden of the Zimbabwe Zoo was invited to interact with the Wildlife Institute in Dehradun. Two senior officials from the Namibian Broadcasting Corporation visited India and were shown Doordarshan and AIR facilities with a view to long-term cooperation between India and Namibia in this important sector of information and communication technology. Mr Patrick Mandago, Namibian Chief of Protocol visited to study the functioning of the Protocol Division of the Ministry.

Sometimes, a study visit is arranged to acquire expertise from the visitors as was the case when Mr J R Muller, General Manager of a South African Government-owned Company called Abakor came to India to advise the Municipal Corporation of Delhi on improvements in its abattoirs in Delhi and Aligarh, also during this year.

Under the Aid to Disaster Relief Programme (ADR), TC Division provides humanitarian aid for disaster relief to various countries, in the form of medicines, clothing, food etc. In the current financial year, medicines and foodgrain were sent to Bangladesh for victims of some of the worst floods that the country has known. Afghanistan's earthquake victims were assisted with medicine, blankets, tents and biscuits. Many other countries such as Comoros, Cambodia, Central African Republic, Sudan, Papua New Guinea, Kenya, Mozambique, Peru, Tajikistan and Kyrghyzstan received quantities of medicines and other forms of assistance depending upon their expressed requirements. Countries in Latin America and the Caribbean affected Hurricanes George and Mitch respectively were also assisted with small quantities of medicines and surgical instruments under the ADR programme. A complete list of the relief supplied by India under this programme in 1998-99 may be seen at Appendix-XXII.

12

Trade and Investment Promotion

The Central Government and the State Governments took several initiatives and measures during the year aimed at encouraging foreign investment inflows, particularly the flow of Foreign Direct Investment (FDI) into India. Major thrust areas included infrastructure development, particularly energy, power, telecom and information technology. It was the task of the Investment Promotion and Publicity Division to actively undertake effective investment promotion and publicity efforts, particularly through the Indian Missions and Posts abroad for attracting foreign investment into the country. Quite often, Commercial Wings in the Missions are the first point of contact for the foreign investor. It is, therefore, essential that the Missions are given full back-up Support in their efforts in the form of providing up-to-date information about the economy, the liberalised policies and the procedures, the project and opportunities available in different sectors, the incentives offered by the Central Government and various State Governments etc. Missions are also approached by investors seeking their intervention in case of delays in respect of clearances for their proposals or in respect of other hurdles faced in the implementation of projects. For all these and related matters the Investment Promotion and Publicity (IPP) Division in the Ministry has acted as a nodal point of contact and coordination to serve as an effective channel of communication between the Missions and the relevant Ministries/State Governments or other agencies, the case may be.

Policy

The Ministry provides inputs for Policy formulations, whenever required, based on investment trends world-wide and based on the need to maintain harmony between foreign policy objectives and our economic policies. Regular feedback was received from the Missions on foreign investor perceptions about India's investment policies or about successful model/policies followed elsewhere for serving as inputs to the evolution of any new policies or to the review of an existing one, if the same was considered necessary in the national interest.

The Ministry also actively participated in the meetings of the Foreign Investment Promotion Board (FIPB), where it was represented by Secretary (Economic Relations). Investments from NRIs were given particular attention. FIPB was also empowered to give a firm 'Yes' or 'No' answer to every proposal involving FDI within a deadline of 60 days.

Promotional efforts and initiatives

The Ministry undertook several initiatives towards suitably projecting the various investment policies and announcements of the Government by co-ordinating with the Missions on the one hand and various economic Ministries of the Central Government and State Governments on the other. Economic news about India was regularly disseminated to all the Missions highlighting major policy decisions and new opportunities, thus keeping them abreast of developments. Missions were also encouraged to hold investment promotion seminars and workshops besides extending investment support services, for which suitable publicity material, speaking points etc. were regularly despatched. Such seminars were held by several of our Missions in identified target countries. Ministry also undertook special efforts to highlight the policies, procedures and opportunities available in the Information Technology sector.

The Missions also provided support to visiting Indian delegations including those sponsored by the State Governments by arranging suitable meetings with potential investors, local Government officials and the local Chamber of Commerce or Products Associations.

The Ministry also assisted, based on information provided by the Missions, visiting foreign investor delegations/groups in having appropriate meetings with concerned Government Departments, the Apex Chambers of Commerce, the State Governments etc. The Ministry also participated in many bilateral or other meetings/ conferences involving overseas investor groups. Among the many delegations was also a 30-member International Public Affairs's Centre (IPAC) delegation which visited India from 17-20 January, 1999. The IPAC is an association of Presidents of multinational corporations and currently has 150 leading business houses among its members.

The Ministry also actively assisted various organisations in the country such as the apex chambers, EXIM Bank, Indian Investment Centre, in organising investment/ trade promotion events in India including the Global Indian Entrepreneurs Conference (12-13 November, 1998), India Economic Summit (29 November-1 December, 1998), various joint business councils and other events.

The Ministry actively participated in the efforts to mobilise good response for the Resurgent India Bond Scheme launched by the State Bank of India to which our

Missions lent full support. Eventually, the scheme proved a success mobilising over US $ 4.16 billion.

Publicity

The following publications were brought out this year by the IPP Division for the use of our Missions and Posts:

a) The IPP Division brought out an illustrative brochure "India - Investment Related Websites" in August 1998. The brochure gives information regarding website location and home page of several of the economic ministries of Government of India, the State Governments and a number of other investment related agencies.

b) IPP Division in association with World Link, which is the magazine of the World Economic Forum and Investor Access, a CD-ROM publisher in UK, brought out a CD-ROM on "India - Priorities for the 21st Century" in August 1998. This is a unique multimedia guide to India for Investors conveying a comprehensive picture about the evolving scene in India as the country moves towards the 21st Century. Industrial and investment policies of all the State and Union Territories have been featured along with analysis of 20 different sectors, each highlighting the potential for growth and the vast opportunities opening up. The CD also has a complete guide for foreign investors on policies and procedures for foreign investment. The hyperlinks given for important websites, the CD virtually acts as a gateway to the larger data base contained in most of the investment related websites of India.

As per the arrangement worked out with World Link, the CD was distributed by them to all the participants of the last Davos Summit of World Economic Forum. Copies of CD were also Sent to all our missions abroad who sent copies to key local chambers of commerce or large corporate groups and are also using it as a presentational aide while addressing investment promotion seminars or other such speaking opportunities.

c) "Investment Avenues for Non-Resident Indians'- a new publication which gave information on investment opportunities including in portfolio investment, investments in debt securities and deposits and investment in real estate while also outlining options for returning NRIs and provided answers to some of the most frequently asked questions on NRI investment and related subjects. The brochure was also circulated to participants at the Global Indian Entrepreneurs Conference held in New Delhi from 12-13 November, 1998.

d) A revised edition of "India Means Business - Perspectives" in a user friendly format and design, giving the updated position about government's policies and initiatives in infrastructure and other sectors to attract foreign direct investment, was brought out in December 1998.

e) IPP Division took the lead in sponsoring a special supplement on the IT industry in India which appeared, the 'Financial Times'. London on 2 December, 1998. This helped to project the outcome of the work of the Nation. Task Force on Information Technology and Software

Development and also the IT policies announced by the various State governments.

Agreements

The Ministry participated in the negotiations for drawing up of bilateral investment promotion and protection agreements that were held in respect of a number of Countries. Such agreements were signed during the year with Turkey, Mauritius Bulgaria, Indonesia, Morocco and Zimbabwe.

The Ministry also participated in the negotiations relating to bilateral Civil Aviation matters with other countries. The Ministry provided legal inputs, as required, and also tendered advice based on the need for increased civil aviation links particularly with our neighbouring regions to evolve in consonance with the initiatives being taken on the foreign policy front.